A
QUESTION
OF
BALANCE

ARTISTS
AND
WRITERS
ON
MOTHERHOOD

A QUESTION OF BALANCE

ARTISTS AND WRITERS ON MOTHERHOOD

EDITED BY
JUDITH
PIERCE
ROSENBERG

PAPIER-MACHE PRESS
WATSONVILLE, CA

04 03 02 01 00 99 98 97 96 95   10 9 8 7 6 5 4 3 2 1

ISBN: 0-918949-53-X Softcover
ISBN: 0-918949-54-8 Hardcover

Cover art, "Family Portrait" © 1990 by Ann Trask
Cover design by Cynthia Heier
Photo by Sarah Putnam
Interior design by Leslie Austin

Grateful acknowledgment is made to the following publications which first published some of the material in this book:

Publishers Weekly, August 31, 1992 for "Interview: Rosellen Brown"; *Belles Lettres: A Review of Books by Women,* Vol. 8, No. 3, Spring 1993 for "Interview: Alicia Suskin Ostriker"; *Sojourner: The Women's Forum,* Vol. 18, No. 9, May 1993 for "Interview with May Stevens"; *Belles Lettres: A Review of Books by Women,* Vol. 9, No. 1, Fall 1993 for "Interview: Mary Gordon"; *Belles Lettres: A Review of Books by Women,* Vol. 9, No. 2, Winter 1993–94 for "Interview: Rita Dove"; and *Ms.,* Vol. IV, No. 4, January/February 1994 for "Creative Tension: Being a Writer and Mother."

Library of Congress Cataloging-in-Publication Data

A question of love : artists and writers on motherhood / edited by Judith Pierce Rosenberg.
     p. cm.
     ISBN 0-918949-53-X (softcover : acid-free paper). —
     ISBN 0-918949-54-8 (hardcover : acid-free paper)
     1. Motherhood and the arts. 2. Arts, Modern—20th century—United
     States. 3. Women artists—United States—Interviews. I. Rosenberg,
Judith Pierce, 1946- .
NX180.M68L33 1995
700'.85'2—dc20
                                                 95-7216
                                                  CIP

Acknowledgments

I wish to thank all of the artists and writers whom I interviewed, those whose stories appear here, and those whom I was unable to include, for giving so generously of their time and experience. Without their interest and enthusiasm, this book could not have been written.

I also want to thank my agent, Liz T. Fowler, the editors at Papier-Mache Press, and the many colleagues who read portions of this manuscript, including Shelley Buck, India Smith, David Bartal, and Jeff Barth; the members of my nonfiction writers group, especially Lynn Liccardo, Vanda Sendzimir, and Wickie Stamps; and those who were enrolled with me in Gail Pool's Writing for Publication course at the Radcliffe Seminars these past few years. I am especially indebted to Gail Pool for her insightful criticism and unflagging encouragement.

I am also grateful to Annika Carlsson, Jenny Bäcklund, and Terese Locking, who lovingly cared for my children while I worked, and to Rachel Travers for her skillful and quick transcribing.

Most of all, I want to express my deepest appreciation and gratitude to my husband, Carl Rosenberg, and my children, Michael and Christina, for their sustaining love.

Contents

Introduction

MOTHERS HAVE BEEN THE SUBJECT OF ART AND LITERATURE for centuries, from the Greek tragedians' portrayal of Clytemnestra to Mary Cassatt's paintings of maternal tenderness. But with few exceptions, the visual and literary images we have of mothers have been created by men or women without children.

In the popular imagination, the artist is a solitary male in his studio while the good mother is in the kitchen surrounded by her offspring. The artist needs to be ready whenever the Muse deigns to speak to him. The good mother must remain available to her children, whose needs must be met before her own. The artist must maintain a core, a center, a sense of self from which to create. But the good mother should be selfless. The male artist creates books or sculptures because he cannot bear a child; a woman's creative drive is fulfilled by motherhood.

Of course, there have always been a few exceptional woman of talent, and often of means, who succeeded in producing art or literature while raising one or more children; writers Harriet Beecher Stowe and George Sand and painters Elisabeth Vigée-Lebrun and Berthe Morisot are examples from the eighteenth and nineteenth centuries. But only in the past few decades have a substantial number of women been able to choose both a career in the arts and motherhood. This book chronicles the struggles and celebrates the achievements of twenty-five of these women.

And yet, these women still face formidable obstacles in combining childrearing and an artistic career. In this they are like their sisters in other professions. But the challenges facing artists and writers differ, in several important ways, from that of lawyers, doctors, and others who work in corporate or institutional settings.

Visual artists and writers generally work alone. The artist must maintain faith in her vision, and the discipline to continue working toward that vision. That discipline separates the professional artist from the amateur.

Even the most talented and dedicated artist may spend years honing her craft with little financial remuneration. In his book *On Becoming a Novelist,* John Gardner bluntly suggests, "If a writer finds himself living, for honest reasons, with someone glad to support his art, he or she should make every effort to shake off the conventional morality and accept God's bounty, doing everything in his power to make the lover's generosity worthwhile."

While several of the older women interviewed here, such as fiction writers Ursula Le Guin and Rosellen Brown, were supported by their husbands when their children were small, few families today can live comfortably on a single income. Consequently, many of the women in this book, including photographer Bea Nettles, fiction writer Perri Klass, and poet Rita Dove, have triple-shift duties, juggling paid employment (often university teaching), domestic responsibilities, and their creative work. For those who are now or who have been single parents—for example, Kate Braverman, Karen Horn, and Linda Hogan—this situation is exacerbated.

With so many demands coming from the outside world, carving out the time and space needed to do creative work requires an inordinate amount of determination. Indeed, while the women interviewed differ in many ways (including age, geographical location, ethnicity, sexual preference, financial means, marital status, number and ages of their children, and artistic medium), they seem to have two traits in common: determination and perseverance. Many spoke of motherhood as an experience they were unwilling to deny themselves. But neither were they willing or able to give up their creative work.

Motherhood itself has only recently become a choice rather than a fact of life. Women today can not only choose whether or not to have children, they can delay childbearing until their work and finances reach a comfortable level. Indeed, most of the women interviewed here recommended that young artists establish their careers first, before having children.

As Erica Jong pointed out in her essay *Creativity vs. Generativity: The Unexamined Lie,* "One cannot become a novelist or poet overnight. Even if the talent is there, it takes years to form the *habit* of writing, the sitting down at the desk in the morning, the knowledge of one's own evasions, one's fears of writing, fears of failure, fears of success." Jong's words apply to my own experience, for although I had begun to think of myself as a writer before I became a mother, I had not yet established the habit of writing. In fact, I was only a junior in college when my son, Michael, was born in 1980, a few weeks after my twenty-fourth birthday.

Intent on a career in journalism, I had taken media courses and reporting seminars and worked for the campus newspaper and radio station. Returning to the University of California, Berkeley, some months after the birth, I interned at a CBS-affiliated radio station and, after graduation, landed a full-time job reporting on a suburban weekly newspaper.

But the long and irregular hours of newspaper reporting proved to be incompatible with raising a child, especially since my husband, Carl, was starting a computer software company at the other end of California. In the interests of family unity, I quit my job after five ex-hausting months and moved four hundred miles south to Los Angeles. In the summer of 1983, I set up an office in the unheated sunroom of the cottage in which we lived, and started freelancing.

Within about a year, I was freelancing on a regular basis for a local newspaper, which I continued to do after giving birth to a second child, Christina, in 1984. But when my daughter was twenty months old and my son was entering kindergarten, I left that paper and soon quit writing altogether.

In retrospect, I can see that the career crisis that followed was primarily the result of losing my office. We had just moved out of a cramped two-bedroom cottage into a ranch house with a fenced yard and a room for each child—but no office. My husband quickly nixed my idea of converting the dining alcove into a workspace, saying that it would look too messy. And I believed the childrearing experts who insisted that my son and daughter were too old to share a bedroom. So my filing cabinet went into Christina's room, my office supplies were stored in our bedroom closet, my books were shelved in the living room, and the computer was placed on a table in the kitchen.

Why didn't I insist on taking my old desk to our new home and using the dining alcove as an office? Why were the perceived needs of my children more important than the demands of my work? In retrospect, I think the reason lies in the fact that I was earning very little money as a freelance writer. In fact, my work was a financial drain on the family since I did not make enough money to cover my work-related expenses, especially child care. It was difficult for either my husband or for me to consider my work as important as his.

With no workspace and no more newspaper deadlines, I began to drift away from writing. Instead, I volunteered: as a Cub Scout den mother, secretary of the board of directors of my daughter's day-care center, cochair of the PTA safety committee.

But I felt frustrated and resentful. Late one night returning from a long drive, I started crying. I felt lost without my writing, but my attention was so fragmented by the minutiae of daily family life, that I was unable to concentrate. Although I had freelanced for several years on a regular basis, I had never really established the habit of going to the desk each morning, year in and year out, whether or not I had an assignment. I still had a lot of ambition, but without a constructive outlet, my energy emerged most frequently as rage.

Tillie Olsen, herself a mother of four, wrote in her book *Silences* of the difficulties women writers face because of the way motherhood is structured in American society: "The circumstances for sustained creation are almost impossible. Not because the capacities to create no longer exist, or the need (though for a while as in any fullness of life the need may be obscured), but… the need cannot be first. It can have at best only part self, part time…. Motherhood means being instantly interruptible, responsive, responsible. Children need one now (and remember in our society, the family must often try to be the center for love and health the outside world is not). The very fact that these are needs of love, not duty, that one feels them as one's self; *that there is no one else to be responsible for these needs,* gives them primacy. It is distraction, not meditation, that becomes habitual; interruption, not continuity; spasmodic, not constant, toil. Work interrupted, deferred, postponed makes blockage—at best lesser accomplishment. Unused capacities atrophy, cease to be."

Olsen did, however, acknowledge that an increasing number of women writers are also mothers. How did they manage? I read and reread the piece on Fay Weldon in Nina Winter's *Interviews with the Muse* and some of the essays in Janet Sternburg's first volume of *The Writer on Her Work,* especially the inspiring "Still Just Writing" by Anne Tyler and the tragic "Creating Oneself from Scratch" from portions of Michele Murray's diary. The latter chronicled the struggles of a poet with four children, whose career was just taking off when cancer cut her down. In Murray's case, work deferred was poetry forever lost.

But while many books and articles had been written about women artists and writers with children, I discovered that there was a dearth of material about how they integrated the maternal and artistic aspects of their lives. Perhaps if I could talk with some of these artists and writers, I could learn from their experience and share that knowledge with other women.

At first, I was driven by my need to find practical solutions to the problems of time and space that seemed overwhelming. But then I became curious about how the experience of mothering affects the content—the images, themes, subject matter—of the art itself.

Artists use their tools and materials to create something new and original out of themselves. They translate visions and ideas into concrete forms—a photograph, a story, a sculpture—that others can look at, read, or touch. Becoming a mother is a process that permanently changes the self. It is a kind of metamorphosis. What happens to the artistic self in the process of becoming a mother? How does that change manifest itself in an artist's work?

As an increasing number of artists and writers who are themselves mothers explore this vast subject, drawing on their own experience of familial relationships, they are creating new images of mothers and children which deepen our understanding of this most complex of human relationships.

While this book presents a diversity of voices, it is not meant to be a definitive survey. My time with each subject was limited and our conversations were generally focused on the topic of combining childrearing and work; consequently, while some of the women discussed issues of sexuality, class, race, ethnicity, and religion, those aspects of an artist's identity are not the focus of these interviews.

In the course of writing this book, I learned to take myself more seriously as a writer. When we moved again in 1989, to the Boston area, we found a house with an office and a spare bedroom for an au pair. I sought out a community of writers, joining first a group of nonfiction book writers, all members of the active Boston chapter of the National Writers Union, and then enrolling in Gail Pool's Writing for Publication course at the Radcliffe Seminars.

I work in the basement now, in a room of my own, with a view of the backyard and the woods beyond. It is a proper office, equipped with bookshelves, a desk, filing cabinets, sufficient lighting, an adjustable chair—and a door that shuts. A portrait of my children hangs on one wall, and their ceramic bowls and sculptures decorate the mantel.

Now that Michael and Christina are fourteen and ten years old, the practical difficulties of combining writing and mothering have eased. Like most of the women interviewed—who spoke with incredible honesty, but were, at the same time, concerned that their words might hurt a loved one—I find that I remain torn between the deep pull of work and the equally deep pull of family. And yet, from the depths of this division, new work continues to emerge.

JUDITH PIERCE ROSENBERG, 1995

To Michael and Christina,
and to Carl,
with all my love

Photo ©, Alejandro Rosas

LINDA VALLEJO

Linda Vallejo

Linda Vallejo, thirty-eight, is a dynamic sculptor and painter who uses the bold palette of her Mexican heritage to create images of women. Inspired by her belief that "woman is the symbol of the earth," much of her work is "an effort to touch the heart of all people to remind them that the earth is our home and we should befriend it," the artist explains.

Vallejo has a BA in painting and drawing from Whittier College and an MFA in printmaking from California State University at Long Beach, where she has been a visiting lecturer. She also did graduate work in lithography at the University of Madrid, Spain, and studied theater in London, England. The recipient of a Latinas Making History Award and a Brody Arts Fellowship, Vallejo has been recognized by a number of organizations, including the National Association of Chicano Studies, the Institute for Hispanic Cultural Studies, and the City of Los Angeles. Her work has been exhibited throughout the Southwest, as well as in New York, Madrid, and Mexico.

At the time of this interview, Vallejo was also working part time as a grants writer for the Long Beach Civic Light Opera and the Long Beach Ballet; she has subsequently opened Galeria Las Americas, a Los Angeles gallery representing contemporary Chicano and Latino American artists. Vallejo lives in Long Beach, California, with her husband of seventeen years, Ron Dillaway, and their two children, four-year-old Robin and three-year-old Paul.

"BEING A MOTHER AND HAVING CHILDREN EMPOWERS MY life," says Linda Vallejo. "That's really the key to the whole idea of being an artist and a mother. Being a mother surrounds me with the kind of love and support that I need to live a complete life as a human being, as a woman, and then as an artist and a worker in the community."

She believes that as an artist she has a responsibility to use her gifts. Vallejo says, "When I was much younger and studying art, I decided that I wanted to have three basic elements in my life. One was to be an artist forever and never let that go. The second was to be a wife and a mother. And the third was to have a spiritual core in my life. And at this point, I have all three, so I really believe that I am living a full life, where no major aspect is lacking."

Vallejo's vision of how she wants to live contrasts sharply with the stereotype of the angst-ridden artist. Her reaction to a retrospective of works by Jackson Pollock (a leader of the abstract expressionist school of painting who died in 1956) exemplifies this contrast: "I have a love-hate relationship with Pollock and his kind. On the one hand, you really have to applaud this human being for breaking all the rules. And when it comes to art, I love to break the rules.

"But on the other hand, I really hate him because he was an alcoholic and he had a terrible personal life. He was emotionally disturbed and somehow or other he's become an artistic demigod. I really resent that, because I think that a lot of the role models artists have today are drug-ridden, alcoholic, emotionally disturbed—socially, spiritually, and physically fragmented people who don't have families, who are ostracized by society and become rich and famous."

Although she flirted with the image of the angst-ridden artist in her early twenties, Vallejo found that being depressed and miserable drained her; she had no energy left to create. Then she fell in love with her husband, Ron Dillaway, and, "the work just started flowing out like so much water." Vallejo determined to live her life another way: "I'm going to have good friendships and people who care about me; I'm going to have strong spiritual support systems, and I'm going to kick ass in art."

In addition to her husband and the woman who cares for her children, Vallejo has a spiritual support system of men and women involved in the Native American religion she practices. She also volunteers in a prison, conducting indigenous ceremonials for Native American women. Her vision of the unity of her roles as wife, mother, artist, and community worker, allows her to pursue her goals apparently unencumbered by the guilt that holds back so many other women.

While Vallejo does not see children as hindering her, she admits that one can travel faster on a career path without them. "If your priority is to become an internationally renowned, famous, and wealthy artist, you can accomplish it much more quickly without children. You can go to all the openings—you're available for travel, for exhibition dates, and for last-minute production without any glitches.

"But that, to me, is not necessarily the only way to accomplish it. Anyone who has children realizes that things move a little bit more slowly with kids. I struggled a great deal to have my children. It took me seven years to have two kids. I had to go through major surgery, and I had two miscarriages before I had my two boys. So they're really like miracle babies.

"In a very human sense, my children taught me that I can accomplish anything. I had to be very consistent about my efforts; I had to watch my health very closely. And because of my desire for children and my initial inability to fulfill that dream, I developed a very strong spiritual sense. So you see, my children have brought a wholeness to my life."

Vallejo slowed down her production and changed her mode of working while pregnant. "One of the things you have to accept as a mother is that things are going to change. You have to hold on to the thread of inspiration. You have to hold on to the thread of dedication. You have to hold on to the thread of discipline. It's kind of like a spider's thread—it's very strong and it will only break if you purposely cut it. But if you hold on to the thread and continue to work, you can learn much about your personal ability to work in the face of difficulty, negative energy levels, and discomfort," the artist says.

During that time, Vallejo continued to go to her studio one or two days a week, regardless of how she felt. "When I was pregnant the first three months, I puked all day, and how do you make artwork when you're puking all day? Well, doggone it, you can make it happen. What became important to me was not quantity, but the thread of the work itself and staying in line with my desires as an artist.

"I found that I could speed up my production. I worked out a process that allowed me to be a mother and artist at the same time. So I'm not developing a process where it takes me 150 hours to complete one painting and I must have twenty-four hours in a row to be able to complete this painting. Instead I started to become highly flexible and create work that could happen beginning to end in a day."

When she is unable to go into the studio, Vallejo uses a technique that she calls "filling the well" to accumulate ideas and inspiration for future work. She explains, "You can't create work—really sensitive, meaningful work—without a reservoir of imagery and beliefs. And you can't create a reservoir of imagery and beliefs and concepts in a vacuum." Vallejo fills her well by going to the country. "It's very easy to find a girlfriend who will drive with you someplace. You might take a small sketchbook and keep a log, write down ideas and begin filling the well."

While pregnant, Vallejo filled her well in other ways too, such as buying books that she had always wanted to read and attending religious services more frequently. "I began to round out my life in the time that I had when I wasn't forced to be an artist. I could develop those aspects of myself that I'd never had time for before. I really took the opportunity to grow on all kinds of levels so that I could become a full human being and make a full artistic statement because of it," Vallejo says.

"And women know that once you become pregnant and have a child, you have the opportunity to become closer to your mother than ever before, closer to your sister and your aunts, closer to elderly neighbors who have had children."

An elderly neighbor took care of Vallejo's first son for a year and a half while she went into her studio one day a week. "I found out I didn't need nine hours in the studio. If I was really centered, I could go in for four hours and accomplish a great deal. So you feed the baby, you leave a bottle, you go to the studio.

"Now I have a woman who comes to my home. She's in her late fifties. She's a Mexican woman, so she speaks Spanish, which I'm very pleased with. She has a lot of knowledge about old ways of taking care of children. She's a masseuse; she's amazing. She's a very good teacher to me, and she's become a member of my family. I helped her get her papers, I got her a dentist and a doctor, I got her some eyeglasses," the artist says.

"She comes to my house five days a week. My children are in Montessori school two days a week. So she basically cleans my house, takes care of my children, and does all the wash. She's taken on a lot of the physical aspects of being a mother and really become a second mother to my kids. And I take on the emotional responsibilities and specific teaching responsibilities with my kids because I have the energy to do it."

Vallejo has developed a system that works for her and is eager to advise others on how to schedule their time. "I tell other women, 'If you only have one day in your studio, make it a day; pack yourself a lunch and go to your studio, even if it's only a corner of a studio you're sharing with somebody else. Spend all day, even if you don't feel like going, even if you don't know what you're going to do when you get there. Go anyway and get this rhythm going. After a while, your creative clock will get in sync with you.'

"You have to set up a real schedule. One of the things I tell people is, 'You cannot fragment your days. You don't want to have an appointment for your art career, a layout job, a meeting at your kids' school, and people coming over for dinner on the same day. Don't divide your day into minuscule pieces. If four hours a week is all you can get, that's your creative time, you stick with that. If you're doing eighteen things in one day, you won't make art.'"

Rather than trying to do a little of everything every day, Vallejo has evolved a schedule that keeps her energy concentrated. She works two days a week as a grant writer for the Long Beach Civic Light Opera and the Long Beach Ballet, and spends the other three weekdays in her studio; weekends are reserved for her family. The only exception to this strict division is that Vallejo accepts business phone calls at home.

"When I come to the studio, I usually don't leave. I come and deal, deal as hard as I can. By the time I get to the studio, I'm so excited and happy to be here that the energy flows very quickly."

Does she ever pick up a paintbrush at home? "Never! I don't expect my children to wait on the sidelines while I'm doing my artwork. They won't anyway, anybody knows that. So when I'm at home, I'm at home. I'm cooking, I'm cleaning, I'm teaching alphabets, I'm driving the kids to a special event. I'm a woman, I'm a wife, I'm a lover, I'm a friend, I'm a mother at home. In my studio, I'm a ragtag, mad-dog artist."

The days she works as a grant writer are also full days. "I don't do any other business at the job—I don't accept any private phone calls; I just do the job. I turn the switch, I'm at the job. I go home at night and cook dinner and massage my husband's back. So I'm not fragmented in a million ways."

How does being a mother influence the content of her work? "I'm real playful with it, that's one thing. Being a mother just balances me out as a human being so that I can do my work. I have done some motherhood images, but I don't tend to do that that much. It's more or less on an emotional level. The happiness that my children, my husband, my family gives me comes through in my work.

"I think the work influences me being a mother more than my motherhood influences me to be an artist because this place is so separate. My children aren't here. I bring them to see my work as often as I can, but this is really my place. This is my place for me."

Having a studio outside the house has always been important to Vallejo, but after becoming a mother, the studio became essential. When her first child was born, her studio was three minutes away from home. "I was very fortunate to have a very inexpensive studio in a very beautiful place. I've never lost a studio. I've even sold jewelry to keep my studio; I've done everything possible.

"Because of my children, I've become highly prolific. I tend to accomplish a lot in a short period of time because I have other responsibilities. And I'm still more prolific than many of the women I know without kids because their time isn't as precious to them. Since I have such a big support system to fall back on, I tend to take bigger risks with my work.

"People say, 'My art is my children.' I don't believe that for nothing. If you have a kid, you know doggone well your art is not your children. You can stack your paintings and walk away. You can't stack your kids and get up and go. My art is my work. It's something I've done all my life. I can't help it. At one point last year I thought I might quit. It was a ridiculous idea. I held it for like thirty minutes and came back three days later and busted out three new paintings."

Does she ever feel guilty about going into the studio? "Why should I? I believe that if you're given a gift, you must use it. If you have the gift of writing and poetry and beauty in any form—sculpture, painting, dance, music, literature, cooking, sewing, any of the traditional arts—you have a responsibility to the symbolic and physical whole to live it out. Because beauty really does counteract ugly."

Photo ©, Sigrid Estrada

MARY MORRIS

Mary Morris

Mary Morris, forty-six, is a traveler, someone intimately familiar with the tension between those who leave and those who stay behind. She is clearly fascinated by the idea, expressed by the late John Gardner, that literature has only two plots: "You go on a journey or a stranger comes to town." In fiction, she portrays the powerlessness and endurance of those who wait for the return of a loved one and the redemption that comes to those who cease waiting and set off on their own journeys of discovery. In her nonfiction travel books, Morris conveys not only the sights and sounds of her destinations, but also reveals her personal responses: fears, hopes, dashed dreams, and new understandings.

Morris was raised in Illinois and educated at Tufts College in Boston, from which she received her BA in 1969. She attended graduate school at Columbia University, completing an MA in 1973 and a master's degree in philosophy four years later. The recipient of a National Endowment for the Arts grant and a Guggenheim Foundation fellowship, Morris is the author of two nonfiction travel books, Nothing to Declare: Memoirs of a Woman Traveling Alone *(1988) and* Wall to Wall: From Beijing to Berlin by Rail *(1991); three novels:* Crossroads *(1983),* The Waiting Room *(1989), and* A Mother's Love *(1993); and two collections of short stories:* Vanishing Animals *(1979), which won a Rome Prize, and* The Bus of Dreams *(1985). With her husband, Larry O'Connor, she coedited* Maiden Voyages *(1993), an anthology of travel writing by women. At the time of this interview, Morris was teaching creative writing part time at Princeton and at New York University; she now has a tenure-track position at Sarah Lawrence College.*

Morris lives in Brooklyn, New York, with her seven-year-old daughter, Kate, and her husband, a Canadian journalist, whom she married in 1989 after a year and a half as a single parent.

GATHERED TOGETHER ON THE MANTEL OVER THE FIREPLACE in Mary Morris's living room are three Zuni bear fetishes, a kachina doll, and snapshots with the desert as a backdrop—all mementos from a year the author, her husband, Larry O'Connor, and her then three-year-old daughter, Kate, spent traveling by car around the southwestern United States. On that journey, Morris says, she discovered, "the way that a child opens doors. Having a child with you is, on every level, an opening experience. It's true that there are all kinds of constraints of time and fragmentation, which are real issues. But the emotional opening and the way other people become available can have a profound effect on one's work and one's life. It certainly has on mine."

Morris began writing in college in the mid-1960s. But after reading the biographies of such women authors as Virginia Woolf, Jane Austen, the Brontë sisters—all of whom were childless—Morris says, "I felt that being a woman writer would be a disastrous mistake for me." Instead, she envisioned her future as a French teacher, married to an orthopedist and a mother of two. But the orthopedist never materialized, and she finished her years at Tufts College "obsessed with writing and literature," but with no clear idea of where she was headed.

"And then one summer I was studying Dante at Harvard, and I had just broken up with this man I was madly in love with, this French economist." While reading Dante's *Purgatorio*, she fell asleep and, Morris says, "I dreamt that I was walking down a street in Paris, and I saw a cafe and the name of the cafe was Leave Behind All Hope Ye Who Enter Here. I thought that was a very strange name for a cafe, but Gertrude Stein and Hemingway and F. Scott Fitzgerald were drinking camparis and sodas in there, so I thought maybe I should go in.

"So I went in and ordered a campari and soda and my chair fell immediately, descending into a deep dark hole, and there was no way out. Six pall bearers arrived and they brought a coffin, and they put the coffin in front of me and they left. And I understood that my fate was in the coffin and that I had to open it. I opened it and it turned into a rolltop desk and paper for eternity."

Waking, she knew that writing "was the only way out for me." She believed that she would never marry or have children, that as a woman writer her life would be "filled with misery and questionable affairs and maybe a certain amount of alcoholism and tobacco and hopefully a few good works of art would come out of it. But I felt that was the pact I'd made with whoever that devil was."

A decade passed with only sporadic publishing success, but then at age thirty-two, Morris received both a National Endowment for the Arts grant and a contract for her first short story collection. The grant supported a year's sojourn in Mexico (later chronicled in *Nothing to Declare*), where she completed *Vanishing Animals*. That book, published in 1979, went on to win the Rome prize and gained Morris a teaching position at Princeton University. Her first novel and her second collection of short stories were published within the next few years. Then in 1986, when she turned thirty-nine, Morris told the man she had been involved with for three years that she wanted a child.

"I really felt for about twenty years that I couldn't be a writer and have a child. And then at a certain point, my life felt empty and alone. It just seemed to me that it was then or never. I'd had some medical problems; I wasn't sure I could even have a child. I certainly didn't think I would get pregnant easily," she says.

While traveling in China with her companion later that year, Morris met an eleven-year-old girl with whom she passed an afternoon, reading and painting watercolors. "Her family, who lived in Fiji, traveled all over the world. I admired this family of intrepid travelers—each child wearing his own backpack—and I knew then that I wanted to have a child to journey with, to see the world," Morris writes in *Wall to Wall: From Beijing to Berlin by Rail*.

In this memoir, Morris not only describes the people she meets and the passing landscape, blending stories of personal travail and tales of empire, she also reveals her inner turmoil, her hopes and fears as her external journey is shadowed by an internal transformation.

"I got pregnant on the Yangtze River," Morris says. Her companion returned to the States while Morris, unaware of her condition, boarded the Trans-Siberian Railway, traveling from Beijing to Moscow. She planned to continue on to the Ukrainian capital city, Kiev, and from there to search for her maternal grandmother's village, to find the site of her childhood stories.

But Morris never reached the Ukraine. Although she had heard about the accident at the Chernobyl nuclear reactor outside of Kiev before leaving home, none of the details had been released. By the time she arrived in Moscow, Morris was not only sure that she was pregnant, but also learned that the magnitude of the nuclear accident was far greater than initially reported. The city of Kiev was still open to tourists, but Morris concluded that traveling in the radiation-contaminated Ukraine was too risky, not only for this but also for future pregnancies. She eventually found a sympathetic Moscow tourist official who was willing to change her reservations.

"I watched as she flipped through my vouchers—the dream and destination of this trip now diverted by the tragic mishap of Chernobyl while perhaps another dream and another destination were unfolding," Morris writes in *Wall to Wall*. As she foregoes the opportunity to fulfill one long-cherished dream in order to preserve another, Morris writes, "I felt thwarted, and yet at the same time I experienced a sense of completion."

Although she considered leaving the pregnancy out of the book, focusing only on the external journey, Morris says, "It seemed as if a layer would be missing. In the end, I think I made absolutely the right choice to write it the way I wrote it, but it was extremely difficult."

While she was traveling, Morris was out of touch with her companion for a couple of months. "I got pregnant assuming I would marry the father. By the time I got back to New York and did a pregnancy test, I was committed to having this child. And it became clear to me that he was not interested in having a child." Although she very much wanted to have the baby, Morris says, "I reached a point where I just felt like I couldn't handle it, financially, emotionally. It was my parents, to their credit, who embraced me and embraced the situation. My father said to me, 'Men come and go, but a child is forever, and you should have this child.'"

Her daughter, Kate, was born in January 1987. Although her writing time has often been constrained, Morris says, "I feel that I've been given the greatest gift that I can imagine. It's almost as if somebody said, 'What's the perfect child for you?' and that's what they gave me."

Morris recalls the validation she felt when she read Ursula Le Guin's essay on motherhood and writing, "The Hand That Rocks the Cradle," in the *New York Times Book Review* two years after Kate's birth. "That just made me feel that one can start to rewrite the history of women writers, that we can look at ourselves as women with children, whose work in some way is informed by and grows out of that," Morris says.

"Where I was extremely lucky was that I had already created that writing life. So it wasn't as if I had to invent myself when I had a small child." While conceding that it might have been easier to have married before having a baby, Morris says that she is "a better mother and a better writer" for having established her career first.

But Morris still feels guilt about the difficulties of Kate's early years. "I was a single mother for a year and a half. I totally supported us financially, and at times I didn't have all the time I would have liked for my daughter and, occasionally, I suppose I was impatient." When Kate was an infant, Morris wrote at the word processor, usually for magazines on assignment, stopping to nurse her daughter as needed. "I loved the first six months of her life because I would just roll her up in a blanket, and she'd lie there on the bed and look at me. And I would just write and I was very happy."

When her teaching contract at Princeton expired during Kate's infancy, Morris and her daughter moved to the West Coast, where she spent the next year teaching at the University of California, Irvine, "a job that I hated." Although the woman she hired to help her was very good with Kate, Morris recalls coming home from work and seeing "smoke pouring out of the kitchen of this little bungalow" she had rented because once again the baby-sitter had burned dinner.

Morris's third novel, *A Mother's Love,* is the story of Ivy Slovak, a woman artist who struggles with both the practical problems of raising her infant son alone on little money and with the psychological difficulty of coming to terms with the loss of her own mother, who abandoned Ivy as a child. In writing that novel, Morris drew on her own experiences to convey "the physical act of being a single parent, the carrying, the schlepping, the logistics, the nightmare of needing to go to the store in the middle of the night. What do you do if your child's asleep and you've run out of diapers? Night after night I made those decisions."

At one point in the novel, Ivy discovers that there is no toilet paper, nothing to eat or drink but cold pizza, and only two diapers left. It's eleven o'clock at night, Bobby is finally asleep and so she takes a chance and leaves him alone in the apartment for fifteen minutes to run to the corner store. "I don't think I ever left Kate alone, but there were many nights when I wanted to," the author says.

Despite such practical nightmares, Morris says, "I think my daughter and I were living out a certain mother-daughter myth, and we were doing pretty well at it. But Larry came into my life at a moment [when] I was so tired; I was so exhausted from everything that I didn't know how I was going to go on."

Married in 1989, the couple divide the housework fifty-fifty. "Our tasks are very delineated," says Morris. Her husband goes to the supermarket while she shops the specialty markets. He does the short-term finances while she takes care of the long-term planning. "It sounds so hokey to say it, but I think that there's a feeling of partnership here."

While she says that her husband "would fiercely dispute this," Morris explains that although the tasks are divided, she is the person who "oversees and delegates" the housework. "I have three careers: I teach extensively to earn a living; I run a household, which cannot be underestimated, just what it takes to organize the lives of three people and a dog; and there's my own writing. I'm at a point where I could almost [afford to] leave the teaching, but the strain it would put on my writing is unbearable to me. I can't stand to think that I have to turn in something to get money. I want the artistic part of me to be pure and not affected by coarse capitalistic concerns.

"My ideal day would be to drop my daughter off at school at eight-thirty, sit down at my desk, and then at two-thirty go to the gym and swim, do my errands, and pick her up after school. But I almost never have a day like that."

During the eight months of the academic year, Morris currently teaches Wednesdays at New York University and Thursdays at Princeton, returning late in the evening, so that "after two days of teaching, on Friday morning, I'm exhausted. Monday is a kind of getting started day, so in terms of my real writing days, I only have Tuesday."

In one sense, she says, "I'm writing all the time. I'm writing on trains, I'm writing on subways, I'm reading things that are generating ideas. I take a yellow pad wherever I go." However, she differentiates between the days when she's writing by hand or typing up those fragmented ideas and a "real" writing day when she turns on the computer and tries to make something from the bits and pieces. "It's one thing to be generating ideas and thinking around your work. It's another thing to sit down and actually enter the work. For me to enter the work, things really have to be physically, emotionally, fiscally, in every way, in order. And I don't come by that sense of order so easily these days."

To achieve that sense of order, Morris says, "The first thing I do when I come home after I've dropped Kate at school is I clean—I organize; I do what the Buddhists call 'cleaning the temple.' A lot of what I'm doing as a writer is taking a chaos of emotions that I've lived with all my life and trying to make sense of it. I have to create outer order in order to deal with inner disorder."

She also needs the quiet of being home alone. "I find it hard to work if there are other people in the house. Even though my studio is on the ground floor, I feel the presence of others. So even if it's a day where my daughter might be upstairs playing or my husband's playing with her, I don't work so well. I suppose it's guilt to a certain extent; I feel that I should be mothering her. I feel that the part of me that needs to be an artist and creative has to be very internally focused, and the part of me that has to be a mother is very externally focused, and they don't cross over very well."

Morris faces formidable internal obstacles to sitting down at her desk and concentrating on her writing. "I wake up terrified every morning. I feel like the terror of the day is beyond belief. By the same token, if you ask me in a rational moment, what is the only thing that will make me feel good on that day, it is to have a good day's work and to write some scenes that I really love."

She describes this sense of "creative depression" as being like a "big, dark pit that I've descended into," filled with self-doubts. But once she sits down to work, all of those feelings disappear. "It's as if I never had a moment of doubt, I never was looking into the deep dark pit of mortality and eternity, and somehow everything makes sense.

"I suppose swimming is the perfect metaphor for me because it's taking the plunge. There's this moment, particularly on a winter's day, you get to the pool and it's cold [outside] and the water's cold and everything feels scratchy, and I think I don't have the strength. Then I dive in and I start to move around and I let myself go. I start to swim and I'm like a fish—I love it; I never want to get out. And I say to myself, 'Why do I resist the things that make me happy?'"

Morris has found that the most successful technique for diving into her work is to get up at six, before the rest of the family arises, and write until seven-thirty. Then, she says, "I can take Kate to school, I can do errands, and I can come back and pick up where I was. I can sit down to work, and eight hours will go by and I don't know it. I can lose myself in a way that I can't really lose myself in anything else. Time becomes meaningless, and I'm completely happy; I'm the happiest I could be."

Before having a child, Morris lived an unscheduled life, where she could write whenever she wanted, for as long as she wanted. Then, she had "free time in the ultimate sense, as opposed to now where free time is always parceled out; it's always scheduled.

"The thing I think I miss the most are those stretches of time where I'm not accountable to anyone or anything," Morris says, adding that much of her work has been generated by travel and a sense of movement and freedom. "I don't work so well when I feel captive. And sometimes I feel quite captive—not by my daughter, just by the reality of parental and domestic life. I think that creativity requires a certain continuous flow. It's very hard to say, 'Between nine and three, I will be a writer, and from three o'clock on, I will run errands and cook and clean the house.'

"On the other hand, I was incredibly lonely, and my life was rather empty when I had all that freedom. And now, in a sense, the fullness of it probably shapes my thinking. The emotional resonance is much deeper in my work because of it."

While her husband is also a writer, "He doesn't have any of this resistance to work that I have. First of all, he's a journalist," with ten years of newsroom experience, Morris says. "Larry can look at a clock and say, 'Okay, I've got three hours' and go down and work."

Morris and O'Connor also have different parenting styles. On the nights when her husband works late and she is alone with her daughter, Morris says, "I try to make Katie's favorite meals, and I ask her what she wants. So, of course, I feel very beleaguered because I'm writing all day and then I have to be a single parent at night; I have to pick her up and I have to cook a nice dinner." When she discussed the matter with O'Connor, "He said that on the nights when I'm teaching, he just takes her out for pizza and they talk. And I thought to myself, 'Why do I have to make mashed potatoes and steak and green beans? Why not take her out for pizza and then just sit and talk to her and not let it be such a big deal?'

"I find it hard to just be with my daughter," Morris says. "At times, it seems easier to think about what a character is going to do in chapter twelve. I wish I were the kind of mother who could make dinner and then play a game and not feel that I had to do the dishes and put things back. I'm sure I'd be a better mother.

"There are certain things we like to do together," Morris says, such as art projects. "We have an art room downstairs—it's a closet, but she can paint the walls, the ceiling, whatever she wants. Every night we read together and sing together for about an hour or so. There are times that are as precious and fulfilling and rewarding as anything I've ever done in my whole life."

Morris finds it easier to focus on being with her daughter when they are out of the house: "When we're on the road, when we're moving, I'm much more able to leave other things behind."

Morris describes a recent family vacation to the Caribbean where she took Kate snorkeling as "one of the best times I've ever had. I was holding her, [swimming] across coral reefs and pointing at tropical fish and discovering this world with her. I felt so close. I remember when we were coming back to shore, she looked at me and she goes, 'It's a magical, magical world.' And I thought, I showed her that magical world and, in a way, I showed myself the magical world."

In her own childhood, Morris says, "nobody tried to show me the world in those ways. My parents did all the things parents are supposed to do, and we had a nice house and lived in a nice place. But I never felt really understood emotionally. And I definitely know that Kate has given me back my childhood.

"It's one of the reasons why, as I see her getting older, I feel very sad." Although she would like to have a second child, Morris says, "it's probably not going to happen. There's a part of me that thinks that I've been given a gift that I never thought I'd have.

"Just last summer Kate asked me if a cow had a different udder for every kind of milk, like the chocolate udder and the buttermilk udder. I literally did not want to answer the question because I wanted her to believe that cows have different udders for different kinds of milk. And the little mistakes with language. She thought I had lemon disease last summer. Of course, she was confusing it with Lyme disease."

Morris is keenly aware of the increasing separation between her daughter and herself, and expects that this will manifest itself in her future work. "As Kate gets older, I'm already feeling the whole issue of letting go of a child. Letting go of a child in the way that one also lets go of a book—the tremendous exhilaration of having completed something, and the terrible sense of loss that nothing else can fill.

"I'd like to write less about family, and this new novel that I'm working on is fairly political," Morris says. "But I guess I have to say that the family is at the core of it for me."

Photo ©, Tom Leeser

ALISON SAAR

Alison Saar

Alison Saar, thirty-eight, carves life-sized demons, divas, zombies, goddesses, and suffering mortals from rough-hewn timbers, covering them with scrap linoleum, discarded tin, pottery shards, or bits of broken glass. In some of her figures, the chest opens, revealing inner light, secret truths. Each piece has a story, each is an embodiment of spirit.

While Saar is often considered a black artist, her heritage is more complicated. Her father, art conservator Richard Saar, is of German and English ancestry, while her mother, assemblage artist Betye Saar, is African-American with Native American and European ancestors.

After graduating with a BA in studio art and art history from Scripps College in 1978, Saar went on to the Otis Art Institute where she completed her MFA in 1981. She has received fellowships from the Guggenheim Foundation and the National Endowment for the Arts. Saar lives and works in Brooklyn with her filmmaker husband, Tom Leeser, and their four-year-old son, Kyle, and newborn daughter, Maddy.

ALISON SAAR AND HER MOTHER, BETYE SAAR, BEGAN PLAN-ning *House of Gris-Gris* (1990) when Alison's first child—and Betye's first grandchild—was only a week old. The one-room structure was their first collaborative piece, for their joint exhibition, "Secrets, Dialogues, and Revelations: The Art of Betye and Alison Saar." For both artists, the piece, constructed of wood and aviary wire and stuffed with feathers, moss, and eucalyptus leaves, expresses home, family, and shared values. The house "looks very much like a nest. To me, it symbolized nesting," Alison Saar says.

In working on the piece, "I was really taken by how both my mother and I work with found materials, and how you come up with this idea and you have these found materials, and the pieces take on a life of their own. You only have a certain amount of influence over them; they have their own personalities."

She also saw how the relationship between materials and artist mirrors that between mother and child. "As soon as Kyle was born, I realized that he had his own personality, his own destiny. And as a mother, your influence on that is in exposing them to different things."

The word *gris* in the title of the piece is French for "grey," and refers to the Creole idea of magic which is neither black nor white. The title reflects both mother and daughter's interest in various spiritual traditions. It could also be a metaphor for the artists' refusal to be bound by narrow definitions of color, culture, or creed.

Asked how she sees racial and ethnic identity, Saar says, "It's very important to me. And it's very difficult because my husband is white. Kyle and I have these discussions about who we really are. I try to explain to him that I'm part black, and he wants to know what part of me is black," Saar says with a laugh. "I look like I'm white, or I guess there's some evidence that I'm mixed, but it's not obvious. But his sitter's black, and so we talk about that, and he recognizes that his grandmother's black. But I don't think he really understands how things dovetail just yet.

"What's wonderful about living in New York is it's not so deeply segregated, a lot of the population here are people from the islands, where there isn't a black-white line because everybody's pretty much mixed."

In her own childhood, Saar experienced racism not only in school but also within her extended family. "People ask why I don't talk about my white heritage. I'm very close with my father, but we were estranged from that side of the family. My step-grandfather was racist and refused to see us. It wasn't until he passed [away] that I met my father's mother. So Thanksgiving and Christmas and Easter were all spent at my grandmother's house, on my mother's side. Those were the cousins that we saw five to six times a year, or during the summer we would live with them. I think that whatever part of the family that you associate with, then that's who you are in a certain sense."

The school she attended was "deeply divided between blacks and whites." Saar recalls how hard her school years were "because I looked so white that it was very difficult for me to break through those barriers." She was isolated, and the students who became her friends "were equally isolated: a gay male; a woman who was part Native American, part white; and a woman who was black but raised in a white community. We all kind of clung to each other because nobody else would accept us." It wasn't until she entered college, on a black fellowship, that she was accepted by other black students.

By contrast, the area of Laurel Canyon where the Saar family lived was an enclave of artists, writers, and musicians, many of whom were racially mixed. At that time, Laurel Canyon was a semirural hillside neighborhood in Los Angeles. Devastated by a fire in 1958, the area "was pretty much wild" with deer, coyotes, rattlesnakes, and raccoons. There Saar developed "an affinity with nature and a belief that there was a spirit aspect to nature" which would form the basis for her later interest in Native American and African spiritual beliefs.

"You couldn't play stickball in the street, so what we did was build huts," Saar recalls. Her interest in making things was encouraged by her parents. Betye Saar supplied drawing paper to keep Alison and her sisters busy while she worked on her printmaking, and Richard Saar took the three girls to museums. When Alison became interested in horses, he gave her a book of Leonardo da Vinci's equine drawings.

At age thirteen, Saar was making and selling dolls. "But they weren't just dolls. Each of them had a story that went with them. The dolls that I made are very similar to the sculpture that I make now, in that they're very narrative; they're an invention of personality and symbolize certain things." Later, as an apprentice in her father's art restoration business, where she worked for eight years, Alison learned to carve, and became fascinated with African sculptures.

At Scripps College, Saar did independent studies in African and African diaspora art, history, and religions, planning on a career in art history. Although she also took studio art classes, Saar resisted the idea of entering the same profession as her mother. Saar says she thought of art as "just something you did; it wasn't necessarily something you did for a living." Then in the midst of writing her undergraduate thesis on self-taught African-American artists, she came to the conclusion that "I couldn't be an art historian because I didn't have a good handle on transferring factual information. I wanted to invent things. It wasn't until that point that I decided that I was going to be an artist," she says.

After receiving her BA from Scripps in 1978, Saar enrolled as a graduate student at the Otis Art Institute. There she was able to take studio classes for free because her mother was on the faculty. Later, her mother helped Saar obtain gallery representation and lecture dates. Although the younger artist moved to New York in 1983, Saar remains close to her mother, who has become even more of a role model since Kyle's birth. As colleagues, mother and daughter critique each other's work, share ideas and materials, and provide mutual emotional support against the vicissitudes of the art world.

Both Betye and Alison Saar are master recyclers, creating art from found objects. Mother and daughter both talk about searching for objects they connect with on an intuitive, spiritual level. But while Betye is known for her very detailed assemblages, constructed from odds and ends found in the flea markets of the world, Alison's wooden sculptures are massive, rough-hewn, incorporating the discarded linoleum, glass, copper flashing, and stamped tin she discovers in city dumpsters.

"The way I carve is very rough and crude. I have no interest in refinement of materials. The materials I use are important, but they're important because they're found materials and they have a previous history." The material she chooses may be "a hunk of wood, but it's a hunk of wood that came out of a building that was a stable in 1910, and it has the horse spirit still in it," Saar explains.

Saar's belief "that different elements have different properties and that those properties are ruled by spirits" clearly influences her work. While she was pregnant with Kyle, Saar did her first major installation of *Crossroads* (1989). A large cross is painted on the floor, with one freestanding figure at each of the four points. A female figure, clad in oxidized copper, represents the mother spirit, while another figure, created from metal taken from a burned building refers to resurrection. Between the points of the cross are stacks of stones, similar to those piled at the sites of fatal car crashes in the Southwest. The piece is about "the intersection between the spiritual and material worlds," Saar says.

"*Crossroads* was very much inspired by Kyle coming, in that I was really kind of mystified at the idea that there was going to be a new life, that somehow a spirit was within me. It was the onset of a series of installations that dealt with life and death, and Kyle really instigated that. Before, my pieces were about people I would see, but I got very intrigued by what the world was made of, so the pieces became very elemental."

In *Clean House* (1992), another installation influenced by her son, a female figure is surrounded by a forest of birch branches. Entering the circle of branches, viewers come to a table with an enamel basin for ritual cleansing. Here they are invited, by means of a sign, to take stock of their lives, to cleanse and thereby forgive themselves. The artist explains, "The idea was forgiving yourself for things you may have done against your own morality. The reason I attribute that to Kyle is that there was a point in time where I felt that I was telling him that you have to be truthful, you have to be this and that. And then I realized that I hadn't always been, and that in order for me to proceed with a clear conscience, I had to forgive myself for those violations against my own morality."

Fertile Ground (1993), an installation piece at the High Museum in Atlanta, brings together the artist's maternal experiences and her spiritual beliefs while exploring the painful legacy of slavery.

The subject of the installation is "Africans' and early African-American slaves' relationships with agricultural society in the South," the artist says. One of the five monumental wooden figures is the pregnant "Terra Rosa," who represents the fertility of the red southern earth. "I started it before I became pregnant [with Maddy], but we were consciously trying to get pregnant that year," Saar recalls.

"I made the actual crops be demons," she says. In addition to the tobacco demon, the installation includes a demon representing cotton, which, she says, is "a very draining crop that leeches the soil and sucks everything out of you."

In the same way that cotton drains the soil, so too did white children drain their black nursemaids, slaves who were forced to abandon their own children to take care of the master's, says the artist, explaining another layer of meaning she sees in the piece.

"I hate to say that I viewed Kyle as this demon that was draining everything out of me, but that piece ended up looking like a four-year-old," Saar says with a laugh.

Six weeks after the birth of her second child, Maddy, the artist was in the throes of readjusting her work and family life. When her daughter was only five days old, Saar had to return to her part-time teaching job at the School of Visual Arts, and within a month, she was back in the studio, preparing for an upcoming show. Saar says she feels torn, "because I wanted to stay home and spend some more time with her."

While Saar does some work from home—drawing and planning and handling business telephone calls—she rents a studio for the actual sculpting. Within walking distance of her home, the studio is in an industrial area of Brooklyn, because her work is "too messy and too noisy to be in a residential area." Setting up a bassinet with her new baby and working while Maddy sleeps would be out of the question; while Saar's working, there are "chunks of wood flying all over the place" from the chain saw she uses to create her life-sized wooden sculptures.

Saar is trying to get back onto the schedule she had before Maddy was born. Then, she worked from ten to five, three days a week in the studio and one day away from the studio, taking care of the business side of being a professional artist. She also teaches one day a week for the equivalent of one academic quarter at the School of Visual Arts, where she has worked for the past two years.

Although it was difficult to return to her teaching job so soon after Maddy's birth, Saar says that, in general, "The teaching is not a big drain on my time, and I intentionally keep it that way. But I like it because otherwise I'm alone in the studio all day, and then I'm at home talking to a four-year-old, and I find that I lose touch with the world out there.

"I'm lucky that my career [generates] enough money to justify having a baby-sitter," says Saar. The family has had the same child-care provider for the past four years, a woman with a flexible schedule who helps with the housework. "She's a godsend. If she ever goes home—she's from the islands—I think we'll leave New York City, because I don't think I could deal with it all," the artist says.

"In some sense, knowing that you're paying someone eight to ten dollars an hour to watch your kids, you maximize that time. Before, I would leisurely show up at the studio and look out the window," Saar says with a laugh. "I just don't do that anymore. I can't afford to hang out.

"Right now, because I have a lot of time at home to think about what I want to do, when I go in there, I really set to work. Aside from being a little bit sore, I feel great now that I'm back in there and hacking away at things. It's an emotional and physical vent for me. I think that's why I work the way I do; I've always needed that sort of relief. Even as a child, I would go around throwing things or digging holes— very physical play."

When she comes home from the studio, Saar says, "I'm filthy and have sawdust falling out of my hair and out of my shoes. I come in the door and talk with Kyle and breast-feed Maddy—and try to change my clothes before all that happens—so there are moments that are just chaos." Until recently, Saar says, "I've been coming home and the baby-sitter's been leaving, but what I'm doing now is to invest in having the sitter stay for an hour." With that overlap, Saar says, "I can feed Maddy, then hand her to Yvonne, while I start chopping onions or carrots. Otherwise, everything ends up happening at ten o'clock at night and it's a total disaster."

Even with the extra hour of help, evenings are difficult because her husband often doesn't get home from his job as an effects director until eight. "And he's totally wiped out because he has horrendous meetings with advertising agents all day. So it's difficult to keep everyone calm," Saar says.

Her husband, Tom Leeser, works for Editel, a postproduction facility, in addition to doing his own film and video projects. His work schedule is "very erratic," Saar says. Sometimes he can get away from the office early, but other times he has to work late.

Her husband is "very supportive" of her career, Saar says. "I think he views it as an investment." She adds that while her husband hopes to be able to quit his job at some point to focus more on his art, Tom's current job gives him access to expensive editing equipment that they could not afford.

When the couple married in 1986, four years after they met, starting a family was not an immediate priority. "Because his career was so demanding and mine was just getting going, it didn't seem like a really great time. We were both pretty busy, but it wasn't like we consciously decided not to do it. And it wasn't that we consciously decided to do it either, to have kids," Saar says with a laugh. "Kyle just happened, and we said, 'Well, why not?' " In the case of their second child, Saar says, "We did deliberately decide to hold off until Kyle was a little older."

When Kyle was born in July 1989, Saar had only five months to finish her work for "Secrets, Dialogues, and Revelations," the joint show with her mother. While she took three months off from the studio, Saar continued to work at home on drawings for the exhibition. After the show opened in early 1990, she took a "delayed maternity leave" for several months. This time she hopes to take some time off to be with Maddy once her deadlines are met.

Saar says her mother "was a wonderful role model in that she was, at a certain point, a single mother dealing with three kids and a career and working to make money at the same time. And you know, I respect that she did work at home. I'm kind of baffled at times, right now, struggling with two of them. How she managed to deal with three of us and everything else on top of it, without a sitter, is really astounding to me."

Comparing their different lifestyles, Saar notes that one key difference is that her mother's working environment was generally safer. Even when her mother did printmaking, Saar says, "we would all be drawing, and she would be doing her drawings" while other pieces were setting in etching acid or drying. "None of it was time-crucial like plaster or concrete drying. It was all fairly neat and not quite so toxic.

"Her career was just picking up when we were very young. When she started getting more recognition, we were all in kindergarten or in preschool. I'm not saying it was easier for her, but she wasn't having to travel all over the country, and she wasn't teaching at the time." In her own case, Saar says, between her travels to install shows and give lectures and her part-time teaching, "there's a lot of times when I can't really be with them [Kyle and Maddy]."

With the exception of one curator friend who has a child the same age as Kyle, Saar says her friends are clearly divided between mothers of young children and artists. Her friends who are artists either don't have any children or they had children at a young age and then went into an art career after their children were grown.

Of her peers in the art world who don't have children, Saar says, "I think a lot of them are thinking about it, and I think they're a little frightened. It's even difficult to deal with a marriage because so much of being a successful artist these days is traveling [to give lectures]—that's how we subsidize making the art. So I think it's very daunting to get the nerve up to [have children]."

In conversations with other artists who want to have children but can't imagine when, Saar tells them that if they are waiting for the perfect circumstances (say, until they can afford to take a year off), they may wait in vain. When she assures other artists that if they take the plunge and have a child, everything else will work out, Saar speaks not only from her own experience as a mother but also as her mother's daughter.

Photo ©, Scott Brown

CRISTINA GARCIA

Cristina Garcia

In her haunting, lyrical debut novel, Dreaming in Cuban, *Cristina Garcia tells the story of a family divided by politics and geography, from the perspective of three generations of del Pino women. Reviewing the book in* Time *magazine, Amelia Weiss notes that in this work, Garcia "claims her own aesthetic identity. Like a priestess, in passages of beautiful island incantation, she conjures her Cuban heritage from a land between 'death and oblivion,' so that she too can fasten on Abuela Celia's drop pearl earrings, sit in a wicker swing by the sea, and watch as the radiant spirits of her forefathers 'stretch out a colossal hand.'"*

Born in Havana on July 4, 1958, Garcia was three years old when she immigrated with her family to the United States. She graduated from Barnard College in 1979 with a degree in political science; two years later, she received a master's degree in European and Latin American Studies from Johns Hopkins University. Although she had prepared for a career in the Foreign Service, Garcia became a journalist, working for Time *from 1983 to 1990. Since publishing* Dreaming in Cuban, *which was a finalist for the 1992 National Book Award, she has received a Hodder fellowship from Princeton University, a CINTAS fellowship, and a Guggenheim Foundation fellowship.*

Married in 1990 to journalist Scott Brown, Garcia lives with her husband and their twenty-month-old daughter, Pilar Akiko, in Los Angeles.

"THERE'S NOTHING I LOVE MORE THAN LANDING IN A CITY I don't know and finding out about it," says Cuban-born writer Cristina Garcia. "So in that sense, journalism was a wonderful career for me because every week was different."

Garcia began her writing career in 1983 as a reporter and researcher for *Time* magazine. She thrived in the fast-paced field of journalism and, within four years, was promoted to bureau chief. From the news magazine's Miami office, the twenty-eight-year-old covered Florida, the Caribbean, and, occasionally, Latin America; she was often on the road two or three weeks out of every month.

Like many journalists, Garcia thought that she might one day write a book. "I just didn't know it would be fiction," she says. "The move from journalism to fiction occurred in a very slow chemical way that I wasn't even aware of and was probably sparked in part by a trip I took to Cuba in 1984," more than two decades after immigrating to the United States.

Several years after this visit to her birthplace, Garcia wrote a poem entitled "Ordinary Seductions," about three suicidal Latina women. "The poem suggested to me another world, a nest of women that I was intrigued by."

Two of the women in that poem became characters in the novel, which Garcia began writing in her spare time. "I just threw myself into it, the way I would throw myself into an article or any other project I had tackled with no idea about the difficulties of publishing. I was more surprised than anyone how it took over my life."

Writing fiction proved to be incompatible with working in the news business. As a journalist, "Your schedule is so erratic—you go in Monday and you could be halfway around the world on Wednesday. There's no way you can plan or do anything. Plus you're writing a lot as it is, and it's very hard to get other writing done. It's such a different part of your brain that you use for journalism. You're very constrained by the truth," Garcia says with a laugh. "That was ultimately very confining for me. It was much more fun to make stuff up."

Taking a leave of absence to work on the novel "was just a drop in the bucket. It became a terrible struggle between the journalism and the fiction, and, ultimately, the fiction won," says Garcia, who finally left *Time* in 1990, the same year in which she married fellow journalist Scott Brown. "I needed to quit to be able to finish the book because it was driving me crazy to nickel-and-dime my way through it, snatching an hour here or a weekend there."

Eighteen months passed from the time Garcia began writing *Dreaming in Cuban* until she shipped the completed manuscript to her agent. "I usually was sitting down and working within ten or fifteen minutes of waking up, before I was fully awake. I had a kind of momentum going from the unconscious to the conscious state." Toward the end of that time, she was working from dawn to midnight. "It got to the point where I used to have to throw a sheet over the computer," to get some sleep. "It was like a voluble parrot—you just have to shut it up."

The novel, which spans forty-five years, portrays three generations of women in the del Pino family: the grandmother, Celia, a staunch supporter of Castro; her two daughters: Lourdes, who becomes a successful bakery owner in New York and Felicity, who stays behind in Cuba with her sailor-husband and slowly goes mad from syphilis; and Celia's grandchildren, especially Lourdes's daughter, Pilar, a punk artist who longs for her grandmother and her homeland.

Relationships between mothers and daughters are at the heart of the novel. The two women who are most separated by time and distance—Celia and her granddaughter, Pilar—share an almost mystical bond. As Pilar muses, "I feel much more connected to Abuela Celia than to Mom, even though I haven't seen my grandmother in seventeen years. We don't speak at night anymore, but she's left me her legacy nonetheless—a love for the sea and the smoothness of pearls, an appreciation of music and words, sympathy for the underdog, and a disregard for boundaries. Even in silence, she gives me the confidence to do what I believe is right, to trust my own perceptions."

The nineteen-year-old Pilar thinks to herself, "I wonder how Mom could be Abuela Celia's daughter. And what I'm doing as my mother's daughter. Something got horribly scrambled along the way." Unfortunately, Pilar does not realize the significance of her observation, for the del Pino women are divided by more than politics and geography. Mother, daughters, granddaughter—each carries a secret locked in her heart. Unwilling to take the risk of revealing her secret shame or betrayal, each becomes isolated from and incomprehensible to the others. For example, while both Pilar and Celia are embarrassed by Lourdes's anti-Communist views, neither her daughter nor her mother comprehend that Lourdes's political fervor is rooted in her brutal experience at the hands of revolutionary soldiers.

Although the relationships between mothers and daughters is a dominant theme of the novel, the author herself had experienced only one side of that relationship when she wrote the book. But by the time her novel was published in early 1992, Garcia was pregnant with her daughter, Pilar Akiko, born in October of that year. The pregnancy had a dramatic and unexpected impact on all aspects—physical, mental, and emotional—of Garcia's life.

"I was extremely preoccupied with what was going on during my pregnancy; instead of reading novels and poetry, I was consuming baby books." That preoccupation helped her to remain on an even keel emotionally in the "whirlwind" of interviews and book touring that followed the novel's release and ensuing critical acclaim. "Somehow, being pregnant, I felt so centered in a different way that it didn't faze me so much. In retrospect, I look back amazed at all that has happened. While I was going through it, it was a mildly pleasant feeling, as opposed to totally excited and out-of-my-mind joy."

But the impact of childbearing on her writing has been much more profound and long-lasting. "My writing's been severely curtailed since I've been pregnant. From the early pregnancy on, I was someone who had to take a three-hour nap in the middle of the day," Garcia recalls. More distressing than the sapping of her physical energy was the fact that "the pregnancy had a dulling affect on my creativity. I wasn't as sharp mentally."

Although she continued to write from morning until late afternoon, Garcia says, "in retrospect, I look at what I wrote, and it doesn't even feel like me; it doesn't even sound like me." She wrote an entire second novel while pregnant, which she struggled to revise in the months after her daughter was born. Garcia finally gave up on this second book because "it made no sense; it was a product of my hormonal derangement."

Shortly before Pilar was born, Garcia received a Hodder fellowship from Princeton University, and the couple moved to New Jersey. Before the baby, "I had this idyllic idea of me sitting at the computer and rocking her with my foot," says Garcia. But, in fact, she found it "virtually impossible" to combine writing and mothering for the first year of her daughter's life, despite the help she had from her husband and the financial support of the fellowship.

Garcia was unprepared for the reality of motherhood, which she describes as "a tidal wave." She had had little experience with children. "I had never even held an infant before. I didn't realize the enormous, almost centrifugal force that my daughter would have for me as a mother. I was just enormously pulled into her and really didn't want to do anything else.

"I remember when my baby was about six weeks old, I had to go to the National Book Awards, which you would think would be a real apogee in your life," says Garcia, whose novel was among those nominated for the prestigious annual prize. "And yet, I didn't even feel like going. The baby was so tiny and I knew that she would prefer to be with me than with anybody else, and that was good enough reason not to want to go. In fact, the whole time I was there, I was swelling up with breast milk and uncomfortable and calling home every ten minutes; it was something I couldn't even enjoy very much—such was the force and the power of the bonding," she recalls.

In traditional Cuban society, the women are in charge of the children, Garcia says. "My mother was the one who brought us up; my father was always away, very busy working. And then, when we got a little older, so was my mother." But in her own case, Garcia says, "I really want to share the childrearing with my husband."

Garcia describes her journalist husband as "a born feminist" who grew up in a family where the father stayed home and the mother went out to work. "So he has no sense of traditional roles the way so many men do. There's nothing that intrinsically became 'your job, my job.' It was just who was better at what."

In the early days of their relationship, when they were both working as reporters, on the road frequently and eating meals out even when they were home, the couple seldom argued over domestic issues. But once the baby arrived, the division of labor became "an enormous issue."

Both Garcia and Brown stayed home with Pilar for the first six months. "He was completely saturated the way I was. I was nursing, but he did just about everything else." Nursing Pilar took up most of Garcia's time and energy, so that Brown was left with all of the mundane tasks—errands, cooking, and laundry—made more onerous by the lack of such amenities as a dishwasher and washer-dryer in their cramped student apartment.

"I think he felt very left out, especially with the nursing. He didn't feel like a father, he felt like a handyman. And then, over time, he realized that his work initially was going to be supporting me so that I could nurse and be with the baby. Every time he held the baby, she screamed and screamed; it was very discouraging for him for a long time. Now she just totally adores him, and I'm the one being taken for granted. But he's earned it; he's put in his time."

Her husband has continued to be unusually responsive to the needs of Garcia and their daughter. When the family moved back to Los Angeles, Brown took a job with flexible and contained hours so that he could spend more time with Pilar. "Part of the problem with other spouses, other men, is that they don't really know what goes on, how you spend your day, how it can really just evaporate being with the baby and tending to her needs." Because her husband was home with their baby for so many months, Garcia says, "When I call him and say, 'Can you get back early; it's just one of those days,' he knows exactly what one of those days is like and is home in ten minutes. He's very responsive that way."

At the same time, Garcia says, "It took a lot of negotiating and misunderstanding and fighting to figure the schedule out. And still there are kinks. What's amazing to me is how much we rely on these schedules, and when they don't go the way we hope, there's a lot of tension. In a way, everybody has to be pulling their weight all the time."

Garcia would tell young women writers contemplating mother-hood, "If you can get some writing done ahead of time—something published, something you feel good about—it's a reference point for yourself and you know you can do it again. Even though it was only two years ago, sometimes I have to pick up my book to remind myself that I did this once. And that helps because sometimes when you're swallowed up in the day-to-day urgencies of being with a small child, it's very easy to lose a sense of yourself."

If she had known what mothering entailed, "the relentless present tense of being with a baby, I would have just said, 'I'm not going to try and write this first year.' I would not have struggled and caused myself as much grief as I did, trying to do both."

And yet, Garcia has not set aside her writing career to stay home full time with her daughter. "Until I actually got started writing again, I was a miserable person. As much as I love my daughter, I was feeling very overwhelmed and not functioning. Now, with the writing back in my life, I have much more equilibrium; I'm more satisfied and can enjoy her even a little bit better."

After Brown went back to work, the couple tried a variety of child-care arrangements, ranging from having live-in help ("I ended up doing a lot of the cooking") to having a baby-sitter take Pilar to the park for four hours. Writing at home while her daughter was also there proved unworkable. "If I'm around, Pilar wants to be with me," says Garcia, who found herself "totally distracted" by every little cry or peep her daughter uttered. Finally, about the time Pilar was sixteen months old, Garcia decided that she had to get out of the house, "something which I had been trying to avoid. But I realize now that, for me at least, it's essential to have that uninterrupted time."

Four afternoons a week, Garcia drives the short distance to her rented office and writes for four hours. Although the arrangement seems to be working out well overall, the transition from work to home is a difficult one. Before she is ready to write, Garcia frequently reads poetry for an hour or more, "because it gets my mind off the domestic track and into another realm. Often, it's just the lubrication I need to start thinking about my own work." On the way home, Garcia spends an additional hour or so running errands, using that time "to dissipate my office self so I can come home and be Mama."

One day a week, the author commutes to the University of California, Santa Barbara, a four-hour round trip by car, to teach a creative writing class. "There are six students, so it's fairly manageable. I love the students; we have a lot of fun in this class," she says. Garcia spends an hour or two preparing the evening before. "I don't find that it's all that much work. I've taught before, and I basically have a game plan for it." She accepted the job "as an experiment, to see if I could add this to the mix and still stay sane—and I can. At the same time, my novel is kicking off now, so I may not do anything for a while and see if I can't get a draft down."

Garcia feels "much more clearheaded" about the new novel she's writing, which is actually her third after *Dreaming in Cuban* and the unpublished second novel she wrote while pregnant. "I'm not as emotionally divided or ambivalent about what I'm doing, and so I feel a lot stronger about it and I think it's reflected in the work."

Although she's writing mostly fiction, she sometimes craves her old life as a reporter—a craving not quite satisfied by freelance assignments and reviews. "I miss the companionship and the office schmoozing and griping. Sometimes when I meet a friend or acquaintance who is part of a larger whirl of things, I do get nostalgic."

But the long hours and travel required in her former job were incompatible not only with writing fiction but also with having a child, Garcia says. At one time she believed that on-site day care would be the answer to combining mothering with full-time work as a journalist. But as a novelist, she has been able to work out a different solution. Lacking the pressure of constant deadlines and being her own boss, she can limit her writing to a part-time schedule. "I'm just having one child. I've waited a long time to have her, and I want to be around."

She sees both writing and mothering as extremely intense in terms of time and emotions, "so in a way, they're in direct competition." While her daughter is at home, "and maybe forever," Garcia's writing career "will be a question of a balancing act rather than a sense of giving way to an obsession. That's the big difference now with the baby."

While she hopes that her writing will be enriched by "my evolution as a mother and a person," Garcia says she is prepared for the possibility that later novels may not do so well financially and that she may have to get another job when her daughter is older. She had no expectations for her first novel, but the book's success "has given me the financial freedom to be home these first years with the baby, which has been an incalculable gift of time."

Photo ©, Suzy Kitman

PERRI KLASS

Perri Klass

Writer and physician Perri Klass, thirty-four, bridges the divide between art and science in her work and in her life. A central theme in much of her fiction and reportage is the very human dilemmas facing doctors and scientists who work on the cutting edge of technology. Klass is the author of two novels: Recombinations *(1985) and* Other Women's Children *(1990); a short story collection:* I Am Having an Adventure *(1986); and two nonfiction memoirs:* A Not Entirely Benign Procedure: Four Years As a Medical Student *(1987) and* Baby Doctor: A Pediatrician's Training *(1992).*

Klass was born on April 29, 1958, in Trinidad where her father, Morton Klass, was doing fieldwork as an anthropologist. The family returned to New York City shortly after her birth; Klass grew up primarily in the Northeast, although her family lived in India for a time where her father did research. Both her father and her mother, English professor Sheila Klass, are published authors, as are her sister and brother. Klass began publishing her short stories, several of which have won O. Henry prizes, while an undergraduate. She received her BA from Harvard University in 1979, and then studied zoology for two years at the University of California, Berkeley, before returning to the Boston area. After graduating from Harvard Medical School in 1986, Klass completed her internship and pediatric residency at Boston's Children's Hospital in 1989.

At the time of this interview, Klass had finished a two-year fellowship in pediatric infectious diseases at Boston City Hospital and was job-hunting for a medical position while working at home on her third novel. Klass lives in Cambridge, Massachusetts, with her companion of seventeen years, Larry Wolff, author and associate professor of European history at Boston College, and their two children, nine-year-old Benjamin Orlando and three-year-old Josephine.

"DEALING WITH ANY KIND OF MEDICINE REMINDS YOU CONstantly that the body is vulnerable, that we are all mortal and that flesh is meat, and that if you are deprived of oxygen for long enough, then all of your precious thoughts and memories go—you, me, our children, everyone," says author and physician Perri Klass. "Medicine brings you up against that reasonably unpleasant, reasonably difficult realization again and again. And you develop, in medicine, ways to protect yourself against it, many of which are a kind of denial—not me, not my mother, not my father, not my husband, not my kids. If you're in pediatrics and you're seeing things happen to kids, there's a very particular need to wall off your own children."

In her second novel, *Other Women's Children,* Klass writes about this issue from the point of view of Amelia, a pediatrician who makes deals with God to protect her own young son from the scourges she treats in other children. "You know, 'I'm going to take care of these children and you're going to keep mine safe,'" Klass explains. "In fact, I've known people in medicine who deliberately went into the fields that they were most afraid of. People whose family members had suffered a lot from cancer found themselves in cancer not so much because they wanted to take care of their family members but because that was the most frightening thing: 'I'm going into this specialty and in exchange, my life is going to be safe and my family is going to be safe.'"

The novel exemplifies the ways in which being both a mother and a physician has affected her writing. "The experience of taking care of a child day by day, that was adulthood to me. The intensity we feel about keeping our children safe, the deals we make with God, the lessons we learn about how we can't keep them safe, the purity of our emotions around small children and how those emotions become more complicated as they grow up—that became the condition of my life and that conditioned my fiction."

Klass wrote *Other Women's Children* during breaks in her pediatric residency. At that time, she says, "In many ways, I was so intensely immersed in big hospital, sick child, tertiary-care pediatrics that I really don't think I would have found it very easy to write about anything else or any other setting." She decided she wanted to write about some of the issues facing her and the other people she was training with, "issues without resolution, which included this paradox: that everyone who goes into pediatrics usually does it out of a very real affection for children, a very real pleasure in their company, and a very real delight in spending days surrounded by children. And your pediatric training involves three years, essentially, of watching children suffer and frequently die.

"I wanted to write about the struggle that I saw in myself and in my contemporaries and also in the people further along to live some kind of life which included that kind of pain and misery and horror but also included normal life. You know, the day is over, you go home, you hug your own kids, you say hello to your husband, you sit down at the dinner table, and [someone says], 'How was your day, dear?' Well, a baby died. It's part of the job and part of the professional scene, but it's not something that you ever come to deal with completely professionally, I think."

In *Other Women's Children*, the character Amelia's son was the same age as the author's son. Klass explains that she chose to write about a four-year-old not for autobiographical reasons but because "It's very difficult to get the dialogue right without having a child of that age around."

Klass had established the habit of writing long before becoming a mother or a doctor. She began publishing short stories ("After amassing two hundred or three hundred printed rejection slips") while still in college. Before entering medical school, she had written, although not yet published, her first novel, *Recombinations*, a witty coming-of-age story about a young woman scientist. While a student at Harvard Medical School from 1982 to 1986, Klass wrote about her experiences for the *New York Times Magazine, Mademoiselle,* and *Discover;* those columns were collected in her first nonfiction book, *A Not Entirely Benign Procedure: Four Years As a Medical Student.* That book includes a chapter on her first pregnancy and the birth of her son, Benjamin Orlando.

Her second nonfiction book, *Baby Doctor: A Pediatrician's Training,* continues the story of her training over the next three years as an intern and then resident at Boston's Children's Hospital. In her nonfiction, which often has the immediacy of a diary, Klass consciously struggles to maintain the outsider's perspective. She gives her readers the inside scoop on how ordinary mortals become doctors while at the same time, unflinchingly reporting on the ways in which she herself was transformed into someone willing to assume responsibility for life-and-death decisions.

In *Baby Doctor*, Klass draws parallels between her two vocations, noting: "Every patient is a story. Every family is a story. Every illness is a story." She goes on to say, "The doctor is like some obsessive novelist who insists on composing full, minutely detailed biographies of each character, biographies that will never enter into the text of the novel, but will inform the actions of those characters, the phrases of their creator; the doctor tracks the innumerable bits of information, sorts them, checks them, looks for something that will help move the story along."

Fiction also allows her to write the happy endings that don't always happen in real life. She explains this idea in her book, *Baby Doctor*: "In fiction, finally I am in control.... So when I turn away from the amoral workings of hospital stories, from the good who die young and the undeserving who flourish, I can allow myself the luxury of rewarding and punishing as I see fit. I can kill for the sake of pathos, or, greatest luxury of all, I can tell a story without a dying child in it, think for a while about a world in which there are other exigencies than fevers, labored breathing, and all the rest."

Klass finished the revisions to *Other Women's Children* just before her second child, Josephine, was born in 1989. "I had this joke with my editor that whichever came first, the baby or the manuscript, she would get it."

What she remembers about that summer, Klass says, "is that it was, physically, extremely difficult to sit still and write. It was difficult, first of all, because sitting was no longer comfortable, especially sitting hunched forward a little bit. Josephine was incredibly active—she did nothing but rhythmic kicking. And second of all, I couldn't sit as close to the computer as I wanted because I just didn't fit in between the chair and the computer anymore. It was July, and then August, and it was just horrible. We had this large armchair with carved arms that come up, and I put an ironing board across the arms of the armchair and put the keyboard on the ironing board. So at least I could comfortably sit back, cushioned, in this chair. It was a little bit more comfortable, but it wasn't very satisfactory.

"The other thing was that it was really hard to make myself write about someone who was not a nine-months-pregnant woman. I mean, I just could not imagine any other physical state for a while, and there I was trying to finish this whole novel I'd written about someone who wasn't even pregnant. What did I know about her, her feelings?" Klass rhetorically asks. She had been very busy for most of the pregnancy, and even with the novel to finish, Klass found the last few weeks went by slowly. "To suddenly find myself at home every morning, subtracting the number of days till the due date and waiting for the hours to pass, was somewhat torturous."

Klass found the periods following the births of both of her children good times for writing because she had a little more time for herself and was "very interested in what was going on in my own life and in the child and my own feelings." However, she says, "That first year, maybe even that first year and a half, maybe even that first two years with each kid, you are so tired. I know about tired—I did an internship, which was all about being sleep deprived. And it's still not like that chronic tiredness of taking care of little babies.

"My natural biorhythm would be to stay up and write until three or four in the morning, and then sleep until ten, eleven, or noon. It was one of the things I had going for me in my medical training, that I liked those late night hours. The hours from 10:00 P.M. to 3:00 or 4:00 A.M. aren't bad hours for me, they're good hours—I can get things done, I can think straight. And then in the morning when [the next shift] comes in and I try to explain what it is that I've done over the course of the night, I become incoherent. But on the whole, that's better for the patients than the other way around."

Klass still gets a burst of energy around nine or ten at night and uses that time to write. "But realistically, if you're going to get up before eight to get two kids to school, you can't actually sit up until three in the morning working, even if you have the energy—it's crazy.

"Someday when my children have all grown up and left the house and I've retired after a long and distinguished career in pediatrics, I'm going to sleep until noon every day. Probably when I'm elderly it will turn out that I no longer want to; you know, people's [biological] clocks do reset."

Her three-year-old daughter also loves the night hours, and is usually awake until midnight or 1:00 A.M. Klass puts her daughter to bed earlier than that, but Josephine sits in her crib singing and talking to herself. "She's very good-natured; I assume she has a rich fantasy life," Klass says. "But she doesn't go to sleep; she's just not tired." Although Klass likes to have time to herself to unwind after everyone else has gone to bed, she says, indulgently, "there's usually a little voice singing upstairs during those hours." As a transition ritual to help get her into the writing mode, she brews tea "in a pot I really don't use for anything else. By the third cup of tea, between the caffeine and the warmth and the quiet, I find I've switched over."

Writing "around the edges" of her life is a strategy that Klass says works well for journalism and short fiction but not for longer fiction. However, she adds, "I'm not sure exactly what the way to write a novel is. One of the disconcerting things about being home for a few months and not working as a doctor is that I find it hard to get started. I find it very easy to waste whole days and let time go by. Whereas when I had a few hours late at night, the sooner I could get it finished, the sooner I could go to bed, and I was up against a deadline, it was a lot easier to get started. That may just mean that that's what I'm cut out for. But it's not a good way to write long things, and there are limits on what you write under those circumstances and how well you write. And it may just be that I haven't yet learned how deal with those big blocks of time that are in my own control."

While some people make a fuss over her multiple roles, Klass rejects the superwoman label as sexist. In fact, while Klass finished medical school and her internship, her companion, Larry Wolff, took over the domestic front and the care of their first child. She has pointed out in print that no one has ever asked Wolff—who is a college professor, a published author, and a father—how he manages to do it all. She says, "What I think is funny is that even when we were in the situation where it was perfectly obvious that I was not around, that Larry was primarily raising the child for a couple of years, nobody ever thought it was evidence of unusual dedication or talent or skill."

The couple manage with little help outside the day-care center their daughter attends and the after-school program at their son's private school. "We're in our ninth year in the same day-care center," says Klass. "We're very dependent on day care." Although having someone come in to clean is one of their perennial New Year's resolutions, Klass says that so far their lives are "a little too chaotic" to schedule such help.

Klass and Wolff take turns watching the kids evenings and weekends so that the other can write. "But it's also nice to do things all together. You don't want to trade off exclusively." Klass describes the couple's current division of domestic labor as "both of us do as little as possible, and we're in constant competition to see who can do less. Which means that we live in a fairly chaotic and messy house, and the children are not quite having the kind of upbringing which might have been deemed in the 1950s to be essential to their future mental health."

Klass has a role model in her mother who was a college professor and author of at least ten books in addition to raising three children. When Klass was a child, her mother got up at five every morning so that she could write for two hours. "Of course, she also set the table for breakfast. She didn't have the kind of children who were trained to go stand on a chair and get the cold cereal down off the refrigerator themselves." Klass says that her mother also "believed that if she didn't cook everyone dinner every night—a hot dinner with a protein, a green vegetable, yellow vegetable, starch, some kind of fruit, and then dessert afterward—that that was basically child abuse, and that they would probably take her children away.

"And she may have been right. I do not remember in my entire childhood ever being allowed to have a TV dinner, even though we begged for them; ever getting pizza for dinner, even though it would have been a treat; ever getting take-out Chinese food. I don't remember my mother ever saying, 'How can I possibly cook tonight? Let's just get in the car and go out for dinner.' And she says so too, that it would have been unthinkable."

By contrast, Klass says, "My child knows every take-out menu in Cambridge by heart. He's extremely proficient with various things that you can pick up on the way to the house. It's a less rigorous way of raising children, I suppose."

Nor do the couple ferry their children around to lessons and other extracurricular activities. "It's not a conscious decision; it's sort of the opposite: it's an act of selfishness and laziness, I suppose. If you wanted to make raising children more of a full-time job, you could do many parts of it more thoroughly and with more enthusiasm than I do."

Weekends in this laissez-faire family are for hanging out together, lying around, and reading. (But not watching TV; the couple owns neither a television nor a VCR. "We're very low-tech," Klass says.)

"Occasionally, if I really feel impelled to do something creative, we will play CLUE, but one game is my limit and I feel extremely proud of myself for that. Things I like doing with my kids: I like cooking with them, I like shopping with them, I like doing things that you haven't invented purely to distract them. I'm better at that than I am at coming up with creative projects," says Klass, who knits for relaxation.

"But the idea of getting up at eight o'clock on a Saturday morning to take one child to some athletic practice and then to 'encourage creativity' lessons, I'm just not ready for it. Saturday mornings are when I sleep late and come downstairs in my pajamas. I suppose, to be fair, if I had a child who cared enough to find something like this [extracurricular activity] out and wanted to be part of it and it mattered, that would be fine, but I've never felt it had to come from me.

"Would I actually do those things if I never wrote another word? I don't know; it may just be that you're the kind of parent you are, and you do it on the level that you enjoy and that you feel is right and that works for you and your kids. It may be that if I had different kids with different personalities, life would be different too. There might be things that other children would need to make them happy."

Asked how her nine-year-old son reacts to her two careers, Klass says he's been to lectures and readings she's given and "he likes it when I tell stories about him." She dedicated *Other Women's Children* to him and "to my incredible delight, he brought it in for show-and-tell.

"I think that kids have a tendency to take what their particular parents do very much for granted. I think that if I were an international spy and the house were full of spying equipment and people were always slipping in the doorway and passing over microdots, that it would probably be a very long time before my son realized that everybody's parents weren't international spies, that everybody's houses weren't fitted out with radar screens. I think he thought for a very long time that all fathers were professors and all mothers were doctors."

Photo ©, Jill Posener

DOROTHY ALLISON

Dorothy Allison

In her fiction and nonfiction, Dorothy Allison, forty-five, writes with humor, pas-
sion, and unflinching honesty about family love and betrayal, sexuality and
violence, literature and class. A lesbian-feminist political activist, who has aroused
controversy with her explicit writings about sex, Allison says that her goal is to
construct fiction that will "literally remake the world."

Like the character Bone in her novel Bastard Out of Carolina, *Allison was*
born in Greenville, South Carolina, to an unwed fifteen-year-old waitress. She
grew up despised as "poor white trash" by the community and treated with con-
tempt by the stepfather who abused her physically and sexually. The first in her
family to attend college, Allison graduated from Florida Presbyterian College
with a bachelor's degree in anthropology in 1971 and went on to receive her
master's in anthropology from the New School for Social Research in 1987. She
is the author of four books: Trash *(1988), a collection of short stories that re-*
ceived two Lambda Literary Awards; The Women Who Hate Me: Poetry 1980–
1990 *(published in 1991);* Bastard Out of Carolina *(1992), her first novel, which*
was a finalist for the National Book Award; and a collection of essays entitled,
Skin: Talking About Sex, Class & Literature *(1994).*

Allison lives in northern California with her partner of six and a half years,
Alix Layman, and their two-year-old son, Wolf Michael Allison Layman.

DOROTHY ALLISON HAS SPENT MUCH OF HER ADULT LIFE TRY-
ing to come to terms with her childhood and the physical, sexual, and
emotional abuse she survived. Writing has been part of the process of
unraveling and revealing the truth of what happened to her as a child,
as well as of affirming her adult identity as a lesbian.

But rather than writing autobiography, she "crafts truth out of
storytelling," using her life as the raw material from which to construct her fiction. Whether she is writing about the world in which
she was raised, where her family was considered "poor white trash,"

or the lesbian community in which she has struggled to make a place for herself, Allison seeks to present the full humanity of those people whom society considers marginal.

While often tender and warm, Allison's work is neither pretty nor sentimental. Particularly in her writings about her childhood, Allison embraces the gritty reality of poverty and despair without neglecting the humor that keeps people sane and the fierce love that binds a family together. Glimpses of that world appear in about half of the short stories in Allison's first book, *Trash,* as well as in a few of the poems in her second book, *The Women Who Hate Me: Poetry 1980–1990.*

In her first novel, *Bastard Out of Carolina,* the author returns to the dirt yards and run-down houses of her native Greenville, South Carolina, to tell the harrowing story of Ruth Anne Boatwright, nicknamed "Bone." The bastard daughter of a fifteen-year-old white woman, Bone begins her life in the care of her maternal relatives, the close-knit, desperately poor, hard-working, hard-drinking Boatwright family. When Bone is five years old, her mother marries the ne'er-do-well son of the town's dairy owner, a man with a quick temper and big hands. Bone has no words for what happens to her: the fondling that begins in the hospital parking lot the night her mother miscarries, which escalates to brutal beatings and finally, rape. Nor can Bone reveal the truth to her mother, who loves her ardently but cannot protect her.

Although the novel is not strictly autobiographical, the outlines of Bone's story resemble the author's own childhood. As Allison writes in the essay, "A Question of Class," from her most recent book, *Skin: Talking About Sex, Class & Literature,* "When I was five, Mama married the man she lived with until she died. Within the first year of their marriage Mama miscarried, and while we waited out in the hospital parking lot, my stepfather molested me for the first time, something he continued to do until I was past thirteen. When I was eight or so, Mama took us away to a motel after my stepfather beat me so badly it caused a family scandal, but we returned after two weeks. Mama told me that she really had no choice: she could not support us alone."

In another essay, "Shotgun Strategies," Allison notes, "When I set out to write *Bastard Out of Carolina,* I wanted to do two things: to recreate the family that I deeply loved and was not saved by, and to put in print everything I understood that happens in a violent family where incest is taking place." Rather than focusing on the details of the abuse, she wanted to examine issues of family love, loss, and betrayal. In particular, she sought to understand and talk about her mother, "about the choices she was forced to make, the impossible grief of her struggle to create a family and care for her daughters."

In that essay, Allison writes that she has made a promise to herself to break the habit of lying that she learned as a child. Not only did the women in her family lie to themselves and to each other to preserve their sanity and keep their family intact, but the world lied to them "about the meaning of what was happening. The world told us that we were being spanked, not beaten, and that violent contempt for girl children was ordinary, nothing to complain about."

Just as Allison could not, at age eleven, tell her mother and aunts that she was being sexually abused, she could not tell them, at twenty-five, that because of that abuse she was unable to bear a child. "Would it have been 'the truth' to hold my aunts and my mama responsible for the venereal infection that was never treated when I knew how hard I had tried to hide my pain from them at the time?" she asks in the essay, "Skin, Where She Touches Me." In fact, Allison finally told her mother about her infertility by writing the short story, "Don't Tell Me You Don't Know," and giving it to her mother to read.

So when her partner, Alix Layman, told Allison, in the first year of their relationship, that she thought she wanted to have a child someday, "My response was bad. I had an enormous amount of anger about it and a kind of contempt that she could do something that would be difficult-to-impossible for me." When Allison last consulted a doctor on the subject, she was told that trying to have a biological child would "probably cost fifty thousand dollars, and the pregnancy very likely wouldn't come to term."

The issue did not really come up again until Layman was thirty-two years old, and she asked Allison to consider the idea one more time. "I don't think I could have done it with anyone else," the author says. "What's hateful and makes me really ashamed of myself is that I needed her to be able to say, 'If you don't want me to, I won't have children.' I needed to know absolutely that I was primary in her life.

That somebody loved me that much made it possible for me to get past some of the anger."

Writing *Bastard Out of Carolina* also helped Allison to release some of her rage, which she considered an essential prerequisite for becoming a mother. "I didn't want to bring a baby into the world and damage it."

Although Allison believed that she had resolved her feelings about motherhood, "once Alix became pregnant, an enormous range of things happened emotionally that I had not thought about or predicted or understood, and that I had a lot of trouble dealing with."

For example, Allison says, "Because of how I grew up and because of all of my complicated fears about children and babies and sex, one of the things that I was terrified of was that I would look at him and not love him—and that I would have to fake it." Allison was in the operating room when Wolf Michael Allison Layman was born by cesarean section in August 1992. She recalls that "Junior" looked like a "huge pink-and-white ball, and this ball unfolded like a flower. His legs and arms opened up and extended; his eyes opened up. I cried for two days because I just couldn't believe that I had looked at this baby and knew immediately that I loved him passionately."

Becoming a mother has helped Allison to continue the process of reclaiming her violated body, reawakening her ability to feel, not only physically but also emotionally. "When I was in my early twenties, I figured out that I had this huge robbery in my life, that I couldn't feel anything sexually," Allison says. With the help of therapy and physical awareness programs such as the Alexander technique, she was able to develop her capacity for sexual feeling and physical trust. But she ignored the emotional damage. "I also developed the attitude that having that emotional numbness was an advantage in the world, a source of protection that I could not afford to give up.

"It's curious how that relates to sex and yet doesn't," says Allison, who has written extensively and graphically about lesbian sex in such essays as "The Theory and Practice of the Strap-on Dildo" and "Her Body, Mine and His." While the controversial author says that she has been "extremely sexually active, almost promiscuous at times," Allison has only had two long-term intimate emotional relationships in her life.

The security and love Allison feels in her relationship with Layman and with their son have enabled her to relax on an emotional level, to let go of some of the fear she has carried inside herself since childhood. Toward the end of Layman's pregnancy, Allison experienced what she refers to as "an almost overwhelming body memory" in which she realized for the first time in her life "how fragile children are—and that meant how fragile I had been at one point. I had never thought of myself that way. I had this image of myself as this incredibly tough, strong little creature who had never been a child."

Allison recalls a conversation in which Alix said to her, "'It's as if he [Wolf] peeled your armor off, and you've got to learn to be in the world without that armor.'"

However, Allison had a "great deal of emotional difficulty" dealing with her newly acquired sense of fragility. She had to set aside the novel she was working on, Allison says, "because when I write, I have an ethic about facing really painful realities, and a lot of my work is concentrated on that. For the first six or seven months of Junior's life, I could not allow my imagination to consider anything dangerous.

"At the same time, I discovered a capacity for imagining a kind of peacefulness and joy that I don't think I had ever had. Up until the baby was six months old, I would rock him and sing to him, and there was something purely physically and emotionally satisfying about that. Better than sex—and I had never found anything better than sex. But when he was about six months old, he started putting his hand over my mouth," she says with a laugh, "so we had to stop the singing part."

During those early months of motherhood, Allison found herself wanting to write "saccharine, love-conquers-all stories, which I'm convinced came right out of his presence in my life. I wrote them in my journal and maybe a decade from now I'll publish them, but it all seemed to me to be really new and untrustworthy. My experiences with how real life affects writing is that there's a long lag time," says Allison, although her son did appear briefly in "Promises," the last essay in her collection. "He crept into it because I can't keep him out," Allison says.

Because she is fascinated by the emotional connections between people, especially those who consider themselves to be part of a family, whether biological or communal, Allison says she knows that she will eventually write more about her son, "but I don't want to write about him in any predictable or easy or saccharine way—and I can get pretty damn saccharine and romantic about my son," she says with a laugh.

Another surprising aspect of becoming a mother is the relationship that both Allison and Layman have formed with their son's biological father, whom they refer to as "the daddy donor." Having never known her own father and wanting to spare her son that painful experience, Allison insisted that the man who fathered their child had to be willing to be a presence in his life. Although he agreed to this condition, "he just couldn't say how much that would be. I think that originally his intention was to have it be very, very minimal," like sending an annual Christmas card, Allison says.

But instead, "We found ourselves becoming more and more of a family with him in a kind of nonlegal, terribly close and caring way," Allison says. "Junior calls him Daddy, and he's always excited to see him," when he comes up every two or three weeks to spend the weekend. Allison attributes this closeness in part to their son's loving nature and in part to the death from AIDS of the man's lover, who was also a close friend of Allison's.

While she wanted her child to know his father, Allison also wanted to make sure that neither he nor his family would try to stake a claim on Wolf, whom Allison is now in the process of legally adopting. She has to go through the same exhausting investigation as any heterosexual, but with the prior knowledge that Social Services "will not approve a lesbian adoption.

"They turn you down but you get a report that says if you were not a lesbian, they would have approved you. And then you have to do the whole thing over again." After undergoing a second investigation and being turned down a second time solely because of her sexual preference, a lesbian can go to court. "And the judge will hopefully approve the adoption because discrimination is illegal in the state of California."

But while the California adoption process is "insulting" as well as expensive, Allison says, "It's an enormous advantage over what I'm watching friends go through on the East Coast, who don't have the legal precedents that we have in California."

This discrepancy in state adoption laws affects Allison directly, limiting her career options. Although the community in which they live is "extremely queer friendly," in this rural area of northern California, there are no teaching jobs, which are "one of the main sources of income for writers," Allison says. She has been invited to teach in South Carolina, but Allison can't imagine accepting a position in her native state because "the legislature there just ruled that it's illegal for queers to adopt children. I will stay in this area and keep my child safe."

The couple have organized their lives to need as little money as possible. Layman is a full-time college student who also works part time. Allison's primary source of income now comes from speaking engagements at universities. For the first seven months of Wolf's life, he accompanied Allison when she traveled. "He loved it," Allison says, but "it was physically a little daunting carrying a baby around the country." When they decided that he would stay home, Allison likewise cut down on both the number of trips she took and their duration.

When she is home, Allison has trouble limiting her writing to the hours when Layman and Wolf are out of the house. "I'm a binge worker, which means that when I start really cooking on a story, my long-term practice was to basically close the curtains and disappear, working for three or four days straight, taking catnaps. That stopped pretty much with the birth of my son, and we're still working out the whole response to that," Allison says.

"Sometimes in the early afternoon, I'll realize that I'm really cooking and I'll move in to the cottage, which is the office outside the house. I'll just leave a sign up that says I'm out back, so when Alix comes home with the baby, which is usually around six o'clock, she'll see the sign up and leave me alone."

Their son, however, is not so willing to let Allison work in peace. "Usually Junior comes and beats on the door. He'll come in and demand, 'What's that? What's doing?' and he'll beat on the computer keys a little bit. I've got to play with him for ten, fifteen minutes before he'll decide to let me go again. It's real hard to get back to work after he comes in," Allison admits.

"For the first time in my life I am seriously considering going to a writer's colony, something I have never approved of for myself. But I'm beginning to think it might just be vital to finishing this book," she says, referring to her novel-in-progress.

By getting up "ferociously early," Allison is able to work for about three hours before the rest of the family awakens. "But it means I'm getting sick a lot. I just don't get enough rest," says Allison, who recently suffered her third bout of pneumonia in three years. Their son started going to day care, "earlier than Alix would have liked," so that Allison could get some work done. But because Allison has chronic bronchitis and a weakened immune system, the little colds Wolf brings home threaten her health.

"A doctor finally pointed out to me that one of the main reasons that I continually get sick is how I treat myself. This binge system that I learned as a writer is also how I live my life. For years, I would literally work sixteen hours a day—no time for rest, no vacations," Allison says. In addition to working full time at various jobs, Allison devoted evenings and weekends to political activities such as editing and grant-writing for feminist journals, squeezing her own writing into whatever time she had left. "Every year or so, I would collapse."

Now that she is a mother, Allison says, "I can't afford to collapse. I no longer have permission to do that because if I can't take care of him, then it falls on Alix, and if she gets sick, there's nobody to take care of Junior."

Although Allison feels more at ease with herself and more accepting of her physical limitations, she adds, "for me, nothing about the body is casual and easy the way it can be for Alix." For example, one time when she was bathing Wolf, "he suddenly grabbed his pee-pee and was waving it, taking an enormous interest in it [and asking], 'What's that?' I went into a total panic; I had to run and get Alix. What are we going to tell him about genitals? What are we going to call them? And she said, 'Oh, well, we'll tell him it's his penis.' So I went back and I explained to him that it was his penis, and then I got him out of the bath and got him dressed and he was on to something else. And I went off and threw up."

Similarly, when he has suddenly shown an interest in her body,

Allison says that she would "seize up in this state of absolute terror. I was afraid that I had been taught so many horrible things about the body and sex that somehow I would pass them on to him." Unable to think about the subject rationally in those moments, Allison would turn the situation over to Layman, "watching her and following the emotional tone that she sets. For her, it's no big deal.

"One of the main reasons that it took me so long to decide to have a child was [that] I was afraid that I would be an abuser." Allison worried that she would hit or slap, as she had seen one of her sisters do to her children. "I was terrified that when I would get tired, especially, that I would react with violence. What I discovered is that that's not what happens to me. When I'm really tired and not able to think, I freeze," Allison says.

Although for the first year of Wolf's life Allison couldn't imagine scolding him, she is now the disciplinarian. "I'm the person who sets the rules and the limits." In the family she grew up in, Allison saw an "alternation between abuse and no boundaries. I watched some of my cousins lose their lives in that struggle because they didn't know what was right or wrong or good or bad."

Having a child has helped Allison improve her relationship with her two sisters, both of whom became mothers in their teens and never finished high school. "There's never been any question in my family but that my mother loved me enormously and that in some ways she was almost estranged from her other daughters." In turn, Allison was, for most of her childhood, "deeply estranged" from her sisters. While "there was at least a decade where we viciously hated each other," over the past five years, the three women have slowly become more comfortable with each other.

"When I told them that Alix and I were having a child, it changed my relationship with them enormously. It was the first time in my life that they decided that I was like them, the first time I did something they knew more about than I knew. My little sister June actually came and spent two weeks with us when Junior was about three weeks old to make sure we knew what we were doing," Allison says with a laugh, adding, "She also rewired the electricity."

Although the couple had discussed having more children, Wolf will probably be their only one. Layman had a severe case of gestational diabetes and was told that if she were to develop the disease during a second pregnancy, she might be diabetic for life. Nor are they sure that they can afford another child, Allison says. "I grew up very poor, and I am terrified of poverty and of not being able to take care of my family."

The pressure to have another child has eased up because they have become part of a network of other lesbian mothers and single mothers, "so Junior has a number of other children that he's close to, almost like older siblings. Although I have to tell you that when he put his hand over my mouth and wouldn't let me sing anymore, I had this deep longing to have another one," says Allison.

At the same time as her personal life was transformed by motherhood, Allison experienced a parallel change in her professional life when her first novel was published four months after the birth of her son.

While finishing the book had given Allison a sense of "completion, healing, confidence," she was jolted by the public response to her work. "I was prepared to be ignored or assaulted; I was not prepared to be appreciated. I was not prepared for the enormous numbers of letters, really loving but painful letters, from people who essentially felt like I had given them a piece of my life, and they tried to give me a piece of theirs back."

Nor was Allison prepared for the critical acclaim she received from reviewers such as George Garrett, who wrote in the *New York Times Book Review,* "Please reserve a seat of honor at the high table of the art of fiction for Dorothy Allison."

The author says, "All of a sudden, I've gotten a great deal more recognition and approval than I've ever had before in my life. And it has triggered in me a painful sense of alienation and fear that I'm only beginning to look at. I'm having to consciously resist a kind of vicious defensiveness. It's very, very difficult to change that inoculation of despisal. I was taught that I was contemptible; I was taught to expect hatred."

Allison recalls the words of a therapist she consulted about the time her novel was released. "She said to me, 'Just keep thinking that all your life you have been leaning into a wind that suddenly isn't blowing on you. In fact, you have a whole new wind coming from a different direction, and you have to figure out how to stand up in it.' Junior's part of the wind," Allison says, "He's a real warm, sweet wind. But I'm still kind of tipping over now and again."

Photo ©, Courtney Winston

SARAH CHARLESWORTH

Sarah Charlesworth

Artist Sarah Charlesworth, forty-five, is concerned with visual language, with the meanings we read into the images that surround us. Influenced by conceptualism and deconstruction, Charlesworth uses carefully researched images, such as Aladdin's magic lamp, a Renaissance angel, or a lotus blossom, isolated and out of context, to challenge our traditional assumptions and interpretations about the world.

Since graduating from Barnard in 1969 with a BA in art history, Charlesworth has received three National Endowment for the Arts grants. Her work is in the collections of the Victoria and Albert Museum in London, the Smithsonian Institute's National Museum of American Art, the Museum of Modern Art in New York, and the Los Angeles County Museum of Art, among other institutions.

Married for eight years to filmmaker Amos Poe, Charlesworth lives in New York City and has two children, seven-year-old Nick and three-year-old Liz.

SARAH CHARLESWORTH'S PHOTO-COLLAGE *ASSUMPTION*, ONE of the most visually compelling pieces in her 1992 exhibition, "Renaissance Drawings and Paintings," exemplifies the way in which this intellectual artist plays with words and ideas. To create this collage, Charlesworth used color reproductions of Renaissance paintings as her raw materials, cutting out selected portions and rearranging them on a plain background. She then photographed the collage and laminated the resulting Cibachrome print onto a wooden board, giving the piece a luminous finish characteristic of her work.

In *Assumption*, the central figure of the Virgin Mary is seen only as a silhouette against a black background, outlined on either side by the outstretched hands of a column of five Renaissance angels, dressed in sumptuous gowns with wings of gold, green, white, and brown. To the left, one angel playing a harp is positioned slightly above the others, breaking the symmetry.

Charlesworth describes the main theme of *Assumption* as the desire for a smooth transition at the time of death. The title, she says, plays on both the dogma that Jesus's mother was "assumed" into heaven and the doctrinal "assumption" that "one will be uplifted by angels and enter the pearly gates at the time of death"—the assumption that there is, in fact, an afterlife.

By manipulating such Renaissance religious iconography, the artist seeks to explore modern psychological archetypes. Just as a psychologist analyzes past familial relationships to understand the patient's current state of mind, Charlesworth says she used the Renaissance as a shared point of memory, "part of the family life of contemporary culture." But these collages have a personal, emotional content as well: they are expressions of the artist's own struggles to deal with such concepts as separation, fear of death and the unknown, male and female sexuality, and family relationships.

Asked how her art has changed since becoming a mother, Charlesworth says, "I've always had a little difficulty giving a clear answer to that because I feel like my work has changed throughout my career. I've been working publicly as an artist for fourteen years—and that doesn't include all the time that I was a struggling unknown artist who didn't exhibit. And during the course of fourteen years, I have matured as a human being and as a woman. There have been a number of factors, both personal and political, that have had a bearing on changes in my work." Having children is only one of those factors, she says. Although she has done pieces, such as her 1989 *Self Portrait,* with a maternal theme, that subject is not her primary focus.

"As an artist I'm concerned with a broad range of experience. I deal and have dealt with a number of different aspects of my life or my experience; motherhood, sexuality, and gender issues are part of that. It's not that they're ever excluded from my sphere of interest; it's just that they've never become a sole, concentrated interest to the exclusion of other things.

"The strongest effect of having children is in terms of the practicality of managing my life," says Charlesworth. "On that level, it's absolutely affected everything about the way I work and the way I think and the way I organize my time. I didn't have my first child until I was thirty-eight years old, and one of the reasons that I didn't even consider having children when I was younger was because I was very committed to my artwork. By the time I was thirty-eight years old, I had a somewhat established career. I had galleries representing me and had a market for my work. I felt if I took a few weeks off and didn't call up my life, my life would still call me up.

"I think if I had been twenty-five years old and had a child, it would have just completely thrown me for a loop for a few years. As it was, it was a complete shock—and I've heard other women say this—the enormous impact of having a young child, an infant, and adjusting to the incredible changes that that entails. I think the intensity of that experience is something that no one could even imagine unless they went through [it]."

Despite that intensity, she says that she cannot claim the experience has made her "a person with a greater heart or more humanity. Perhaps that's true, but I notice it more in terms of a natural process of maturing. Becoming more thoughtful, I'm more interested in issues of the unconscious—not only with explicit political issues, but perhaps more spiritual things—than I would have been at twenty-five or thirty years old. But I don't think that has necessarily only to do with having children."

When her first child was born, Charlesworth worked at home but found she could only concentrate while the baby was out at the park with the baby-sitter or when he was sleeping. "It required juggling not only actual time but also the way in which I directed even my thoughts, my mental space. It was sort of like, 'Whew, he's asleep. I can think my own thoughts for three hours.'"

It was when she became pregnant with her second child that Charlesworth decided she had to get an outside studio. "During my pregnancy, I went searching for a studio, contracted a studio, renovated a studio, moved—at the same time I was getting ready for an upcoming show. It was a nightmarish experience. I felt, emotionally, I couldn't cancel a show that I had already committed to [just] because I was pregnant; on the other hand, I felt like I wasn't going to be able to concentrate working at home, and the pressure to get my setup organized before the birth became enormous."

But she did manage to move, albeit in her eighth month, into her new studio a few blocks from home. She recalls a moment a few months later when she was sitting in the studio, "doing what I always do, staring at pieces of paper I'd pushpinned to the wall and rearranging images, and nursing the baby at the same time, so I was literally nursing and working at the same moment. And I felt so completely fulfilled and happy and like I had the best of both worlds."

Above and beyond the pressures of show deadlines and such exigencies as moving, both of her pregnancies were "extremely difficult work periods," she says. "It wasn't so much from a purely physical point of view; it was more how the physicality of pregnancy affected my mental state. Being an artist involves a great deal of projection: it's taking yourself and your views and your opinions and your emotions and casting them out into form. And I felt that a lot of what was going on biologically in terms of the pregnancy was a kind of turning inward of energy; it was a very internal experience. I found I felt very conflicted in terms of my energy." She explains that while a portion of her energy was wrapping around her and turning inward, at the same time, "another part, the part of me that was wanting to get the show ready and get on with the work, was wanting to cast out.

"The work I generated during the time of my first pregnancy, I consider relatively weak in terms of the overall body of my work," Charlesworth says. During her second pregnancy, on the other hand, she attempted to accept and describe "the internalized process," to use it as a starting point for her work.

In that series of photo-collages, called "An Academy of Secrets," Charlesworth says, "Even though all the artworks do not deal specifically with pregnancy, the pregnancy—the womb-like state, the internal psychology—enters all the works," directly or indirectly. *Self Portrait,* together with *Of Myself* (also completed in 1989), is one of her few works explicitly about pregnancy. At the center of *Self Portrait* is a giant Classical Greek or Roman urn supported by three little feet. "Arrayed over the top of the urn in an arc were a hand, an eye, and a breast, artifacts *ex-voti* or something, and down below, a foot and an ear, forming the shape of a human body. But the urn is just giant in the middle, and the appendages are just floating out there. I felt like this giant thing, and while I was collaging, I could barely move my hands to cut paper and glue. I felt so much like this thing, with my eyes and my hands and my feet way out on the outskirts of things. So I was attempting to actually make an image of my physical/mental state."

Now that both of her children are in school—her son is finishing first grade and her daughter goes to nursery school—everyone is up and out of the house by eight-thirty and Charlesworth gets to the studio within an hour. The baby-sitter arrives in the early afternoon, does housework and errands for two or two and a half hours before picking the kids up from school, and stays until 6:00 P.M.

The family has had a baby-sitter more or less full time since their first child was four or five months old. Charlesworth says, "I found that to be one of the best investments I ever made in my life." Economically, though, it has been a struggle to maintain a baby-sitter and, now that the children are in school, Charlesworth says she's always on the verge of deciding she can get by with less help. "I probably could make do with somebody really just a few hours a day to pick them up from school, but I keep thinking I really would not be able to keep pace with my work as much as I'd like to if I were to undertake doing all the laundry and the housekeeping and what have you."

The fact that she makes a living from her art helps her to justify the expense. In the beginning she tried to do it all: the housework, the child care, and her art. "After my son was born, I was trying to take care of him and continue to work, and I wasn't getting any work done at all and was feeling completely snowed under with all the responsibilities of a newborn baby. I finally realized that actually, at that point in my career, I could make more money by hiring a baby-sitter and going to the studio, even though at that time the amount it cost to hire a baby-sitter just sounded astronomical."

As a new mother, Charlesworth also "began to feel that I was losing myself in diapers and nursing. I felt I was actually in a position to enjoy being with my children more when I had some time to myself and could pursue my own work and not feel that it was an either-or question."

Asked about the division of domestic labor between her and her husband of eight years, Charlesworth says, laughing. "Well, basically, when it comes to economics, we split everything fifty-fifty and then I do all the child care, except the part the baby-sitter does. In my opinion, I still do a vast majority of the household work and organization. I do all the cooking and a great majority of the shopping and organizing doctor appointments and birthday parties. Even though it doesn't seem fair to me, I've never been able to pass this on to him."

Charlesworth says that her husband loves spending time with their children. "He's very good about being willing to baby-sit. But he has no capability in terms of running the household or shopping or keeping things under control while he's baby-sitting. I'm constantly going home to find, you know, my son has made a magic potion and poured it in my bed, or my daughter has dragged her dollhouse across the floor and scratched up the newly sanded floors. Things don't stay so well under control when I'm not there," she says with a laugh.

Both Charlesworth and her husband plan to be home at 6:00 P.M. when the baby-sitter leaves. "That way, we're planning to have a regular family dinner and a quiet night at home, and if either one of us is tied up with our work, then we always have the option of calling the other and saying, 'Listen, can you carry on while I continue finishing up on something that I'm in the middle of?'

"But I also plan to pace myself into a schedule where I expect to go home. I don't like to not see them those few hours in the evening. Usually by the time six o'clock rolls around, I'm looking forward to going home and playing Mom for a few hours. By the end of two hours of that, I can't wait to get in bed and go back to my musings.

"Once I get the kids in bed, I do have a few hours before I go to sleep, which is time that I do more contemplative work: just daydreaming, reading, thinking about things, doing drawings for projects."

Asked if it is difficult to switch her creativity on when she arrives in the studio and off when she goes home at night, Charlesworth says, "I've lost the ability to just go with the flow that I used to have, to sleep as late in the morning as I wanted and do whatever I wanted with my daytime, and suddenly wake up in the middle of the night and say, 'Oh, I know what I wanted to do about that,' and go into the studio.

"On the other hand, I can remember, before I had children, being in this constant state of low-level anxiety that I really should be doing something. No matter whether it was Sunday afternoon or the middle of the night, I always had this, 'I should be working' feeling. Now I feel that my time is more clearly bifurcated." Since moving her studio out of the house, she limits her art endeavors while at home to "quiet thinking, brainstorming, and reading," and then, during the workday, does absolutely no housework. "There's a certain pleasure in that, in knowing that when I come to the studio, I don't have to worry about doing the laundry and the cooking.

"I still have the feeling that I never know when inspiration itself is going to take hold, or when an idea is going to gel for me, and I'm still dependent on whatever complex circumstances bring that about. I mean, I can't just sit down and say, 'Well, now I think I'll think of a good idea.' Good ideas come by immersing myself in the problem and throwing it around in different ways and trying out different things.

"I also design my days to be different types of days. If I know I have a meeting or two during the day, I'm apt to decide that that'll be the day that I do these three errands and sort the file and write the letter. And if I have a wide-open day, and perhaps a wide-open day where I've made arrangements with my husband to work late in the evening, I'll allocate that day for brainstorming, and that day I'll play with my images, play with my ideas, and try to invite inspiration or decision."

Although at this point in her career she no longer needs to make the rounds of galleries to drum up business, Charlesworth says, "There's no doubt that I would have more time to spend on my work if I didn't have children. I would definitely be having more dinners with collectors or dealers from out-of-town or with other artists or going out to meetings in the evenings: the schmooze level of promoting. I don't have as much time to go out and socialize and build contacts on that level. That's one thing that I notice: the night life of an artist that I used to have—sitting around bars and talking art theory all night—that doesn't go on anymore. Nightlife has been something that's sacrificed. I go out once or twice a week, but nowhere near as much as I used to."

Many of the friends whom she would otherwise be seeing are

similarly trying to juggle young children and art. "I think that as my kids get older, they become my closest friends or my strongest human contact. I even show my artwork as it's developing frequently to my son. 'What do you think of this? How do you like this picture?' I like his feedback."

Pointing out that her husband is also in a creative profession, filmmaking, Charlesworth says their involvement in art has affected her children positively. "My son is extremely creative and imaginative himself: he draws beautifully, he builds things, he writes scripts, he does woodworking. My daughter has a different personality: she's very social, and her creativity is expressed more in terms of her personality. She likes to engage people, and she's a storyteller like my husband— she spins yarns and performs to a large extent. She's not as interested in traditional art projects, at least not at this age.

"I think the pleasure of creativity is something that I've been able to share with my children ever since their infancy." Charlesworth was so eager to share that joy, she remembers, that she pinned collections of pictures of babies or baby animals onto her son's bassinet when he was only weeks old and made an alphabet book for him long before he was ready to start learning the letters. "I just couldn't wait—he must have been about one when I ran out and bought the first set of finger paints."

That playful attitude toward art is particularly evident in the photographs Charlesworth created for her 1993 "Natural Magic" exhibition. Bent forks and spoons float in space in *Proof of Telekinesis*, while in *Materialization*, yellow smoke pours out from an Aladdin's lamp, suspended in midair.

With their round or oval black backgrounds, vivid-colored foregrounds, simple shapes, and lustrous textures, these humorous photographs have an arresting quality typical of the artist's work.

In the introductory note to the "Natural Magic" show, Charlesworth writes, "At once a poet's denial of the authority of reason, and a humorous philosophical discourse of the assumed veracity of photography, these original photographs explore the boundaries of conventional logic." By conjuring images such as these, Charlesworth challenges us to rethink established truths and to see the world anew.

Photo ©, Joel Glanzberg

ROXANNE SWENTZELL

Roxanne Swentzell

*Clay is in Roxanne Swentzell's blood. "I'm a mud person," she quips. On her
mother's side, Swentzell was born into a family of potters and a tribe famed for
ceramics, the Santa Clara Pueblo Indians, and so it was only natural that she
grew up playing with clay. Now thirty-one years old, Swentzell continues to
spend her days surrounded by clay. Using the coil-and-scrape technique usually
associated with pots, Swentzell creates people: small, squat figures, a foot or two
in height, of men, women, and children, alone or in family groupings, with faces
so expressive as to look uncannily alive even within a glass case at the Heard Art
Museum in Phoenix, Arizona.*

*She was born and raised in Santa Fe, New Mexico, where her European-
American father, Ralph Swentzell, teaches at Saint John's College, but frequently
traveled to the Santa Clara Pueblo reservation to attend ceremonies and visit
her maternal relatives. Educated at the Institute of American Indian Arts in Santa
Fe and the Portland Museum Art School, Swentzell has won a number of first
place awards in the Santa Fe Indian Market, a major venue for Native American
artists, and is represented by several galleries, including Studio 53 in Manhattan.*

*Although she has made a living from her art since the age of seventeen,
Swentzell has eschewed the high-powered art career path. Instead, she has chosen to lead a simpler, more integrated life on the Santa Clara Pueblo reservation
in New Mexico with her husband, Joel Glanzberg, and two children, ten-year-
old Porter and nine-year-old Rose.*

ROXANNE SWENTZELL VALUES RELATIONSHIPS: BETWEEN
herself and the earth, between her work and her family. That sense of
connection, Swentzell says, "is why having children isn't a matter of
having time for them set aside and my work having a time set aside.
It's all mingled together."

Her philosophy of everything being interrelated is, she says, "a
very Indian view," which she shares with her mother, Rina Swentzell,

and her mother's sister, Nora Naranjo-Morse, both of whom are also ceramic artists. "The way we see the world is that it is connected, and the more connections you have to all of it, the bigger and fuller you become as a person."

One of Roxanne Swentzell's best-known sculptures, *The Emergence of Clowns* (1988), illustrates this sense of connection with the earth. The piece is based on the religious myth of the Santa Clara Pueblo in which four black-and-white striped sacred clowns, called *koshares,* emerge from the earth. According to the tribe's creation story, the clowns, who symbolize the four directions, led the people from the underworld through the earth's navel into their present home in the middle world.

The four figures in Swentzell's piece seem to represent the process of awakening, ranging from a sleepy clown lying down with only his head raised, to a kneeling figure who is almost ready to stand. Although the figures are not life-sized, the tallest being about twenty-three inches high, their gentle, comic faces appear startlingly realistic.

Swentzell, whose mother is a tribal elder of the Santa Clara Indians, explains that Pueblo culture honors both the male and the female. "The whole Pueblo world was concerned with keeping things in balance: keeping themselves in balance with nature, keeping themselves in balance with their female and male sides. If you were a man and you were called a mother or a woman, you were being told something very good about yourself. You were a whole person, you were a much bigger person than just a man.

"They really honored the female. The earth, being the mother, was continuously being remembered in the dances, in the kivas, in the ceremonies. The clowns come out of the mother, the earth; they were the first into this level of the world. That sculpture was trying to get people to remember: we're from this earth, we are creatures of this earth, she is our mother. Remember where you come from. She is the one who gives you life, and if you destroy her, then you destroy yourself." The Western cultural concept of "being independent and separate from things," Swentzell adds, "is very unlike Pueblo culture, where what makes you strong is your connections and your interdependence."

The Emergence of Clowns was shown in the Heard Museum's exhibition, "Shared Visions: Native American Painters and Sculptors in the Twentieth Century." While related to the traditional storyteller figures made by the Cochiti Pueblo people, Swentzell's work is also part of the Native American Fine Arts Movement. This revitalization of Native American visual arts is rooted in folk art but often has a more political content and is created by artists trained in modern as well as traditional techniques.

Describing the Native American Fine Arts Movement in the "Shared Visions" exhibition catalog, Dr. Rennard Strickland and Margaret Archuleta of the Heard Museum write: "Twentieth century Indian art is about survival—the survival of the spirit. In a way, this art was the counterbalance to the federal effort to destroy all that was Indian. The Indian artist knows the lesson of building and rebuilding a civilization, of adapting, of changing and yet of remaining true to certain basic values regardless of the nature of change. At the heart of those values is an understanding and appreciation of the timeless—of family, of tribe, of friends, of place, and of season."

One of Swentzell's earliest influences was her maternal uncle, Michael Naranjo, who became a sculptor after being blinded in Vietnam. She recalls an evening at her uncle's when she was about six years old: "He went into his work area, and he said I could play with some clay. The door was shut, there was no lightbulb in the room, and it had no windows. It was pitch black. It made me realize the world he was living in and probably deepened my feelings of how you express things through clay."

Her parents returned to find the two of them sitting in the dark, sculpting. "He was teaching her to see with her heart, not with her eyes," says Swentzell's dealer, Ellen Silverberg of Studio 53.

A shy child, Swentzell found she could express her emotions in clay. "If I was depressed, I would make these figures depressed, or if I was upset about something, I would make these little figures being upset."

At the age of sixteen, Swentzell was accepted into the Institute of American Indian Arts in Santa Fe where she studied for the next two years. She then moved to Oregon to attend the Portland Museum Art School, but left in frustration after a year. She felt that the students and faculty focused on technique "to the point where they stopped seeing the world around them. I felt like my surroundings and what was happening around me were so very important to what I was making, that to block that out would make art for art's sake or empty art. I always think of it as just masturbating over art. There's no depth, there's no meaning. I got really disgusted at that.

"The funny thing is that when I was leaving art school, everyone was saying, 'Rox, you're going to get behind; we're going to beat you, we're going to win.' [As] if there was some kind of competition, that you're supposed to get a degree, and if you don't go along with the program, you're going to be left out. I was still going to make my stuff, but I needed to be in a place where what was around me mattered. I came home and I had children and I continued [making art]."

Her son's father left her when Porter was born. "He just disappeared," Swentzell says. Soon after that, she married her daughter's father, but the couple divorced after two years. When she moved to the site of her present home, Swentzell says, "There was nothing here except a little old shed that didn't have a roof on it. I had two babies in diapers and no husband. I lived in the shed and that's where I worked. I made enough money [from selling her work] to fix the shed up and start building a house." It was while building her house that Swentzell met Joel Glanzberg, her present husband, who works as a consultant in the field of permaculture, a system of agriculture that emphasizes the use of renewable natural resources.

"My working area has been my living area for a long time. And since the house was built, the shed that was our house has become my studio. But when it gets cold, I'll just move into the kitchen."

Her work methods are well suited to family life. "I'll put some clay down, and I'll work on that for a while. Then it needs to dry some, so I'll go off and we'll make lunch and eat or do something else. Then I'll go back and work on my piece for an hour more, and then I have to stop again. I can go wash clothes or do work outside and then I'll go back." Swentzell says of her art, "It is just mixed in with everything else I'm doing."

Swentzell admits, "Before I have a show, it sometimes gets pretty hectic where I'll be doing nothing but sculpting just to get some things done if I've procrastinated enough. I don't like those times at all; I don't like it when I'm forced into a corner.

"There are times when I really enjoy just getting into the work, and that's how I want it to be all the time. Those times I don't like being interrupted, but it's not like I'm totally involved for days on end. I may be totally involved for maybe two, three hours, and then I'm ready to go water my plants or something. Maybe I don't need to have [the art] be so consuming; there are other things in life I enjoy."

Swentzell and her husband are teaching Rose and Porter at home rather than sending them to school. Consequently, "the kids are here all the time," the artist says. "I think they think every mom sculpts.

"They've never gotten in my way," she adds. While Swentzell is working, her children can "walk up to me and ask questions, and even if I'm involved in it, I can certainly turn and answer them, or they can come up and hug me, or I can throw some clay at them. And if something is really pressing, then I can always stop."

Rose shows signs of following the family tradition. "My daughter loves to get her hands into things, and a lot of times she'll want to help me make my sculptures. She'll stand there, and I'll turn around to get some more clay and she's changed it while my head was turned," Swentzell says with a laugh. "I'll tell her to go make her own."

Swentzell prefers the coil-and-scrape method she learned as a child, although she has tried other ways of working with clay. She rolls the clay into snake-like coils, then winds the coils into concentric rings, building the piece in a spiraling motion. She then scrapes the piece to smooth out the ridges.

Painted in earth tones, Swentzell's figures appear heavy but are actually lightweight, being hollow inside. Their fragility can be a drawback in selling the work to collectors. "I think some people get nervous because it's clay. They think, 'Oh, it will break.' I laugh because sometimes I'll break them just to fit them into the kiln, and then I'll glue them back together afterward."

Swentzell is reluctant to use bronze or stone because of the very permanency of those materials. "My pieces, if they break, are like pottery shards, and that's okay with me." She says that some people think that ceramic work that can break or dissolve so easily is not worth as much as a piece cast in bronze or carved from stone. She believes art should be valued according to what the artist has expressed, not in terms of the material used. "If you don't like what is being expressed, you shouldn't have the piece at all," she says. "There's that whole mentality that everything has to stay the way it is instead of letting it be affected by its surroundings. Maybe the piece wanted to die. It's hard to die if you're bronze," she says with a laugh.

Her work is still a vehicle for communicating her emotions, Swentzell says. "I haven't grown up. I think that language goes so far and then another aspect has to take over, and I think that is the feeling world. If I can make those [emotions] clear, so that other people can see them and go, 'Ah-ha!' because they can relate it to their own selves, then we have another kind of communication that goes much deeper than words. It becomes a way of helping us feel that we are not so alone in the world and that we are okay inside."

Swentzell has found that no matter what she plans to make, the piece will reflect her moods. If her sculptures were all put in chronological order, she says, "You could probably tell when I was very depressed and when I was happy or what part of my life was a struggle and what part of my life was easy.

"I remember one day I was working on this piece that I had had in my mind for days. It was going to be a cheery figure. Days went by and I had gotten really depressed. I was trying desperately to put a smile on this sculpture, and it wasn't working. I finally managed to put a smile on it and then I stood back. I couldn't help but crack up—the smile was so forced and it looked so sad and depressed. I thought, 'What are you trying to do, Rox? You're trying to force something to happen that is not true to itself.'"

That struggle for authenticity can also be seen as "a search for the true self. I feel that what's happening with the Indians and what's happened to most cultures of the world is that they've lost a sense of themselves. My whole thing is trying to remember who we are, way inside, so that we can start being human beings again." Instead of seeing ourselves in terms of what we do, such as banker, carpenter, or artist, Swentzell wants us to recapture what she calls the "original self."

A connection to nature is part of that original self, Swentzell says.

"Nature is what we should be aligned with, and the way society is now, everyone is pulling away from nature. Even if they're deciding in their head to go back to nature, it's still ideals of going back to nature, it's not going back to our base self that will allow us to be connected to nature again. We are animals of this earth and we need to remember that. This is our mommy."

Photo ©, Joyce Ravid

MARY GORDON

Mary Gordon

Mary Gordon, forty-three, explores the concepts of love and duty—filial, mater-
nal, and spousal—and the limits of familial obligations in her fiction and es-
says. She is the author of four novels, including: Final Payments *(1978),*
nominated for the National Book Critics Circle Award; The Company of Women
(1981); Men and Angels *(1985); and* The Other Side *(1989). Gordon has also*
published a short story collection, Temporary Shelter *(1987), a book of essays,*
Good Boys and Dead Girls *(1991), and a collection of three novellas,* The Rest
of Life *(1993).*

Gordon was born on December 8, 1949, in Far Rockaway, New York. Her
father, David Gordon, a writer and publisher who converted from Judaism to
Catholicism, died when she was eight years old. Gordon grew up in the New
York City area, attending parochial schools in Long Island and Queens. She
graduated from Barnard College with a BA in 1971; two years later, she com-
pleted her master's in the Writing Program at Syracuse University. Gordon has
taught at Dutchess Community College in New York and Amherst College in
Massachusetts; she is now McIntosh Professor of English at Barnard College.

In 1979, Gordon married her second husband, Arthur Cash, who is an En-
glish professor at the State University of New York in New Paltz and literary
biographer of Laurence Sterne. Gordon lives in Manhattan with Cash and their
two children, twelve-year-old Anna and nine-year-old David.

"MY CHILDREN ARE THE GREATEST PASSION OF MY LIFE AND
nothing gives me the joy and intensity of feeling and pleasure that
they do," says Mary Gordon. "And, of course, nothing calls up one's
fears or rages more, either. But I would never *not* have children, never;
it would be almost half a life for me. On the other hand, I would never
not write. That would be half a life too, so it doesn't seem to me to be
an either-or [choice]."

Gordon had already published one novel, *Final Payments*, before becoming a mother; her second novel, *The Company of Women,* came out when her daughter Anna was an infant. "Oddly enough, when they were littler, it was not so much of a conflict. When they were both about four months, I sent them to a baby-sitter in the mornings. And I was very vain in saying, 'Well, four hours [writing] is fine, and that's more than most people really do: people waste time going to lunch and sharpening pencils and having coffee, and I don't do that. I just go and work, and then I go and pick up my children.' I was sort of stinking of virtuousness.

"As they got older, maybe I just got tired of being so virtuous, or my creative life got more explosive. I found it more and more frustrating to have to stop at four hours. I began to really yearn for long days, days in which I didn't have to stop either at twelve or at three. The first year that they were both in school full time was when we moved to New York, just two years ago. So from 1980 to 1990, that was ten solid years—that's a long time—of being interrupted.

"So I began to say, first with enormous guilt—still with enormous guilt but less—I have to go away either for a long weekend or a week by myself occasionally." Gordon then does what her son's godmother, Toni Morrison, calls 'binge writing,' where "I would just be by myself and work very, very hard for a long time."

Gordon and her husband, Arthur Cash, have a commuter marriage: he spends three days in the middle of each week in upstate New York where he teaches while she manages the children alone in Manhattan. "That has given me enough guilt chips to be able to say occasionally, 'I'm staying down here; you take them for the weekend.'

"Also, I started getting up really early in the morning; before children, I was a night person. The trouble is that now that my daughter has to get up at six-thirty to get to school, there's really not much point getting up at five-thirty because you have to stop at six-thirty, and you're both tired *and* interrupted." Gordon still rises early on weekend mornings to write for a few hours before her children awaken.

When her children are in school, Gordon can work on a schedule, preparing for and teaching classes three days a week at Barnard College and writing at home the other two days. But when they are home, working is much more difficult. Gordon says, "I can write anywhere, but I can't write with them around.

"School vacations in the middle of the year [are] a disaster; I just lose it," she adds. With family members attending or teaching at four different schools, midyear vacations seldom coincide.

Summers are another difficult time. "This year, they went to day camp and they stayed at home. My daughter was underemployed this summer, under-entertained. We always go to the Cape for a month, and this was the first summer I didn't have any baby-sitters. That was a real mistake. I believed that they [the children] could entertain themselves, and they couldn't—I entertained them. I just resigned myself to getting up really early, and I figured if I worked from five-thirty to ten-thirty, that was enough. It wasn't, but it was okay and I actually had a lot of fun with them. Next year, I'm going to try to send them to sleep-away camp at gunpoint," she joked, adding, "We'll see; they've refused to go thus far.

"The children go through phases where they'll really respect my work, and then sometimes they won't. My son did something classic this summer. The place where I was working was upstairs in an attic in a house that we rented. He went to the bottom of the stairs and said, 'Are you busy?' And I said, 'Yes.   And he said, 'Are you too busy to be interrupted?'" After she answered affirmatively, her son responded, 'But do you know that I'm crying?'

Gordon adds, "Another mother might be able to say, 'Well, just deal with it,' but I couldn't, I just couldn't.

"Even though [my husband] is tremendously helpful and wonderful, still, I'm the one that remembers everything. I'm the one that knows what everybody's shoe size is and who everybody's friends are and who you call to invite and what two kids you can't have in the same room at the same time and what would be a good thing to do with the children so that they don't sit watching the VCR."

She particularly does not want her children to sit passively in front of the TV. "If I could endure that, I could probably get a lot more work done. It's just like a poison that seeps into my work room; if I hear that TV on I have to go bouncing out."

Having to keep track of all those details is the biggest distraction to work, Gordon says. "It often takes me a very long time sitting at my desk before I can get all that crap out of my mind, all those details of who has to be where and who's doing what and who's not doing well with this and what teacher I should speak to." To clear her mind, Gordon says, "I read and listen to music; I sometimes need to do that for an hour or two to decompress. That's a big difference between what's happened to my writing since children: I used to be quite sparky and intelligent when I sat down at my desk, and now I have two hours of real stupidity."

Before motherhood, Gordon unplugged the phone while she worked. "But I'm always afraid school will be calling saying that they're sick, so I don't feel I can do that." Her fantasy office would be a hotel room, "where I could call room service and everyone could clean up after me—that would be perfection. I think all mothers love hotels."

Gordon has someone come in to clean two mornings a week. She acknowledges, "I'm quite untidy; that falls through the cracks. I just can't be after them to tidy up all the time, it ruins the relationship between parents and children." As long as she can close her office door, Gordon says, "I endure a certain amount of domestic chaos, which my husband truly hates.

"Many of my most vexing problems could be solved by Mary Poppins. It's not the spiritual or emotional demands of motherhood that I find exhausting, it's keeping track of everything."

The "non-scut work," that is, her relationship with her children and "the kinds of conversations that we have and the sense of having a stake in life, have really fed my work enormously," Gordon says. "And also, I'm just in love with my children. I really needed to have children. I'm one of those boring people that played with dolls and wanted babies. I never had any conflict about that; I would have been miserable without children."

Asked what advice she would give a young woman about trying to combine writing and motherhood, Gordon says, "Do it. Don't ever not do it. Don't ever think that you should wait until some magic time because the magic time won't come. Also try to find a friend who has children your children's same age who really respects your work." Another piece of advice, which she admits she can't follow, is to "really believe that your work is important enough to occasionally say no to your children for. Not all the time. On the whole, I'm not convinced that it's such a terrible thing to say no to your work for your children because in the end, children are so fragile and neglect can harm them. I think the trick is figuring out when they really need you and when you just think they need you. Sometimes you can take a risk and [then] find out that they really did need you and you blew it. But the whole game isn't up if you blow it once, twice.

"My daughter thinks it's a really stupid question that I would say, 'Do you feel I've neglected you for my work? Do you think I shouldn't have worked so hard?' She just thinks that's such a boring ridiculous question that it's not answerable." Despite such assurances, Gordon says, "I think it's very hard for women to believe that their work has anything like equal claim."

Teaching has a paradoxical effect on her writing, Gordon says, "because it takes a tremendous amount of time, and yet I feel that I have more creative energy, and my work, in an odd way, is more satisfying and exciting to me now than it ever has been: I feel like there's some dreadful joke, that I have less time than ever and more ideas than ever."

Does she find that there is a maternal aspect to teaching undergraduates? "Very strongly. But at least I don't have to buy socks for them," she says with a laugh.

Gordon wrote about the dilemma of the working mother in her third novel, *Men and Angels,* which also draws on the persona of one of her students. "I actually had a quite mad student at one point who was fixated on me. She was quite crazy, and she told me she had a job as a live-in au pair. I thought, 'Oh my God, what would it be like to have her as your au pair?' "

What was the inspiration for Anne, the mother character in that book? Gordon says, "I was interested in someone who had been very fortunate and felt kind of guilty about her good fortune. And [I was] interested in the collision of a fortunate person and an unfortunate person and what that would be like."

Both Anne and Laura feel rejected by their own mothers, but Anne has the love of her father, husband, children, and friends, while Laura has no one. Novelist Rosellen Brown, reviewing *Men and Angels* for the

New Republic writes, "What binds all of Gordon's work together, whatever its differences, is her unique fascination with the idea of love and its derivatives, the lovable, the unlovable, the unloved, subcategories as ineluctable as election and damnation.… In Gordon's work, loving is not so much a process as it is a state, given like grace; a condition, like beauty, into which one is born."

The protagonist, Anne, rediscovers the joy of intellectual work when she returns to her career after several years at home with her two children. But the novel can also be seen as a cautionary tale—Anne becomes so focused on her work that she ignores both her own intuition and her children's fears about their baby-sitter, a psychotic young woman who believes herself to be chosen by God to save Anne and her family from themselves.

Although Gordon wrote about children and parents before becoming a mother herself, she says, "I think I write more darkly about them now. I think that I'm more aware of the darker feelings that children bring up. The tremendous possessiveness—I think I had no notion of the depths of maternal possessiveness—and also fear. And the difficulty of placing a child in the world, and the conflicts that that creates I think were not clear to me before I had children. What is the child's relationship to the rest of the world? What do you want for the child in terms of other people? How does the fate of the world touch upon the fate of your child? How are your moral standards tested by having children? For example, you might not care about your own success or personal comfort or well-being or luxury, but you don't want your children to suffer. That creates interesting moral questions.

"As I've moved in the culture of mothers and children, I've been able to observe more mothers and children at close range," Gordon says, resulting in such stories as "Separation," a favorite of hers, which was anthologized in *Best Short Stories of 1991*. Novelist Margaret Drabble, in a review of *Men and Angels* for the *New York Times Book Review* comments that Gordon's, "rich, informal, imagery-packed prose beautifully reveals the poetry of domesticity and her language dramatizes the small inner movements of the maternal heart."

In an excerpt from her journal, published in *Good Boys and Dead Girls,* Gordon writes of the sensuous, physical aspects of mothering a small child: "It is the first hot day of the year. A drugged and meager light sifts through the haze; almost as in a dream I see the chestnut tree through the window, its flowers set within its leaves like little candelabras. I can see the chestnut from the bed where I lie with my baby, skin to skin. The pleasure of this is like the pleasure of a drug; it prevents activity. Only I *am* active. I am feeding. Perfectly still, almost without volition, I nourish. A film of moisture covers my flesh and my son's. Both of us drift in and out of sleep."

She says, "I just love those little bodies. I always think they could have a bottle of perfume called Baby Head; it would make a zillion dollars. I love the way they smell and feel, and I love their warmth. I love it when they're sleepy. I really like it when they're a little bit sick—not very sick—but just kind of slowed down, loving and needy. And I love seeing them run and move. I love seeing the way light falls on them, the way they move through water. Just seeing them move independently and realizing that they really move in the world without you is always exciting."

But for Gordon, those years of cuddling babies have passed into the realm of memory. Her daughter, Anna, is entering adolescence, a tough time, Gordon acknowledges. "On the one hand, she's just enchanting because she's such an interesting companion and she's very smart. In some ways she's really different from me—she's someone who has a tremendous sense of herself, and she's not obsessed with pleasing the way that I was. But I see her making many of my mistakes, and I want to say, 'Don't be friends with that girl, she's not going to be nice to you, and don't wear that and don't eat that and don't join this club.' And I can't tell her and she won't listen. Knowing that I have to stand back and let her make many of the same mistakes that I made is very painful. Even though she won't make some of the mistakes that I made, she'll make some that I was convinced I was going to be able to prevent a daughter from making.

"And then I see her looking at my body these days, looking for clues like a prosecuting attorney. The other day she said to me, 'Did you ever think of wearing lip liner?' And I said, 'No, absolutely never.' And she said, 'I have to tell you, there's only one word for the way you put on lipstick, and that is *pathetic.*'

But her daughter can also be empathetic. The *New Yorker* recently published Gordon's essay about her father dying when she was eight years old. When Anna read that story, "she came in to me, weeping, because, she said, 'I know that's about your childhood, and it makes me cry to think that anyone would have had to go through that, but that you had to go through that breaks my heart.' So, the same person who thinks I have a lipstick problem also weeps for me.

"I occasionally wake up with a terrible pang and say, 'I'm only going to have my daughter in the house for six more years.' I think I'll really miss their presence and their sweetness and their humor and their richness—they're great human beings to have around. I will have a tremendous amount more time [when they're gone], and I look forward to that at the same time that I fear it—supposing it's this big hole I fall into. When I see my friends whose children are grown and how much freer their days are, I can see there's something enviable in it. And yet the fact that I wouldn't be in [daily] contact with these growing people anymore seems like a terrible loss."

Portions of this interview were previously published in the Fall 1993 issue of Belles Lettres: A Review of Books by Women.

Photo ©, Fred Viebahn

RITA DOVE

Rita Dove

Rita Dove, forty, is the youngest writer to be appointed Poet Laureate by the Library of Congress. A concern for the individual experience of ordinary people is one of the hallmarks of her writing. "Her lean and exquisitely crafted poems, sharp with contemporary attitude are filled with ideas that even a newcomer to poetry can reach out and grab," writes poet and arts critic Patricia Smith in the Boston Globe.

Winner of a Pulitzer Prize for Thomas and Beulah *(1986), a collection of poems telling the two sides of her maternal grandparents' love story, the African-American writer has published three additional books of poetry:* The Yellow House on the Corner *(1980),* Museum *(1983), and* Grace Notes *(1989); a short story collection entitled* Fifth Sunday *(1985); and a novel,* Through the Ivory Gate *(1992). Among her many honors, Dove has received fellowship support from the National Endowment for the Arts, the National Humanities Center, the Guggenheim Foundation, and the Andrew W. Mellon Foundation. She teaches creative writing at the University of Virginia as Commonwealth Professor of English and is also associate editor of the African-American literary journal,* Callaloo. *Dove lives in Charlottesville, Virginia, with her husband, German novelist Fred Viebahn, and their ten-year-old daughter, Aviva.*

IN HER POETRY AND FICTION, RITA DOVE IS CONCERNED WITH the individual experience, her own and that of her characters. Asked to briefly characterize her work, Dove replied, "I think that up till now, I could safely say that one of my predominant preoccupations is the theme of the ordinary individual, the unknown individual, caught up in history. Not in the sense of Napoleon's aide-de-camp, but people like Thomas and Beulah who live their lives against the flux of larger history," she says, referring to her collection of poems about her maternal grandparents. "So in that book, we get a clear picture of their lives, whereas all those events that are happening around them, like world wars and depressions, we only see filtered through their every-day lives.

"I'm very interested in getting inside a person's head, with all of those intricate thoughts; then that person can never be lumped into a stereotype again."

Dove's struggle to avoid stereotyping is evident not only in her Thomas and Beulah poems, but also in her novel *Through the Ivory Gate*. On one level, that book is a portrait of the artist as a young black woman trying "to create artistic space for herself to grow in." But when the protagonist, Virginia, gets a job teaching puppetry to fourth-graders in her old hometown, memories of long-ago family scenes surface, and she is left with the mystery of why her family suddenly left town, and why her mother is so hostile to her father's sister. At the heart of the novel lies Aunt Carrie's secret: the consensual incest between a teenaged boy and his older sister.

"What was important to me was not to have people recoil in horror and say, 'Oh this is awful.' I did not want to play upon the standard and acceptable reactions but to look at it in terms of the two individuals and how it happened," the author explains. "And then to have Virginia discover that actually she wasn't as shocked as she 'should be,' that she could see how it came about and that it wasn't an ugly and horrible thing. I didn't want easy judgments to be made."

Even in dealing with the mythic, Dove is concerned with individuality. She is currently working on a cycle of poems, many of them set in modern times, which explore the ancient Greek story of Demeter and Persephone. "The Persephone and Demeter poems are trying to look at mothers and daughters without just dismissing the terms of the myth but really talking about what it's like to lose a daughter, to have her abducted. What is it like to wait and not know where she is? And what is it like to have her come back?

"I began writing these poems as a response to [Rainer Maria] Rilke's *Sonnets to Orpheus*. 'Why don't we have sonnets to a female deity?' I thought." Dove did not consciously choose Demeter and Persephone in order to explore mothering issues. On the contrary, she began writing the sonnets, she says, "without thinking of the deeper implications of the goddesses I happened to choose. I have to admit I was very dense for a long time."

In fact, it was her daughter, Aviva, who, after reading a book of Greek myths at school, pointed out the connection between the poet's personal life as the mother of a daughter and her choice of subject matter. "She read the myth again and then she said, 'Oh, yeah, that's like you and me.'

"In terms of writing, I know that there are certain things that I would not have been able to imagine had I not had Aviva, if I didn't have her now." While she might have tried to write about it, Dove says, "I could not have imagined, really, what it is like to be pregnant, to bear that responsibility. After she was born, for the first time in my life I felt completely vulnerable to the world. I mean, we all feel vulnerable at certain times, but with a child there is this feeling that you would do anything to save her or protect her. And that makes you a hostage to reality, so to speak.

"Sometimes the emotion is fear: 'My God, I hope nothing happens to her.' Sometimes it's just an enormous feeling of vulnerability, having to be open. I don't think I could have imagined what that was like. I see it in my friends who don't have children or who have not been responsible for a child: they can be the most compassionate and caring people in the world, but they don't have that odd fragility that parents do."

In her poem "Weathering Out," in *Thomas and Beulah,* Dove says, "There's a description in there of how Beulah feels when she's pregnant—she feels that she's floating, because she can't see her feet. That's taken from my experience, something I think I wouldn't have come up with had I not gone through that."

Beulah's nightmares about misplacing or dropping the baby are the subject of another poem, "Motherhood." Dove writes: "She dreams the baby's so small she keeps / misplacing it—it rolls from the hutch / and the mouse carries it home, it disappears / with his shirt in the wash. / Then she drops it and it explodes / like a watermelon, eyes spitting."

In "Pastoral," one of seven poems in *Grace Notes* that deal with Aviva as a young child, Dove writes about her daughter breast-feeding: "Like an otter, but warm, / she latched onto the shadowy tip / and

I watched, diminished / by those amazing gulps. Finished / she let her head loll, eyes / unfocused and large: milk-drunk."

As her daughter grows up, Dove faces "the bind you get in between writing about your children and then getting to the point where they will be embarrassed by what you write," a problem she has discussed with other women writers. "What do you do? It's a tough call. Up to this point, Aviva has read 'her' poems, and some of them, I could imagine, she will someday be embarrassed by. I mean, there's one where she is exploring her own vagina. At the moment though, she thinks it's all pretty neat."

In the case of Dove's novel, *Through the Ivory Gate,* many of the childhood flashbacks and classroom scenes had already been written before her daughter was born. But during the final revising, when Aviva was in the third grade, the author says, "I remember gleaning little telling details from the social interactions she was having with her classmates, and that was very helpful." For example, the personality of the ten-year-old girl, Renee, who is befriended by the protagonist, Virginia, "how she acts but doesn't talk much, how her mind works—which Virginia doesn't understand because she's not a parent—those passages came from interacting with Aviva."

Asked if her daughter is interested in writing, the author says, "She loves to write short stories. But she wants to be a veterinarian—that's all I know."

In her own case, Dove says, "I've been writing all my life. When I was a child, I wrote for fun. We weren't allowed to watch a lot of television, so reading and writing were my chief pleasures—reading first, of course, and always."

Growing up in Akron, Ohio, Dove spent her summers writing radio plays with her brother, who is two years older. "My father hooked up a microphone you could play through the radio, so we would stand in the kitchen and make up these plays and they'd have to listen to them, poor souls." In addition to the radio plays and writing books together, the pair also started a neighborhood newspaper. Her older brother was the editor and she the reporter until she quit to start her own magazine called *Poet's Delight.*

"When puberty hit, I stopped writing as much—what little I did write were usually soppy poems that I didn't want to show anybody. It wasn't until college that I really started up in earnest, revising things and wanting a poem or a story to be understood and felt by someone else."

Dove majored in English at Miami University in Ohio. "My parents wanted me to be a lawyer, and I really hated anything to do with law, so this was my subterfuge; English was perfectly acceptable as prelaw. I was taking creative writing courses and loving every minute. When I was a junior in college I decided at Thanksgiving to tell them that I wanted to be a writer—a poet, in fact—rather than a lawyer. And to their credit—both my parents' credit—they didn't really get upset. They took a deep breath, but they didn't blink," Dove says.

"Reading was always encouraged, but no one in my family wrote. So I feel now, looking back on it, that it was remarkable that I did not get any resistance, and in fact, they trusted me enough to just let me do that and help support me through college."

She recalls that her father, a chemist, basically told her, "I have never understood poetry, so please don't be upset if I don't read it." She adds, "I thought that was fine because I really didn't want him to read it anyway."

After graduating summa cum laude in 1973, Dove spent a year as a Fulbright fellow at the University of Tübingen in Germany, translating German poetry and studying modern European literature. She then enrolled in the University of Iowa's Writer's Workshop and received her MFA in 1977. "Up to that point, I was writing mainly poetry, but when I got to Iowa, it became exclusively poetry. There was a real separation between fiction writers and poets there. It was rather uncanny how severe the separations were—they went to different bars," Dove recalls with a laugh.

"When I graduated from Iowa, I remember feeling that post-graduate kind of panic: I was suddenly cutting loose on my own, and every poem seemed to have the shadow of graduate school over it. So I wrote prose; that's when I began to write short stories in earnest, with a feeling of relief and intense excitement because, though it was a different genre, it had similarities to poetry."

In 1979, Dove married German novelist Fred Viebahn. While he taught at Oberlin College, she established herself as a writer. "I look back on those years of genteel poverty as idyllic. We had a lot of time." She had time not only for music lessons, but, in those two years, Dove wrote most of the poems in her first book, *The Yellow House on the Corner.* Some of the short stories that she wrote during this period, such as "Aunt Carrie" in *Fifth Sunday,* later became scenes in her first novel.

"What was important about that time was that I got into the habit of writing, of making my own schedule and sticking to it. I think that really has come in handy because you really have to be disciplined as a writer if you have a young child. It certainly helps to have a spouse or a significant other who is understanding—and in my case, who's going through the same thing. But it's still a juggling act. So I'm just grateful that my self-discipline was nailed down during those years right after graduate school."

Dove acknowledges that many women "don't feel the need for a child and that's fine. They shouldn't feel guilty; just say, 'Hallelujah!' and go on." But if a woman writer does want a child, "I'd say she should do it. I think that if she decides not to have children in this age, when it is possible to manage both, though with difficulty, she may regret it all her life. She'll feel impoverished because she did want to have that child.

"But I would also tell her, she should try to wait as long as she can—at least until she has her whole habit of writing in place. She has to get some sense of self-discipline in terms of her writing and get in touch with how she works best as a creative person."

Dove adds, "I think whoever is her significant other, whoever she chooses to live her life with, that she should be very clear from the beginning with them about what this life is like and what they have to put into it—which is more than half the battle if you have a child."

Although she had already published one poetry book and completed her second collection before Aviva's birth, Dove says, "I remember right after my daughter was born in 1983, I was already working on the poems for *Thomas and Beulah;* and I was so panicked that the pit of parenthood was going to suck me under and I was never going to write again. And then I thought, 'I'm not going to let it happen.'"

Having received a Guggenheim fellowship, Dove was on leave

from her teaching position at Arizona State University the year Aviva was born. Dove and Viebahn set up an elaborate schedule, with the two of them alternating care of their daughter in four-hour shifts from 8:00 A.M. to 8:00 P.M.

"Obviously, I couldn't have done that if my husband hadn't been a freelance writer and had a flexible schedule; it was an enormous help. And then I went back to teaching. What happened then is, I think, the story of many women who have three full-time jobs: you teach, you do parenting, and you try to write, too. I was tired all the time. I remember days when I came back home and fell asleep over dessert."

Growing up in a family of four, Dove had imagined herself having two children. "But after Aviva was born," says Dove, "I learned some basic things about myself—that for all these systems and itineraries, I was not naturally organized. And that I was not good at adjusting to changes of schedules. I mean, I could do it, but I didn't adjust inside, psychologically. I know people who will simply say, 'Oh, I can't do that right now? Okay, then, I'll do it in an hour.' And they don't waste much time worrying about it. But I'm a worrywart, and I will say, 'I planned to have this day free and now it's all screwed up, and what will I do?' I have difficulty getting rid of that extra baggage—something I didn't know about myself before because there was always enough time.

"Fred and I both realized we couldn't handle another child. Other people have more than one and will have learned from the first how to manage their lives. But we would just kind of bumble through again; it would be that many more years of not knowing what we're doing."

Despite the difficulties of motherhood, Dove says, "As they say, I wouldn't trade it for anything. For all of the time that is lost to writing, I feel that there's a window that I've gained, a window back into my own childhood. It's a constant amazement to me. So I find myself being torn—pushed and pulled—between frustration and elation. On the day I think I'll be free to write, school is called off because of snow—but on the same day, Aviva and I have a great talk, or she discovers something that changes the world for both of us. It's a real roller-coaster."

Dove tries to set aside three or four hours, three times a week, for writing, but her schedule is constantly changing in response both to Aviva's needs and the demands of academe. "As a consequence, it's much harder to pick up the thread and keep going," she says.

"I find that I cannot really write if I only have an hour. I need at least two hours." Even when she does have time set aside to write, Dove says, "I can't start immediately. Part of the writing process is to settle into it, which is why it also takes so long, why I need such huge stretches of time. What I'll do is make coffee and take it up to my study, though I rarely drink it. It just goes cold, but I have to go through the motions anyway. I'll put on music, usually either classical or jazz, something without words in it."

Dove closes the door to her home office and eases into the work, cleaning her desk, leafing through notebooks, or reading for a while. "I tend to walk around a lot and will occasionally wander out of the room and go do something—fold clothes—while I'm thinking, and then go back in," she says.

"It can take me an hour or two before I really get started. I find that no matter how much time I allot myself in my study, that it's in the last hour that the real writing happens—and I don't seem to be able to trick myself in order to speed things up."

It's always difficult to stop writing, Dove says. "I feel like I'm coming out of another country, like stepping out of the wardrobe in *The Lion, The Witch and The Wardrobe,* saying, 'Oh my gosh, here's real life again,' and not being in sync. Which is one reason why I can never write in the mornings of the days that I teach, because I would not be able to get back into sync to teach, to be articulate and purposeful."

Dove has taught creative writing for twelve years, eight at Arizona State University and the past four at the University of Virginia. In some ways, she says, being a professor has more of an effect on her writing than being a parent does. "I find that teaching is probably the most serious obstacle to writing. I love being in the classroom and talking about writing and poetry to the students and discussing their poems.

"What's difficult about teaching is that it can spill into your personal life at any moment, that it is not a nine-to-five kind of structure.

It's not even a structure where you can say, 'I'm teaching these hours, and then I'm having office hours these hours.' There's always an emergency somewhere. There's always a letter that has to be written right now or the student's not going to get this grant. Or someone is coming to town who has to be entertained, which you really want to do, except that it then throws these schedules out of whack."

Dove keeps a notebook handy for those times when a line or a word comes to her, unbidden, while she is doing something else. "I wish I could say, 'Okay, when an idea strikes, I'm going to drop everything.' And yet I don't think I could live with myself if I didn't go to Aviva's talent show or things like that. So I try to devise a system where I can allow for inspiration by jotting the basic details down as quickly as possible so that when I go back to them later, I really don't think I've lost anything substantial; usually I can recall it, I can recover the spark.

"If I were to wait for it to hit me out of the blue, I think I would have written a lot fewer poems. Very often, I will go into my room thinking, 'I have nothing to say. I'm tired. I really don't want to do this,' and then something hits me out of the blue. So I'm a firm believer in going in there and sitting down and seeing what happens. When I began writing these poems about Persephone and Demeter, I wrote nine poems in about eleven days—and then didn't write anything for two months, of course, because I was exhausted somewhere inside.

"When I'm writing poetry, I tend to work in fragments; I always have. I don't sit down and write a poem or even a stanza from beginning to end. What usually happens is that I'm juggling quite a few poems in various states of undress; I work on them almost simultaneously."

Whenever Dove can set aside four or five hours for several days in a row, she can usually finish several poems at a time. "The system works well for my lifestyle, this grabbing a little time here and a little time there. But it does depend on having time enough to get it all together."

In the beginning stages of her novel, Dove again wrote in fragments. "I could go in for two, three hours and get some work done."

However, she says, "When it came to putting everything together and projecting the trajectory of the plot and the development of the main characters within that plot, I needed enormous amounts of time for extended periods. In the last stages of the novel, there were times when my husband had to take over the entire household."

In addition to sharing the child care and housework, Viebahn acts as a business consultant for his wife, using experience he gained working with the German writers union. Although Dove says their marriage is "not always" ideal, she adds, "but it is, in a sense." They fight, but they manage to confine their arguments to the shared bookshelf.

"The emblem of this marriage is our bookshelf. When we moved to Virginia, we were attracted to this house for the upstairs hallway, which is very wide; the first thing we thought of was books. I started at one end [of the hallway] with my books and he started at the other end with his books. I had a different ordering system than he did. As we neared the middle, we got into lots of arguments, and so books in the middle shelves are jumbled and each of us changes the order. We fight in the middle of the bookshelf. I will pick out a book and then put it back where I think it should be. And if I can't find a book, I know he has put it back where he thinks it should be."

Portions of this interview previously appeared in the Winter 1993/1994 issue of Belles Lettres: A Review of Books by Women.

Photo ©, Jean Lannen

KATE BRAVERMAN

Kate Braverman

Fiction writer and poet Kate Braverman, forty-four, conveys a visionary's sense of the illusory nature of reality, evoking a world in which the most ordinary moments are charged with cosmic meaning. Her writing is rich in metaphors and lush sensory details, her narratives propelled by a pulsating rhythm.

Braverman is the author of three novels: Lithium for Medea *(1979),* Palm Latitudes *(1988), and* Wonders of the West *(1993); a short story collection,* Squandering the Blue *(1990); and four books of poetry:* Milk Run *(1977),* Lullaby for Sinners *(1980),* Hurricane Warnings *(1987), and* Postcard from August *(1990). Braverman portrays women living on the edge, both psychological and continental, buffeted by the Santa Ana winds and their own self-destructive impulses. She chronicles their struggles to regain control of their lives—often with the support of their mothers or daughters—from the men who seek to dominate them.*

Although she was born in Philadelphia, Braverman considers herself "a native daughter of Los Angeles." She received her BA in anthropology from the University of California, Berkeley, in 1971 and her master's degree in English from Sonoma State University in 1986. A single parent for nearly a decade, Braverman now lives in Beverly Hills with her scientist husband, Alan Goldstein, and her twelve-year-old daughter, Gabrielle.

"WHEN I HAD MY DAUGHTER, I LEARNED WHAT THE SOUND of one hand clapping is—it's a woman holding an infant in one arm and a pen in the other," says Kate Braverman. "I came to realize, after I had my daughter, that to be an artist and to be a mother simultaneously was truly to walk on hot coals. The days I stood there, heating formula and having the bottle in one hand, literally, and a pen in the other, I realized what is necessary for a woman to transcend the pure literal level of obstacle that a woman has to transcend to be a mother and an artist.

"There's nothing natural about motherhood and there's nothing natural about writing. In fact, they're both inhuman tasks and what's required of a person to do them well is unspeakable. And to do both of them outside the protections, real and imagined, of the patriarchy is an ordeal of monumental proportions."

Before her daughter was born, Braverman knew that she would leave the "very marginal" relationship she had with the child's biological father and raise her alone. Gabrielle was born in December 1981, "right before midnight, in the rain, under a full moon." In "Falling in October," a story of a single mother's search for meaning amid the alienation and desperation which seems to surround her in Los Angeles, Braverman writes, "We are alone. We even have our babies alone, like contaminated animals. We barely manage not to eat them."

The author recalls, "That was something I thought about when my thinking became coherent enough for me to realize that langurs and baboons do better; at least they live in troops and share food and have patterns of affection. But the idea that I existed in a realm so isolated that I could have had a baby alone was a horrifying startlement." As a single mother, Braverman says, "I had to go through all the terrors that you go through—all the being up at night and functioning during the day—without anyone else to go through it with me.

"But on the other hand, I had a great sense of freedom that this was my baby and I could raise her exactly as I chose, and I never had to compromise; I didn't need to have anyone else's approval. I also had a great sense of honor and dignity that I was functioning outside the patriarchy in this set of circumstances. It was terrifying and horrible, but there was also a great sense of power in it."

Braverman needed that feeling of power to deal with the disapproval of the outside world. "Being a single parent was the first time I was ever truly marginalized. To encounter the sort of discrimination that I, a very well-educated woman, encountered as a single mother was brand-new to me. It had never dawned on me that I would be discriminated against [because I was] a single parent—that I would be treated as if I were wrong, a bad woman, somehow promiscuous, almost criminal, and that I would be perceived that way by people in preschools, by doctors, insurance companies, police, by whatever bureaucratic agency I had to deal with."

The economic consequences of raising a child alone were as un-expected as the discrimination she faced. She had already published two books of poetry and a novel, but the income from her royalties and sporadic teaching was not sufficient. Although she earned some money writing book reviews and doing performance art in rock-and-roll clubs, and received financial help from her family, Braverman says, "I felt I would have to do something monumental or we would both starve. That's what compelled me, that was the catalyst, to try to write a major novel that would get me out of the Bohemian squalor in which we both existed.

"I had no concept of what having a baby would require on any level. I'd never thought about anything other than my art. It could be Tuesday morning or Sunday in the middle of the night—I had no idea, I was just on poem time. I lived a completely unconventional, ren-egade life, and then suddenly I had a baby."

Living her "romantic ideal of a poet as burning the candle at both ends," Braverman did not expect her art or her schedule to be com-promised by the presence of a child. "It was a rude awakening," she recalls. "I think being a mother and being a poet is a contradiction in terms. They're both efforts that require 100 percent at all times—they require all that you have." Believing that writing and mothering were mutually exclusive, Braverman saw two choices: adapt by some miracle or die. "It was certainly the most difficult thing I ever did. I had to learn to write on a schedule, which was anathema to me. I had always done it my way, which is you write until you drop and you know something's finished when you're in intensive care. I had to stop doing all that.

"I was in love with self-destruction before I had my daughter. And it was very difficult to find myself in the position of having this narcissistic personality disorder and being in love with pain and per-sonal ruin and also to be in love with the little life that I had created. I created her with the idea that she was mine; I always knew that I would have a daughter. I had to make a decision, and I don't know how I had the capacity to make this decision and pull it off.

"What I actually had to do was make a choice: whether I was

going to be a writer or a mother. I made the decision that it was more important that I be Gabrielle's mother than that I be a writer. If that meant that fifteen years of ruthless deprivation and incredible hard work were going to be for nothing, then so be it, and it would just be over. And after I made that decision, very shortly thereafter, I learned how to write on a coherent schedule; I learned how to do both."

Braverman started working on her second novel soon after reaching her nadir. She hired a baby-sitter and finished the first draft in 1983. After a year in Maui with her then two-year-old daughter, Braverman returned to Los Angeles to rewrite the book, which she completed in 1984.

"I threaded my daughter into the text itself so that the whole novel culminates with, 'for my daughter,' rather than having the dedication at the beginning. The struggle to try to protect my daughter from what I then perceived as the life-threatening evils of our economic situation was so intense that I felt it might very well kill me trying to do both of these things. While I was writing *Palm Latitudes,* I was on a schedule of work all day, work all night, work all day, sleep four hours. I saw it as a survival textbook for my daughter, right down to menus she could cook for dinner parties and what books she should read."

The novel, written in three parts, portrays Los Angeles through the eyes of three Chicanas: Francisca Ramos, a prostitute whose idea of luxury is a closet filled with flowered sheets; Gloria Hernandez, a dutiful but alienated young wife and mother of two sons she no longer understands; and Marta Ortega, an old woman with a magical awareness of nature. Writing about women such as these was one goal of the author, who lived in the barrio for ten years; she also wanted to experiment with making language more feminine and "tropical."

Braverman achieved those goals, but the book did not bring her immediate success. Rather, it was rejected by twenty-two publishers. "I had agents who wrote back and said, 'Well, this may very well be a masterpiece—it's certainly a tour-de-force—but I don't have time for something like this,' 'I'm not interested in Mexican women,' and agents who said it just wasn't 'commercial' enough for them to bother. I ended up leaving LA with *Palm Latitudes* in a hatbox," Braverman says. "My daughter and I got in a car and drove north. I lost everything; I was entirely bankrupt. I couldn't find anyone to buy that book; I couldn't find anyone who even wanted to read that book.

"I felt that I was finished as a writer. I'd done everything I possibly could do; it was a 110 percent effort, and it failed absolutely. I had some vague notion that I would get a master's degree and join the teaching profession somehow."

Braverman headed north in 1985 to Sonoma State University, nearly fifteen years after obtaining her BA in anthropology from the University of California, Berkeley. She chose the state college in part because she liked the campus's day care center, which her daughter attended for free. "I got my master's [in English] while Gabrielle went to preschool, and that was wonderful to be on campus together like that," Braverman recalls. Returning to southern California after graduate school, Braverman was destitute. "I had no money at all. We had to live with my mother for two years, which is rather a major defeat for one to encounter in her late thirties. Nobody would answer letters from me; I couldn't get any readings. It was like I didn't exist. It was like *Palm Latitudes* was the black hole in space, and I had been sucked into another dimension."

Although she thinks there are a number of reasons why her novel was rejected by so many publishers, she says, "My vision is just unconventional, and people think in terms of their demographics and their sales departments, and I'm just too much of an outlaw."

Finally published in 1988, the book turned Braverman's professional life around and brought the economic security she had sought. She was in demand for readings, she built up her private teaching practice, and then was asked to join the faculty at California State University, Los Angeles.

In 1990, she published both her book-length poem, *Postcard from August,* and her short story collection, *Squandering the Blue.* One of the stories in that collection, "Tall Tales from the Mekong Delta," was selected for the 1991 edition of *Best American Short Stories* and won the O. Henry award the following year.

Braverman also married for the first time in 1991 after nearly a decade as a single parent. She now lives in Beverly Hills "in an apartment one block within the Beverly Hills school district," with her daughter and her husband, Alan Goldstein, whom she describes as "a molecular biologist and research scientist by day and a rock-and-roll guitarist by night."

Through all of the turmoil of those early years, her daughter has thrived, Braverman says. She proudly describes Gabrielle's accomplishments: "My daughter is a straight A student, she's the star of her theater arts program (Miss Hannigan in *Annie*), she played [Beethoven's] *Für Elise* at her piano recital. And my daughter is incredibly sturdy. She's not like me—addicted to the brutal, dark night skies—she's a sunny, amiable child. I find it curious how she's turned out. People always told me she was gifted from her first preschool, but I've raised her so unconventionally. This child has literally grown up at poetry readings. We lived in the jungle without electricity for a year in Maui. I've raised her as the daughter of a poet, and I must say she's flourished."

Asked if her daughter, who had just won a Los Angeles County environmental essay contest, is an aspiring writer, Braverman says, "Oh God, I hope not. No, I think my daughter has a different kind of intelligence. She seems to have a more integrated intelligence; she seems to be proficient at many things. I'd like to see her become a doctor."

Braverman uses her daughter as a model in her fiction. "I'm attempting to 'dive into the wreck,' as [poet Adrienne] Rich says, and reclaim my girlhood." In depicting the little girl characters in her short story collection, Braverman says, "I've taken entire scenes of our life and put them into work I'm doing. So I find that I've threaded her as I thread everything into these fictions."

Bringing children to life on the page is pioneering work, Braverman says, "a second act of the creation, merging motherhood and the artist." Writing about children is also a challenge. "What is the angle that you need to make children interesting? One thing that I do with my children, with my little girl, is I always write her up, not down. I always write her as if she were a functioning individual. And then, of course, I like how she just keeps getting older, as I get older, as we grow old on the page together."

The title story in her collection, *Squandering the Blue*, is told from the perspective of a girl whose mother dies of breast cancer. Braverman explains that the piece "came about when I was imagining what it would be like for my Gabrielle if I died. Recently, whenever I read that story at poetry or prose readings, Gaby's taken to crying. It's a tragic little story. I made myself cry when I wrote it, and it makes me weep when I read it."

Whereas the child characters in her second novel were peripheral figures, the main character in Braverman's third novel is an adolescent girl named Jordan.

Set in Los Angeles in the early 1960s, *Wonders of the West* is about the lure of the open road and what happens to a girl whose mother has gambled all and lost. Jordan is eleven years old when her parents break up; she and her mother, Roxanne, head west to start life anew. They arrive in Los Angeles, broke, only to discover that the brother Roxanne had counted on to rescue them, a bookie with forty phones, has lost everything to cancer. Jordan is physically sheltered but otherwise ignored by the adults around her, who are too caught up in illness and poverty to nurture her. In the end, what saves the young woman's sanity is the promise of the open road and the courage to leave home.

"I was able to understand a little bit about how to think that way by being as close to my daughter as I am," the author says. Indeed, relationships between mothers and daughters is a central theme in Braverman's work. "I think that the mother-daughter story is the great story for a woman to tell. One of the fantastic aspects of being free of the patriarchy is that I've been free to tell a woman's story. The woman's true story is that of her relationship to her mother and her relationship to her daughter. I want to tell stories that are not influenced by one's relationship to a man. I'm married now and very much in love with my husband, but I continue to think that the great story a woman writer can tell is the story of the tragic relationship with her mother and her daughter," Braverman says.

"The patriarchy would have us believe that the central story that a woman has to tell is the story of her relationship to a man. For me, a woman's real story is not about the men that come and go and the marriages and the divorces that come and go, but they're about what is eternal—and that is the mother and the child. Your mother and your children are the permanent acts of your existence; the others are volitional."

Asked whether male children are part of the men who come and go, Braverman says that never having raised a son, she is not in a position to say, although she believes that "the investment would be different because you know a son is leaving, and you know that part of your job is to prepare him to leave. But I don't think a daughter truly divests herself."

At the same time, Braverman does not envision her own daughter as clinging to her. "I think my daughter's going to be the kind of child that says, 'Well, I'm going to Berkeley now. I'll see you at Christmas.' And, you know, waves good-bye. I think she'll be able to be an independent functioning entity, which I wasn't."

As for how her work may change in the future as her daughter gets older, Braverman says, "My work will probably get more fictional. I feel that I can inhabit vast terrains now. I don't feel so bound by the details of my personal history. I feel I've transcended some of them."

Braverman resigned in 1992 from her teaching post to devote more time to her writing. She calls her newest direction in fiction "Exploded Moments." Braverman explains the concept behind these short stories: "They're just a point in time and space, and that's all they are. They don't necessarily resolve and they don't necessarily have a structure. Who's to say that plot is necessary for literature? Just men who have been involved in plots and boundary disputes. Does that really have anything to do with me?"

Braverman has long been interested in the boundaries between forms and sees those boundaries as one way women are ghettoized in literature. For example, if a novel is described by critics as a poetic novel, it isn't taken seriously, she says. "Men are hung up on these absolute forms—where the short story ends and the novella begins. Someone once told me that my novels were epic poems and my poems are miniature novels."

Although she has published four books of poetry, Braverman says that at this point, "I'm using my poems as fodder for longer works of fiction. What I tend to do with my poems is, whenever I get lost in a larger work, a story or a novel, I just throw poems in. They flare up, and in the sudden illumination, I'm able to see where to go in the longer work."

In the poet's life, her daughter is a source of illumination. One of Braverman's favorite scenes from her work is in the short story, "These Clairvoyant Ruins," where the little girl, Annabell, and her mother hold hands as they venture into the dark parking lot after a school Christmas performance. She writes, "Diana Barrington is thinking if they hold hands they can see in the darkness without their eyes. There is no darkness." The author says, "That is how I feel. When I hold my daughter's hand, I feel that I can see in the dark."

Braverman no longer believes that writing and mothering are mutually exclusive. "Once you have been skinned to death and have reassembled yourself, there's no death that you can die again that will ever be as agonizing as the first.

"I know that there are times when I am going to lose a scene or a story because I choose to let my daughter have that moment. I am learning a kind of flexibility. I was always very inflexible with my work. I was just maniacally driven to succeed with my work, and I did feel that the universe was talking to me and that all I had to do was sit there and decode these transmissions. I felt I had a calling.

"I've learned that there are times when I'm not going to be able to receive these stanzas from Alpha Centauri because I'm going to be with my daughter. But I choose to do both of these things. I recognize that there are moments when motherhood will take precedence over sitting at my computer. But I feel that all of this has made me more human; it's certainly made me more compassionate and flexible. It's probably given me more stamina. It means a lot to me that I have so many young students who consider me a role model. It's very curious that it should have turned out this way. I never planned on that. I never planned on doing anything other than being locked away receiving transmissions from other universes, but here it is."

Does she think her writing is better or worse? "I've never written so well; that's the bottom line."

Portions of this interview were previously published in the January/February 1994 issue of Ms.

Photo ©, Robbie Steinbach

BEA NETTLES

Bea Nettles

Throughout her career, photographer Bea Nettles, forty-eight, has worked almost exclusively in an autobiographical vein, visually delving into the places and people that have special meaning in her life. Though she photographs such ordinary objects as bread, children's school work, a pile of laundry, a bowl of apples, she arranges them to reveal the subtle texture of domestic life. Many of Nettles's pieces include self-portraits and photographs of her children as elements of the still-life composition, giving a layered quality to the final photograph.

Nettles has twice received National Endowment for the Arts fellowships, and her work is included in the collections of such institutions as the Metropolitan Museum of Art, the Museum of Modern Art, and the National Gallery of Canada. She started her own publishing company, Inky Press, to print and distribute her photographs in book form; those books include Breaking the Rules: A Photo Media Cookbook *(1977),* Flamingo in the Dark *(1979),* Corners: Grace and Bea Nettles *(1988),* Life's Lessons: A Mother's Journal *(1990),* The Skirted Garden *(1990), and* Complexities *(1992).*

Chair of the photography program at the University of Illinois at Urbana-Champaign, Nettles lives with her husband of twenty-one years, businessman Lionel Suntop, and their two children, fifteen-year-old Rachel and twelve-year-old Gavin.

FROM THE AGE OF SEVEN, BEA NETTLES KNEW THAT SHE wanted to be an artist. She grew up in Gainesville, Florida, where her father, Victor Nettles, was a professor of horticulture at the University of Florida, while her mother, Grace Noble Nettles, cared for five children. When the youngest entered kindergarten, her mother went back to school, becoming a college English teacher and a poet.

Nettles discovered photography in the late 1960s when she was an undergraduate painting major at the University of Florida. She continued studying photography on her own and in elective courses while working toward her MFA in painting at the University of Illinois at Champaign-Urbana.

In her last year of graduate school, Nettles boldly found her own ground as an artist: she began to experiment with printing etchings onto fabrics and with stitching hand-colored photographs together to make collages. "In my photography class, hand coloring was considered a way to disguise poor print quality. Cutting and sewing photographs was seen as an outrage," Nettles writes in *The Skirted Garden: 20 Years of Images by Bea Nettles.* She found herself ostracized and literally locked out of the campus darkroom her final semester, "because my working methods seemed so radical at the time."

Nonetheless, within a year Nettles was teaching photography, first at Nazareth College in Rochester, New York, and later at the Rochester Institute of Technology and the Tyler School of Art at Temple University. In 1984, she returned to the University of Illinois, as head of the photography program that had been so hostile to her work fifteen years earlier.

As a photographer who frequently works in an autobiographical vein, including self-portraits, Nettles's subject matter has altered as her life has changed, but certain themes reemerge. "I see my career as a spiral with my ideas of late circling around and picking up reflections of earlier thoughts," she writes in *The Skirted Garden.*

When she became a mother, it was therefore natural that she would focus on that experience. Some of her work, such as her series of photoetchings called "Rachel's Holidays," celebrates the joys of childhood. But much of her work exposes the fears, anxieties, and threats that all parents and children must face.

For example, *Snake Through the Window* (1982) is a photograph of a large, striped stuffed toy snake that seems to emerge from beneath the lace curtains of an open window, creeping forward on the carpet. Together with *Bad Laughing Frog,* it is one of two pieces that Nettles created in response to her then three-year-old daughter's descriptions of nightmares; both were shown in her 1982 exhibition, "Close to Home."

Nettles's preoccupation with the fears and anxieties of childhood and parenthood continued in two subsequent exhibitions, "Landscapes of Innocence" (1985) and "Life's Lessons: A Mother's Journal" (1988). "Landscapes of Innocence," a series of twenty-one photoetchings, deals with "the first entry of the real world into the lives of my children: going out to day care, hearing about the bomb, hearing about missing children, even simple things like learning about ET," Nettles says.

In the introduction to *Life's Lessons: A Mother's Journal,* her book based on that exhibition, Nettles writes that as her children get older, "Parenting keeps getting harder. The worries at home begin to compound with continued sibling rivalry, adjustment to public school, oppressive materialism, gender identification, struggles with discipline and limits. In addition to this, add the very real fear of harm to one's children at the hands of strangers, concerns for their health (drugs, pollution, AIDS), and the ever-present fear of nuclear destruction."

Ordinary objects, artfully arranged into still-life compositions, convey Nettles's sense of foreboding. In one black-and-white photograph, for example, a knife blade threatens to slice another piece from the already-exposed round loaf of raisin bread.

For *Missing* (1986), a triptych of images from "Life's Lessons," Nettles uses the milk cartons printed with photographs of missing children to evoke the fear of separation and the fear that one's children will be harmed. In one of these pieces, Nettles places, at the center of the composition, two silhouettes, white paper cutouts of her son and daughter's heads. In the foreground is a Beatrix Potter china bowl filled with cereal. To the left is a glass, painted with stars, and, ominously lurking behind, a carton of milk printed with photographs of a missing boy and girl.

In another image from *Missing,* four milk cartons stand in a row against a black background. Each is printed with two photographs of missing children. On one carton, FOUND is stamped below the photograph of a girl who was rescued. While this carton and the two to the viewer's left are in focus, the fourth carton, adjacent to that with the "found" girl, is blurred as a hand grasps the top of that carton, caught in the moment before the carton is lifted up and away.

In the accompanying text, Nettles writes, "When the milk carton girl was 'found,' Rachel was delighted and wanted to know all the details of her homecoming. I've quit buying milk in those cartons.

The endless stream of boy-girl, boy-girl was just too much."

Several of the pieces in "Life's Lessons" deal with her children's developing sense of gender roles and identity. As her daughter approached her first menstrual period, Nettles created "Twenty-Eight Days," a deck of cards with an image for each day of the lunar month. She explains, "I was remembering my situation and marveling that things really hadn't changed that much in terms of society's recognition of this as an important transition in women's lives. It's still very secretive and almost, in some cases, considered embarrassing and shameful."

But this was not the first time Nettles had worked with images of menstruation. In 1972, she created *Koolaid Hearts,* a series of eight clear vinyl hearts, each filled with colored liquid, and individually framed. Beneath each heart was a toned photograph, small portraits of herself and her two sisters at various ages. Growing up in the South in the 1950s, before home air-conditioning became common, Nettles remembers freezing Kool-Aid into Popsicles to keep cool in the summers. "So for me, a Kool-Aid heart is a metaphor for childhood and innocence," Nettles writes in *The Skirted Garden.* "The piece dealt with growing up, losing one's Kool-Aid innocence, with a reference to the onset of menstruation."

In her more recent *Faces/Phases* (1989), a triptych of three black-and-white photographs, Nettles deals with menstruation in terms of phases in a woman's life. In the center photograph is a self-portrait of the artist, representing the full moon of the childbearing years, flanked by her daughter, Rachel, as the new moon of premenarche, and her mother, Grace Nettles, as the waning moon of menopause. Beneath each portrait is bread in a different stage, from yeasted to risen to fully baked, another symbol of the life cycle.

Nettles and her mother have collaborated on four "emblem" books since the mid-1970s. "Emblem books are not meant to be illustrated books of poetry," Grace Nettles explains in the preface to *Corners: Grace and Bea Nettles.* Rather than the photographs being subordinate to the text, each artist works independently; Bea Nettles then does the layout and printing, combining her mother's poems and her own photographs.

For their most recent endeavor, Nettles had almost twenty years of her mother's poetry to draw upon; after organizing the poems into four seasons, the photographer chose the accompanying pictures. "When the right photograph appears for each poem it is because the minds and spirits of the two women are on the same wavelength," Grace Nettles adds in the preface to *Corners.* "That the book exists at all should show the enduring closeness of mother and child in a time of unprecedented high tension."

While admiring her mother's intelligence and late-blooming career, the photographer says of her mother, "First and foremost, she was an amazing house cleaner. Everything was polished and clean and beautiful. And she instilled in me a desire to be surrounded by that sort of order." While she is, in fact, very organized, Nettles says, "there is a lot of unpolished brass in our house, and the windows are not spotless."

Several of the images in her 1992 book, *Complexities,* illustrate her desire for domestic order—a bowl of shiny apples, a self-portrait of her hands kneading bread—and the reality: a pile of dirty laundry. Uncomfortable with paying for someone to come in and clean, Nettles struggles to enlist her family's cooperation and at the same time lower her expectations.

"I don't think we're terribly mismatched, but I'm certainly neater than my husband," she says. Despite this difference in sensibility, Nettles says her husband, Lionel Suntop, is not only supportive of her work, but as a trained photographer, he understands her art. Suntop had been working on his master's degree in photography, but left school in 1970 to open his first business distributing photographic books. He now handles all of the mail orders for Nettles's books. "He appreciates a lot of the technical and theoretical kinds of issues that I deal with, but he's been very respectful of my need for privacy. He's never presumed to come into my studio or offer criticism until I'm ready to show him something."

While Nettles craves order in the rest of the house, she finds that her studio is an exception. "I do find that some of my projects lie around for months and months as they gestate," she says. Sometimes having work tacked up on the wall "in odd juxtapositions" will suggest new ideas to her.

In the case of *Complexities,* Nettles began the project while on a two-week sabbatical at Penland School in North Carolina. She returned with about a dozen finished images, "then I started to look around my studio and realized there were lots of other components I had done over the years that I could combine to create that book. There were little direct quotes from my journal, and things that I had written about in the journal became issues in the book."

While family life continues to be Nettles's dominant theme, the emphasis in *Complexities* is her ongoing efforts to juggle domestic, artistic, and academic responsibilities. *Complexities* marks a shift in Nettles's focus, away from her children and back to her own image. In the foreword to that book, Nettles writes, "I have had to struggle with the demarcation between our family's private life and what I will make public. I have drawn a line beyond which I'm not willing to drag my family members. I feel comfortable revealing myself and have returned to creating self-portraits for this very reason."

Nettles says the shift was, to some extent, unconscious. But, she adds, "there were at least two artists that I knew personally, and others that I'd heard of, who had pretty intense run-ins with the legal system" for photographing their children nude.

"These were preschool kids," Nettles says, adding that young children "still do run around like that, and I don't think that's the least bit unusual." Of the two artists she knew, one was a woman photographing her young daughters with their father in the bathtub, and the other was a man photographing himself with his preschool son.

"I think their motives were different, but they were certainly above-board," Nettles says. "And that was very disturbing; in the woman's case possibly a little more so because she actually had to defend herself legally. I don't believe it ever went to trial, but her daughters—she had twin daughters—were old enough to get the drift, to sense that all this uproar in the family had something to do with the photographs of them. The climate today certainly does promote self-censorship and this sort of fear."

Nettles herself has felt the chill of such accusations. When "Life's Lessons" was recently exhibited in upstate Illinois, a local newspaper ran a photograph of Nettles's *Feminine/Masculine,* and a reader complained that the piece was "child abuse." In that black-and-white photograph, two columns of words, masculine and feminine titles such as "prince-princess" and "hero-heroine," printed in childish letters, are superimposed on a portrait of the artist's daughter. Although Rachel appears to be shirtless, only her head and shoulders are actually visible.

While the complaint directed against her was not serious, "it could have led to something painful," Nettles says. "That's the sort of thing that I don't want my children to have to deal with. And since it's not an all-encompassing major thrust of the work, I don't think it's necessary. I mean, if that was absolutely what I was intent on doing, I might still do it, but I think there are other images that I can use to get a lot of the same ideas across without involving them specifically."

Whenever she has completed a major project, such as *Life's Lessons* or *Complexities,* Nettles says, "it's almost like childbirth and [afterward] it is almost a postpartum depression that I go into. It takes me a while to figure out what to do next," says Nettles, commenting that "this year has probably been the worst in terms of getting my own work done.

"I think as an artist, the stakes get higher and higher. I look back at what I would have considered a new project in the '70s, and I look at it now and I think, that's nothing. Ten photographs in those days would have seemed like a project. Now I do things that involve forty, fifty images and a much longer-range kind of working," she says.

Nettles is now working on *Grace's Daughter.* While in some of her earlier books she has used written text, usually diary excerpts, the new book will include a series of connected short stories. The first of these, "The Passage of the Ruby Ring," concerns a ring that was passed along the maternal bloodline from the artist's great-grandmother, Rozetta, to the artist's daughter, Rachel.

Nettles says that she sees this red stone as "a metaphor for menstruation." The story talks about the personality traits and talents that have passed from one generation to the next. At the same time, the story questions the patriarchal system under which all of these women have different last names and do not pass their names on to their children. Instead, they are remembered by heirlooms such as the ruby ring.

Like many other artists, Nettles also teaches. Early in her academic career, Nettles considered leaving the profession so that she could devote more time to her art. "But something in the back of my head told me I would really be a fool to give up a full-time tenured job," Nettles says. After her husband lost his business in 1982, she supported the family for a number of years while he reestablished himself in the business world.

Chair of the photography program at the University of Illinois at Champaign-Urbana for the past decade, Nettles now teaches three days a week; the other two days "get chopped up with committee meetings." Although as chair she has one less class to teach, "there's a lot of administrative things that I do that my colleagues don't. It's not a huge program, but there are four full-time photo faculty and nine graduate students, and we service close to two hundred students a semester in our various classes."

In addition to administering the program, Nettles also advises students. "I think that I've inspired and been a role model for a lot of younger women and younger men, too, [who] have much more of a concern about participating in their family. A lot of them are interested in the fact that I've used my own life experience and especially the family as a subject matter for the work."

At the same time, Nettles says she is glad that she waited to have children. She had just received tenure at age thirty-one when Rachel was born. "I see colleagues of mine who are on a tenure track with little children, and the pressure on them is just enormous."

Although she says she is more relaxed than some of her colleagues, between juggling her full-time job and parenting responsibilities, Nettles has little time for her art. "Frankly, I don't get that much creative work done during the school year," Nettles says. "My best month is May, when the university is out but the high school and middle school are in."

Ever since her children were born, Nettles says, "I've constantly been seeking out processes that can be dropped and returned to. I do a little bit whenever I can and come back and pick up where I left off. I'm not saying that's a great way to work, but right now, if I want to work, that's pretty much what I have to do."

When Rachel and Gavin were little, Nettles lacked the blocks of time required for her previous method of creating with multiple exposures. So she began to set up still lifes at home and photographed them with a pinhole camera. Essentially, a box with a piece of photographic paper at one end and a tiny hole at the other, the pinhole camera tends to produce dreamy images with an exaggerated perspective. Not only was the new method better suited to her time constraints, Nettles also liked the aesthetic affect. "Some of those early pinhole images were an attempt to create images that I thought might be similar to the way little kids would see things from the ground level and crawling. The pinhole distorts things and makes toys, for instance, larger than life and brings certain items in the foreground into sharp focus."

Nettles photographed and processed film while her children napped. "And then when I'd start to hear them wake up, I would just stop work. Later, I would select the negatives that I really liked and begin to print them. It was a process that could be done in little bits of time, which I have found is really critical in terms of keeping oneself going," Nettles says.

"Most recently I've used Polaroid film a lot because I can take pictures and get the negative instantly and a little proof print. I can file that away and feel comfortable and confident that the negative is there, that the film turned out." Weeks may pass before she returns to enlarge the image in the darkroom in the basement of her home.

Although her children are twelve and fifteen years old, Nettles tries to limit her professional life to the hours Rachel and Gavin are in school. Being a morning person, Nettles says that on the days when she can get to her studio, she can get a lot done between eight and three. But now that her daughter walks home from school for lunch every day, her days in the studio are even more fragmented than in previous years.

Her children know better than to barge into the darkroom. But developing film is a kind of "manual labor" that isn't disrupted when one of the children interrupts with a question over the intercom. "The times that really bother me are when I'm trying to collect thoughts and get ideas going. That's the time that it's really tough."

The sense that she may be interrupted at any moment is as bad as being constantly interrupted, Nettles says. "I get very upset when I get interrupted when I'm doing my artwork, and so I find it's almost safer not to do it than to be angry or feel upset."

On the few occasions when Nettles has had commercial projects with tight deadlines, she has been able to enlist her children's cooperation. But, in general, Nettles would not feel comfortable telling Rachel and Gavin to leave her alone so that she could work for an extended period of time in her studio, for instance, on a school vacation day. She acknowledges that guilt is a factor, adding, "It's not just my guilt, it's the culture. I think a father could go in and lock the door and not be considered a bad person. I think a mother doing that is still probably considered neglectful somehow. It's going to take a long time for those changes to occur."

Photo ©, Audrey Bethel

JOYCE MAYNARD

Joyce Maynard

Joyce Maynard, forty, is a reporter on the domestic beat, specifically her own life as a mother of three children. In the weekly syndicated newspaper column, "Domestic Affairs," she chronicled, for six and a half years, both the everyday ups and downs of her family life and the deeper losses of growing up with an alcoholic father, the death of her mother, and the breakup of her marriage.

A former reporter for the New York Times, Maynard is the author of two books of nonfiction: Looking Back: A Chronicle of Growing Up Old in the Sixties *(1973) and* Domestic Affairs: Enduring the Pleasures of Motherhood and Family Life *(1988), a collection of her columns; two novels:* Baby Love *(1981) and* To Die For *(1992); two children's books, illustrated by her former husband, painter Steve Bethel:* Campout *(1987) and* New House *(1988); and numerous magazine articles.*

Divorced in 1992, Maynard lives in Keene, New Hampshire, with her three children: sixteen-year-old Audrey, twelve-year-old Charlie, and ten-year-old Willy.

SUCCESS CAME EARLY TO JOYCE MAYNARD, WHO BEGAN entering writing contests when she was ten years old. At age sixteen, Maynard was a winner in *Seventeen* magazine's annual short story competition. Three years later, in 1972, she entered the national spotlight when the *New York Times Magazine* published her article "An Eighteen-Year-Old Looks Back on Life," as a cover story. The piece attracted the attention of novelist J. D. Salinger; Maynard dropped out of Yale University to live with the author of *The Catcher in the Rye,* and during their year together expanded her essay into a book, *Looking Back: A Chronicle of Growing Up Old in the Sixties.*

Although her first book included many of the cultural details of growing up in the 1960s, Maynard notes that she left out the central fact of her own childhood: that her father was an alcoholic. Years passed before she was able to write about those painful memories.

With the money she made from the sale of the book, Maynard did something rather unusual for a young, single woman: she bought a house in rural New Hampshire. The house was "a two hundred-year-old cape with four fireplaces and a Dutch oven for baking bread. Roses climbed the rock walls, blackberries grew out behind the porch, and just down the road was a waterfall," Maynard wrote in "End of the Road," one of the last of her *Domestic Affairs* newspaper columns.

But more than a house, Maynard bought a home to have a family in. "I was alone the day I moved into that old farmhouse. But from the day I set my rocking chair on the back porch, I pictured rocking babies there," she wrote in that column.

While waiting for Prince Charming to arrive on her doorstep, Maynard supported herself writing articles for women's magazines and doing political commentary for CBS Radio. "Which really tells something about the times, that they'd be asking this nineteen-year-old college dropout to be speculating on world situations," Maynard says. After living alone for several years, "just before I went round the bend, I rented out my house, went to New York City, and got a job as a newspaper reporter."

As a general assignment reporter for the *New York Times*, "the whole city was my oyster," Maynard recalls. With a plum job and a great apartment, "I seemed to have everything that a young woman journalist would want. But for me, the most elusive and desirable goal was not a career one, it was a personal one. There was nothing that I wanted more than to be part of a happy family." Her dream seemed to come true when she met Steve Bethel. Within two months of their meeting, Maynard had married the twenty-five-year-old painter and then quit the *Times*, "an extremely politically incorrect action for a twenty-three-year-old woman in 1977." Maynard and Bethel moved into the New Hampshire house where Audrey, the first of their three children, was born in February 1978.

The dream of a happy family was for many years the leitmotif of Maynard's life. It was something she herself had never had. Maynard now describes her late parents, Max and Fredelle Maynard, as "extremely sidelined, frustrated parents placing onto their children their dreams for themselves. My father was an artist who wasn't painting.

And I remember him saying almost every day of my growing up life, 'Children are hostages to fortune.'"

Her mother, a PhD from Harvard, couldn't find a job in academe in the '50s and '60s. Instead, she tutored English and Latin, sold encyclopedias door to door, and eventually wrote for the baby magazines and *Good Housekeeping*. She was also a ghostwriter for Dr. Joyce Brothers for a number of years, "at a pittance," Maynard says.

Her parents raised both of their daughters to be writers, says Maynard, adding that her sister, Rona Maynard, is now an editor in Toronto. "Whenever my sister or I wrote something, we'd bring it downstairs, and my mother would make a pot of tea. My mother and father would sit there with these 3 x 5 cards and yellow legal pads." While she read aloud, her parents would note her mistakes. "That's probably why I write in only one draft because it all happens in my head, this horror of hearing my mother's voice," Maynard says, as she brings out a notebook of essays, written by her mother's students, which Fredelle Maynard had corrected—her red-ink comments nearly covering the pages—in the same way she corrected her daughters' writing.

The psychic cost of such strenuous criticism was high. Maynard says that when she reads a paper written by sixteen-year-old Audrey, she can't help but "register all the stuff that my mother would have said, but I am not about to say it to her. I'll tell her I like it or I think it needs more work, and that's about as far as I'll go."

However, Maynard's ability to write without revising did enable her to support herself and her family while still having time to spend with her children. When she married, Maynard recalls, she hadn't given much thought to where the money was going to come from. While she believed that her husband would eventually achieve financial success as a painter, in the meantime, "the reality was that I had to work." Writing again for women's magazines such as *Family Circle* and *McCalls'* after having worked at the *New York Times* was more than a letdown. She had no desire to follow in her mother's footsteps, knowing that her mother felt that in writing pop psychology articles for the women's magazines, "she [Fredelle] had sold out in a lot of the work that she did.

"I had come to feel that I was a journalist, and this work was the poor relation of serious journalism," Maynard says. "I did attempt one piece of serious, hard reporting right after Audrey was born, which was a disaster." Years later, in the introduction to her collection of columns, Maynard wrote about that assignment, investigating houses of prostitution in midtown Manhattan, which she attempted to do while carrying her six-week-old daughter in a front pack. "I tell it as a funny story, but at the time it was a real turning point in my whole thinking about my work life—that this baby could not just be integrated without missing a beat into my career as Nellie Bly, girl reporter."

Maynard says she never seriously considered moving back to the city and hiring a nanny so that she could resume her career, although the family did return to Manhattan for some months during Audrey's infancy to further Bethel's career. "I was very clear about the sort of parent that I wanted to be. And although we always had baby-sitters in our lives, I wanted to be a very present mother. I shaped my work life around the requirements of that, and I'd say I have the career to prove it, which is to say, what I consider a sort of underachieving career."

When Audrey was two, the family had "a rare moment" of being ahead enough, financially, so that Maynard could take a couple of weeks off from writing magazine articles. Having written for money since childhood, Maynard decided, for the first time in her life, "I would write what I wanted to write." She put her daughter in twenty-four-hour child care for two weeks and began writing a novel at her kitchen table.

"I didn't have a clue what it was going to be about." But having recently interviewed writer Ann Beattie, whose novel *Falling in Place* had just come out, Maynard had a model and a method. Beattie had written a novel in three weeks, Maynard says, and "that made me feel that this was physically possible to do, that you could type that many pages at least. I did exactly everything that Ann Beattie said that she had done. I opened up Ann Beattie's novel, and I said, 'Ah, she writes in the present tense. I'm going to write in the present tense. Let me look at her first sentence. Her sentence describes a scene.' I closed my eyes and said, 'I'm going to describe a scene that interests me, and then I'll find out what happens in this scene.'"

Baby Love opens with a group of teenagers hanging out at a laundromat in a small New Hampshire town. Three of these girls are mothers, the fourth is pregnant. Maynard explains that the most autobiographical parts of the novel are "the feelings about having babies. I loved being pregnant. I loved nursing babies. I even loved giving birth.

"One of the things that was going on in my life when I wrote *Baby Love* was that I very much wanted to have another baby, and my husband was saying no," she says. "I discovered, for the first time, the way in which I could comfort myself with my own writing abilities, that I could write myself to happiness. I would write myself some babies. And in more logistical terms, I earned us a baby. We didn't have enough money and then I wrote *Baby Love* and then we had enough money."

While Maynard did manage to write her novel in two weeks, she says that doesn't mean she could write twenty-six novels a year. The reason she was able to write a novel in such a short amount of time is because "there was so much energy and frustration brewing."

At first, Maynard thought that she had found a new way to write, until she realized that this method was not integrated into her day-to-day life but depended on her being apart from her family, which she wasn't prepared to do on a regular basis.

Maynard is proud to have made a living from her writing for twenty-three years, "but it was artistically—if you can even call it artistically—a work life filled with compromise. It was almost nothing but compromise for a long time. I didn't even keep copies of most of the things that I was writing.

"But over the years, something did change, very fundamentally, in my approach to the magazine work. I came to have more respect for the audience," she says, and to see the possibilities inherent in writing about family life. "So I decided, if I'm home with these children and this is my world, that I would consider it my beat, as if I were a reporter, and I would try to invest it with the dignity that so-called more important work possessed for people. Gradually, I began to write more pieces that I felt were true reports of domestic experience."

In 1984, after writing a second series of "Hers" columns, Maynard was invited by the *New York Times* syndicate to do a weekly newspaper column for national distribution. Writing the column, Maynard discovered pride in her work, "not every week but cumulatively; I felt that I had a really important assignment." The column was never a best-seller, peaking at about forty subscribing newspapers, "but I loved the readers, and I loved the connection with them. I felt that I was doing work that really mattered in people's lives, which was a wonderful feeling."

In retrospect, Maynard sees that one of her aims was to present "a revisionist history of the American family. I didn't want some woman in Ohio or Oregon or wherever to open the paper and read my column and somehow feel, 'What's wrong with me?'" the way Maynard remembers feeling as a child, watching the sitcoms and wondering why her own family never measured up. "And so I began to try to tell an honest story," moving beyond telling funny anecdotes to revealing more of her feelings about family events.

But while readers encouraged this new direction, Maynard was still reluctant to reveal some of the key aspects of her life. "Although I talked about a lot of difficult subjects in the column—rage and frustration and fury, wanting to run away from home and looking at another man, bursting into tears and throwing dinner down the sink and pouring my beer over my head—there was one large lie that I wrote around. I portrayed myself as the ditz, as an erratic, emotional, hysteria-prone woman who was constantly being reeled in by this strong solid man without ever telling the rest of it," Maynard says, her voice constricting to a whisper, "which was that the person who was putting bread on the table—and it's hard for me to say it out loud still—was me.

"My husband never read my work; we didn't talk about it. I went by my married name in town—I kept a very low profile. On purpose, I kept myself down so that I wouldn't be more threatening," Maynard says.

"I'm very troubled by the perception I think a lot of young women have that they can have everything, the children and the career, with nothing forfeited. I don't believe that. My situation was probably exacerbated by the fact that I was the sole financial support of the household and I was not married to a particularly domestically supportive man." If one of the children got sick, Maynard would nurse him or her while Bethel would go out to his studio and paint.

But "quite apart from the physical tasks of caring for children," Maynard says, she was also left with the responsibility for what she calls "the most demanding and distracting activity—keeping in mind the ten million little details of their lives," which are "so seemingly unimportant, except that, cumulatively, they add up to a child's world."

The first person to suggest that Maynard and Bethel's marriage was in trouble was a Portland, Oregon, reader who wrote a guest editorial for the local newspaper on the subject, illustrating her point with little details from past columns and sparking a heated debate among the columnist's readers.

"I began to read my own columns," Maynard recalls. "It became increasingly apparent to me how dysfunctional and imbalanced this marriage was and to what an extraordinary degree I had given myself over to the needs of everybody around me at the cost of my own self."

But the turning point in Maynard's life came on Mother's Day, 1989 when her mother was diagnosed with an inoperable brain tumor and given only a few weeks to live. "I did something that under no other circumstances would I have felt that I had permission to do; namely, I left home to care for her. My mother and I had been experiencing a considerable amount of alienation and distance for years that was inexplicable to me because I knew I loved my mother—I knew I had a wonderful, extraordinary mother who'd sacrificed so much for me, and yet I was incredibly irritated by her, to the point where I could barely be around her. I had thought that I had all the time in the world to make up with her, because, if anything, I was going to drop before she did, she was such a powerhouse."

Maynard made arrangements for baby-sitters to care for her three children, then five, seven, and eleven. She recalls leaving pages of notes for her husband, "mostly with telephone numbers of all the mothers who would step in, as mothers do, to do all the stuff that I didn't do." There were detailed instructions, like which drawer to put the tooth fairy present in and admonitions to sign up for swim lessons, but not the 9:00 A.M. lesson because the water was too cold, and a reminder to buy flowers to give Audrey after the play she was going to be in. "He said, very openly, he didn't read any of them; he just threw them out.

"Over the course of that summer, I got some distance on my life." She had time alone, to swim or read or just think, "something I had not had since my children were born. Although it's an odd thing to say about the summer when you're taking care of your dying mother, it was the most peaceful, restful, restorative time in lots of ways for me."

She had time to talk with her mother, who had left her unhappy marriage after Maynard and her sister were grown. Both of her parents had blossomed after the divorce: her father had resumed his painting career; her mother had moved to a new city where she hosted a television show and wrote a couple of books.

Pushing her mother's wheelchair through the park, and later sitting at her bedside, Maynard had plenty of time to contemplate their relationship. "One of the things that I came to recognize was that the root of my anger and resentment of her was her own self-sacrifice, and the fact that she had failed to provide any kind of model of a woman who takes care of herself, so that I found myself in my thirties with no guide. The set of rules for myself that I had taken on from her was that every child's birthday requires a homemade cake and an extravagant party, and that you spend the entire month of December doing Christmas, and that nobody ever goes to bed without songs and stories. Amazing excesses that had a lot to do, in both our cases, with all the kinds of pain that we were not able to shield our children from," Maynard says, referring to the pain of having an alcoholic parent and the unhappiness in both her own and her parents' marriages.

"It's not like this came all in some lightning bolt recognition, but for the first time, I glimpsed another way of life for myself." But when Maynard returned home, she did not suggest separation. She was determined to try harder to keep the marriage going. "I actually went home to my husband and said, 'I want to have another baby,'" Maynard recalls. But to her surprise, "It was my husband who said the marriage was over because he also had experienced life without the constant tension. I'm very grateful to him for deciding because I don't think that I could have, on my own, at that moment."

At the time, however, she was devastated. "I knew that if the marriage was ending that I had to leave the house. It would be too hard and too lonely and too wrenching to stay in that place that was all about my domestic dream, my family dream." She also knew that her husband was attached to the place where he had built his studio and that he could do all the repairs needed to maintain the antique house. "I really wanted to be friends with him, at any cost, and I knew that if there was a battle over the house, that that friendship would be forfeited, so I left."

Five days after her mother died in October 1989, Maynard moved into a Victorian house in Keene, New Hampshire. Although she had had time that summer to rest and reflect, the death of her mother and her husband's sudden decision to end the marriage left Maynard so depleted that she felt there was nothing left for her to give to her children. "I was just spent," Maynard says. So the children stayed in the old home with their father for the rest of that school year while Maynard regrouped and "rediscovered" her voice.

She had continued writing her column while caring for her mother. But when Maynard announced her separation and the fact that her children were staying with their father until the end of that school year, she was surprised that many newspapers dropped the column that she had written for more than five years. "This was 1989, and editors were saying, 'Joyce Maynard is no longer qualified to write on family matters.' When people learned that my children weren't coming with me, they said I wasn't a good mother; that phrase must have been in three hundred letters easy," she recalls.

"Many people were indignant that I would have left Steve. I never said that he was the one who actually demanded the divorce. They would write and say, 'How could you leave this wonderful man that we've been hearing about for years?' And, of course, I was the one who had told them what a wonderful man he was."

Some newspapers dropped her column without explanation, Maynard says, "and since my separation came so close on the heels of my mother's well-documented dying, a lot of people assumed I'd had a nervous breakdown."

Losing contact with so many readers was "very painful," Maynard says. "There were people that I'd been hearing from for years. I knew their handwriting on the envelopes, and I knew their children's faces."

Maynard felt compelled to continue writing her column for those readers who remained. "I felt a responsibility not to leave the story in the middle. One of the big themes of the column always had been how to stay married—two people struggling to stay together even when they clearly have a lot of difficulties."

In those final columns, some of which Maynard has collected into a booklet entitled *No Longer Married,* one can see the author's evolution from a self-sacrificing young woman consumed by her desire to create a happy family to the mature woman who, no longer caught in the perfectionist trap of Supermom, has learned to nurture herself as well as her children.

For example, in "Christmas in a Broken Home," Maynard writes about the holiday that most epitomized her desire for family happiness. During her marriage, she knocked herself out trying—to find the perfect tree, to make not a gingerbread house but a gingerbread town, to sew a complete wardrobe for a child's stuffed animal—all in the vain hope that by creating the image of holiday perfection, holiday cheer would follow. But when her marriage ended and she faced spending every other December 25th alone, she realized that the performance was over. "And once you stop trying to make Christmas the most perfect time of your family's life, I've discovered, you can start allowing it to be simply a good time."

Although she ended the column in 1991, Maynard has continued to write about her life in the *Domestic Affairs* newsletter she started in 1992, the year her divorce became final. The newsletter includes letters and stories submitted by readers. "One of the things about my newsletter is that you get to talk about secrets," says Maynard, adding that some of the pieces that appear anonymously were actually written by her.

Maynard faces the same privacy issues as other artists and writers who draw on their family lives for their material. While Maynard says that she feels good about what she has written about her family life, "there's a lot of other stuff that would make this an even truer and more resonant body of work if I were willing to have no friends and totally alienate myself from my children. Of course, I'm not going to do that.

"My husband made this pitch in court to have me forbidden to write about the family. What I said to the judge was that there are constraints on me restricting my total freedom to tell my story that are far more compelling than any a judge could impose, and they have to do with what would be good or not for my children. I don't write anything that I don't think they could deal with reading," Maynard says, adding that her children almost never read what she's written about them.

While he asked the court to bar her from writing about the family after the divorce, Bethel used the positive things Maynard had said about him before the separation to bolster his case when he sued for alimony, custody of their children, and half of her mother's estate. "My book *Domestic Affairs* was entered into evidence, and passages read by his lawyer [were] read into the record as examples of what a fine father he'd been.

"We had a trial—something that rarely happens in a divorce— and a lot of the testimony surrounded this whole issue of who took care of the children. His contention was that he'd sacrificed his career for mine. He was taking the traditional woman's position, that I had been the money earner but he'd been the one at home, that I had taken all these trips promoting books and he'd been holding down the fort." However, Maynard says, "I knew that if you asked him even very basic questions like what was the name of their dentist, he wouldn't have known."

Noting that she could have sent one of her children to college for what she spent in legal fees, Maynard is reluctant to discuss the exact details of the settlement, other than to say that the judge did not bar her from writing about the family and that Bethel did not win custody. The children continue to live with Maynard during the school year and spend summer vacations and some weekends with their father.

In terms of her writing time, Maynard says that the divorce, "was as distracting as if I'd had a baby, and a lot less fun. It's very hard to sit down at your typewriter with a clear head when you're full of anger and rage and bitterness and filling out financial interrogatories."

When Maynard wrote *To Die For*, she was not only dealing with the divorce but also with the breakup of a subsequent love affair. "I was so deeply pained and grieved that I just wanted to exit my own life." It wasn't that she wanted to kill herself, Maynard says, "but I didn't want to be me for a while—I didn't want to feel my feelings." So she chose a story that was as far removed from her own life as she could imagine. The novel is a fictionalization of the case of Pamela Smart, a high school teacher who convinced several of her students to murder her husband. Maynard says, "I chose the first person voices because I just wanted to enter their bodies. I wanted to be a sixteen-year-old boy, not a thirty-six-year-old woman. It didn't make me happy, but I discovered the enormous restorative powers of creative endeavor."

Now that her children are older, Maynard has more time to write. But while she goes in to her home office every morning, she is often so fragmented by the time her children leave for school that she finds it almost impossible to concentrate enough to write. Similarly, when they come home from school at two-thirty, Maynard says, "there is a kind of energy buzzing around them. My concentration is gone.

"I tend to feel that if I don't have a chunk of at least four hours clear, forget the day. Luckily, when I do have four hours, I can get so much done that if I get a day like that once every five days, I'm in pretty good shape. I don't feel that it's a wonderful solution, it's just the way that I get through. The solution is eventually they grow up."

As to her future direction, Maynard says, "I'm still a journalist and as I have more physical latitude, I hope to see the world and go places again." Recently she checked into a motel room for six days and polished off another novel. As her children get older, she also looks forward to having the time to embark on a more challenging course in her fiction.

One reason she has chosen to write about young characters is that their dilemmas are less complex and can be easily resolved in the kind of novel which can be written in a week or two, she says. "But the problem of two fundamentally decent people who are in a tortured relationship—that's much more subtle and complex, and you need more than six days in a motel to address it.

"I have a lot of affection for those novels, but they were unabashedly commercial. I wrote novels that I'd want to read, but I don't kid myself about what they are and are not. I'm not regarded as a serious literary person, and that's okay. I know that I can do a completely different sort of work, and I'm not filled with any regret that I haven't done it."

Photo ©, Frank Cieciorka

KAREN HORN

Karen Horn

Karen Horn, forty-four, is a realist, in her watercolor paintings of flowers and in her life. After graduating from the California College of Arts and Crafts in 1969, she joined the back-to-the land movement, at one point living in a school bus in rural northern California. Divorced while her daughter, Zena, was still in diapers, Horn survived on food stamps and welfare for a time.

Although she eschewed the traditional career path for a young artist, Horn continued to develop artistically during her child's early years. In the nontraditional settings of a china painting class and a stained-glass business, she discovered a love of flowers and transparent color and had the opportunity to work with design, color, and composition.

Horn began working in watercolor in 1983. Her daughter was ten years old and less needy, and, at that point, Horn was ready to embark on a professional career. She lives with painter Frank Cieciorka in Alderpoint, a hamlet in northern California. At the time of this interview, seventeen-year-old Zena was spending the year in Italy as an exchange student.

"GROWING UP AS A LITTLE KID, I ALWAYS KNEW I WAS GOING to be a painter. When my mother was trying to have me choose a college, I said, 'If I can't go to art school, I don't know where I'll go, I don't know what I'll be,'" Karen Horn says.

But after graduation from the California College of Arts and Crafts, Horn dropped out of art. The conceptualism and minimalism of art at the end of the 1960s interested her but, "It seemed to me that all you needed to do was think about these things or maybe talk about them with a few other artists or collectors. The idea was so central, so important that art had become the realm of the poet-philosopher. I knew I was somebody that needed something to do, that I wasn't so cerebral that I could live completely in the rarefied art world of the mind."

The back-to-the-land movement of the time appealed to Horn

because, by contrast, it was concrete. "It was, you're going to do something real, make something real. And probably in that vein, I also made a baby to do something real, that mattered, that was concrete."

However, the loss of solitude with a new baby was a shock to Horn. "I could be removed from society, I could live out in the woods, that was fine. For all I said that I wasn't cerebral enough to deal with the art scene as I perceived it after I came out of college, solitude and a lot of time to think about things were really very important to me. And suddenly I had this baby that gave me no time at all.

"Everything was fractured, everything was broken down. There was no continuity; anything you started you knew would never be finished, or at least would be finished so much later as to be irrelevant. That was almost torturous for me. Mothering was very hard for me. I didn't take to it, even though I love my daughter. There was nothing, and still is nothing to my mind, wonderful about sleep deprivation or diapers or childhood diseases," she says.

When her marriage fell apart, Horn moved to town to be near a laundromat and so her daughter could have friends. Within the small house she rented, Horn created a studio space. In her bedroom she built a bunk bed four feet below the ceiling with a desk underneath the bed. The other three walls in the room were lined with work tables. The room had a linoleum floor for easy cleaning and fluorescent lights. "It was much more important to me to have a place to work in than a bedroom. And I guess I was making a statement, too, about the situation of men in my life. I was going to have a baby and I was going to work, and that was it.

"I plugged into the welfare system, and that's how I survived for a while. I had no support whatsoever, and coming out of art school, no job skills. But that also really changes your perspective on life. And certainly in terms of painting, I became much less enamored or even interested in the progression of male-dominated art history—the Renaissance to now as this series of things white men have done by themselves being special and isolated geniuses," she says.

"I started examining anonymous art, late medieval things, Indian art, Rajput miniatures and women's art, Amish quilts, and then finally, of all things, china painting. It was a class I could go to. It was something to go to and be together with other women, like going to a quilting bee. You get so isolated in your home with your child, and you just need things that will get you out of the house because there's always something at home that needs to be done.

"It was completely anti-male, anti-art. China painting is probably the least legitimate [form of painting]; this is nice ladies' art. This is what you did if you really weren't an artist; you were a putterer and you went and did china painting and it was genteel. But I found that I enjoyed it just for the company, for the certain period of time that was set aside: you were going to use a brush during these hours," she recalls.

Unexpectedly, the china painting affected her imagery. "I started loving flowers, which have never been taken seriously by Western art, but I didn't care by then. And I have ended up building a career of being a still-life painter."

Horn also embraced realism because she sees it as separate from the "genius syndrome" of traditional art history. "I love paint. I love colors. I love forms." Realism, she feels, is a way to be a painter and not be isolated and removed from everyday life.

While Zena was young, Horn couldn't get involved in ideas that needed to be developed or considered over a period of time. "Because I had no time at all to consider art, to think about or develop a continuity, I would copy paintings out of books that I liked. I could do this because it was an isolated act, something I could pick up and put down," she says.

"One of the things that I learned by copying these paintings—and this has really been integral for me—was that there were certain things that I couldn't help but do. I would try to make this look exactly like the thing I was copying because I wanted to learn what this artist was doing and how they were working on it. And yet the image would come out not quite right. All those things that were not quite right were my own.

"They were the things that I couldn't help but do. Not because I was technically incompetent; it was just part of my nature. Forms would become more solid, for instance. Everything was very subtle, very tied down. I realized, 'This is something that means a lot to you.' The arabesque is not in my vocabulary; something spinning off dizzily into space is not something I care about. That was very interesting for me and was a way of learning about myself that was definitely brought on by the fact that I had a child and had to work within severe constraints."

This new self-awareness gave Horn confidence in her own ability to create original work. "Although I always painted—I couldn't live without it—it was also this very frightening thing. All through high school and college, people talked about creativity, and it always seemed like this incredible burden that I had to be more brilliant, more intuitive—I had to come up with something that nobody else had ever done or thought of.

"Once Zena was a little older and I did have some time, I did stained-glass work because that was pattern work. I could stay up late at night and be by myself and work out a design of what I was going to do. But from then on it was like making a dress—a very complicated and difficult dress, but nevertheless, you could be interrupted all the time. You could keep going back to piece 150 or 152, whatever piece on your pattern you were working on. After doing stained glass—which is something I wouldn't have normally done if I was 'an artist'—I found that I loved transparent color and light and have become a watercolorist.

"All these experiences that were essentially not part of the art scheme, the career, that were sort of forced on me as the best I could do at the time, became very valuable and helped me learn a lot of things that I rely on now," Horn says.

"A friend of mine said, 'Have a kid, lose ten years.'" Her daughter's ninth year was a watershed in Horn's life in terms of both her mothering and her art. "Frank [Cieciorka], whom I'm living with now, gave me the watercolors and said, 'Here, try these, you'll probably like them,' because I had worked in oils and acrylics. They were small and intimate; you didn't have to have a big studio set up to start with, so they fit the constraints of motherhood.

"I'd been doing the stained glass, so it was possible for me to keep up with design, color, and composition when Zena was younger. But painting is, for me, very obsessive. I don't think you're allowed personal obsession when you have young children.

"In terms of being a mother, I can remember nine was when it changed. I can remember having a conversation with her when she was nine. She was suddenly far less maintenance; she was really neat, she was fun. I could talk to her, we could do things together. Nine was good, and from then on it's been good. I'm one of these women who loves teenagers. I can remember people saying, 'Oh, treasure your little baby because they grow up so soon.' Well, I'm really going to miss my teenager. That's going to be the hard part."

Her teenager still needs her emotionally but not constantly, Horn says. "When they need you, it's very intensely. But very often, teenagers come home and you say, 'How's it been? What's been going on at school?' and you get a three word answer and they eat their dinner and go do their homework. Other than being there to supply the dinner, you're not really too necessary. But you do need to be there because there are some very intense times that have to be worked through, and then you need to be absolutely available.

"This year is my first year alone. Zena's in Italy. I find that life isn't terribly different. If I concentrate flat out and work on my painting four or five hours a day, my brain is tired after that; I'm not making good decisions. I'll be putting in unnecessary time and accomplishing very little with it. It's much better to come back fresh another day and bring renewed sight and energy to what I'm doing. So I really am not putting in that much more time in the studio. It's not like with her being gone I've got this huge sense of liberation. That's come gradually ever since about age nine."

How does she foresee her art changing in the coming years as her daughter becomes an adult? "I think that my focus on the art will become even more intense. When you talk about the emotional needs [of teenagers], they also give a lot when they get older. I think I'm going to miss her a whole lot, and then I'm going to have to fill that spot with something else. I'm assuming that will be the artwork. So I'm expecting changes in my work, but I don't know quite what they will be. If this year is any indication, it seems to be that the work keeps taking on more development. I'm working much, much larger than I used to be even a year ago. And I take on projects that I think would have been unmanageable before," she says.

Although she has become successful as an artist, Horn has not forgotten the difficult years when she survived on welfare. Instead of being treated as "pariahs," she would like to see women in her former situation valued for their work as mothers.

"I'm making a living off being an artist; I have a very good career going at this point. I'm a contributing member of society. It's too bad it was so damn hard; that didn't help at all. Poverty is just debilitating. It puts everything off, it makes it take longer and maybe not happen at all."

Photo ©, Kalman Zabarsky

PATRICIA SMITH

Patricia Smith

In an earthy voice, full of poignancy and humor, Patricia Smith, thirty-six, writes poetry about growing up black under the glittery, deceptive sway of Motown music, of blues and bars, love and longing, and headline-gripping deaths. Collected in two volumes, Life According to Motown *(1991) and* Big Towns, Big Talk *(1992), these are poems that are meant to be read aloud, dramatically. Indeed, Smith writes her poems with the intention of performing them in the "slam," a competitive type of poetry reading.*

Winner, in the individual category, of the 1990 and 1991 international championship poetry slams, Smith has given poetry performances in Osaka, Paris, and Stockholm, as well as in the United States. She was sent to Japan as Chicago's cultural ambassador after winning the "Poem for Osaka" contest and has also received an Illinois Arts Council Literary Award. Together with her European-American husband, Michael Brown, Smith hosts a weekly evening of poetry reading, including a slam competition, in the Boston area.

Smith grew up on the impoverished west side of Chicago. She attended Southern Illinois University and then, in 1977, became a reporter, first at the Chicago Daily News *and then at the* Chicago Sun Times. *Since 1990, Smith has worked as a reporter and arts critic for the* Boston Globe. *After thirteen years as a single parent, she married Brown in 1990; the couple and Smith's fifteen-year-old son, Damon, live in Medford, Massachusetts.*

PATRICIA SMITH DOESN'T JUST RECITE HER POETRY, SHE PER-forms it, moving about the stage with a fluid grace. The African-American poet mesmerizes the audience with her words, telling stories in a language that is visceral and immediate, but also spare and elegant.

Smith is a champion of the "slam": a competitive type of performance poetry, an avocation she shares with her fifteen-year-old son, Damon, and her husband, Michael Brown.

In the slam, pairs of poets compete against each other, with dramatic readings of their original works. Several members of the audience judge each reading on a scale of one to ten on the basis of content and performance. The poet with the highest score wins that slam.

A slam team of four or five poets representing a particular city evolves through a series of playoff slams during the course of a year. While most of these teams hail from US cities, the slam is spreading to foreign cities such as Stockholm, which has fielded a team in the annual international slam competition. This international championship includes a category for individual participation which Smith has twice won.

She explains how slam poetry is different from other kinds of verse. "A really good slam poem is one that pulls the audience in immediately. They forget that they're watching someone read a poem, and they're pulled into the story of the poem. It's pretty confrontational. You don't let the audience escape the poem, whether you have to leave the stage and go down and get into people's faces with it, or ask a question in it and have them jolted by that. But you can take a well-crafted, well-written poem that doesn't have any of those elements and deliver it well, and it will work."

The attraction of performance poetry can be summed up in one word: *adoration*. Smith says, "Once you start hearing the applause and you start hearing it regularly, it's like a fever—you want to hear more of it. It makes me see how people who perform on Broadway feel.

"There's a poem that I have called 'Chinese Cucumbers.' It's about a man whose lover is dying of AIDS, and he goes around chasing all these insane cures that he sees in the *National Enquirer.* The poem makes people cry. It makes me cry when I'm doing it because I pull back all the feelings I had when I was writing it. My husband, who has heard it twenty times, cries every time. He has gotten to the point that when I start the poem, he leaves the room.

"To be able to elicit that type of response in people with something that basically is just words on paper, you want to do it and you want to do it again. You think that you're changing the way people not only think of poetry but the way they look at day-to-day life. That's a heady feeling. You know that people walk into a poetry reading one way, and you just hope that they don't feel the same way when they leave."

While poetry is a passionate avocation, Smith supports herself and her son by working full time as a newspaper journalist. She has covered a variety of subjects in her lively writing style, from interviewing Toni Morrison and Spike Lee to reporting on the aftermath of the Los Angeles riots, as well as doing more personal pieces on such topics as sexual harassment and her mother's emigration from Alabama.

Some of her most powerful poems originated in the tragedies, such as rapes and murders, which Smith encountered while reading the news wires or the newspapers. She says she felt "very disturbed or angered or saddened by them and would have a hard time dealing with them on my own. So I would put myself into the story and write my way out, taking the perspective of someone in the story, [such as] the murdered person right before the murder or the police who found the body." One example is "Headbone," a seventy-four-line poem which conjures the horror of the rape and murder of a young girl from the perspective of the assailant, a thirty-five-year-old "pillar of the community," as he destroys his four-year-old daughter. The poems ends, "And that's how they found him, / crouched over his greatest sin, / staring at the bright, slick statements / she'd left on his fingers / and waiting for the one word / that would make it all right again: / *Daddy?*"

Smith's "Medusa" poem is in a similar vein, but here the tragedy is mythological. Medusa, the lusty mortal woman, tells how she seduced the sea god Poseidon in Athena's temple as she is metamorphosed into a monster by the enraged virgin goddess.

Discussing the poem, Smith says, "I'm a fanatic of fantastic movies. One of my top ten movies of all time is *Clash of the Titans*. One of my favorite parts of that is Jason going after Medusa's head; Medusa is really ugly. I was watching it once and then I thought, 'They make her out as being this evil, terrible, bad thing, and she was just a regular woman before all this stuff happened to her.'" Smith researched the details of the story, and then, "I imagined what she thought, knowing something was going to happen, but not knowing what it was going to be, and what she was thinking about as her body was going through the changes."

Smith had written poetry earlier, but it wasn't until she attended the annual Chicago Poetry Festival in the mid-1980s that she became involved with the poetry community.

"I had poems that I'd written and kind of stuffed in kitchen drawers and would take out and read when I needed to read them. So I said, 'I'm going to go to this thing and see what real poets are doing.' And when I got there, I found out that what real poets were doing wasn't that different from what I had stuffed in the drawer.

"It was a nice, warm, inviting community. They said, 'Well, hey, bring your stuff, come on out, there's a lot of open mikes where you can read.' And I finally got up enough nerve to do it, and once I did it, I said, 'Oh, this is what I've been looking for, okay.' And I've been writing pretty steadily since then."

When she left her native Chicago in 1990, Smith organized the first Boston slam team. Together with her husband, she cohosts the Boston Poetry Slam, a twice-weekly gathering at a local cafe that includes an open mike (where anyone in the audience can read), a featured poet, and a slam.

Although both Smith and Brown are involved with slam poetry, there is an atmosphere of cooperation rather than competitiveness between them. Her husband, a European-American who did his dissertation on African-American literature, teaches writing at the University of Rhode Island and at Suffolk College in Massachusetts.

Smith says, "We run the venue together. He's the best press agent I've ever had. He was on me to get my book printed again, and he sells them [copies of her first book] out of the trunk of his car if he has to. He's great about that, real supportive.

"My husband, who's a lot older than I am, has a lot of poetry with beautiful, extended metaphors that I really wish I could write. My writing's always been more immediate than that." Smith says that one of the first things that attracted her to Brown was "that we were both impassioned about poetry. By really listening to a person read his or her poetry over a period of time—whether or not it's an intensely personal poetry—you can learn a lot about that person. That was a unique way to meet somebody and learn about somebody. And I think it formed a stronger base than any of the other relationships I've had."

When she met her son's father, Don Lewil, she was attracted to his passion for the performing arts. "He was a theater major and really full of life, full of fire. He got out of college and decided he wasn't going to pursue the theater—which was basically the most attractive thing he had going for him. He wound up as some kind of computer operator or consultant, which I thought was a real waste of what he was passionate about. He was a really good actor. I'm attracted to people who have that kind of passion, and when he compromised that, I just lost a lot of respect [for him]. He wound up being incredibly dull."

Smith and Lewil grew up in the same poor neighborhood of Chicago, but didn't meet until college. Their son, Damon, was born in 1976, but they never married. "The farther I got in my career, the farther I grew away from him. We didn't have that much in common," Smith says.

"I was pretty much self-sufficient; I was never one who asked for money. My mother still thinks that I should have taken him to court, but that, to me, signaled that I would always have some kind of tie with him whether I wanted to or not. And I was making enough money to do what I wanted to do. It was a little strain to keep Damon in private school for a while. And if I really got in a bind and Damon needed clothes, I'd call and say, 'He needs clothes.'"

Smith describes her son's father as having an on-again, off-again relationship with Damon. "He was one of those people who was a father when it was fashionable. When he was around his friends, he'd go, 'This is my son here.' But he could be gone for months at a time, and then he'd pop up again and he'd want to go out and buy school clothes."

In Damon's early years, Smith had little interest in getting married. She was young and writing a singles column. With each new date, her son wanted to know why she didn't settle down with that man. "I had awful bad luck with relationships for a while, and I think he was buffeted about a little more by that. My son has old-fashioned values. I think he really wanted a nice, neat little family unit—which may have come from television."

Although Smith was a single parent for thirteen years, the experience was not a negative one. "I'd like to say being a single parent was a real hardship, but it wasn't. I had my son when I was twenty, and we grew up together. There never was this big authoritative thing where I felt that I had to lord over him the whole time. We were buddies."

From an early age she involved Damon in her professional life as a reporter. "I always made sure he was aware of what I did for a living, what it entailed. If I wasn't at home, he knew where I was; if he had to stay with someone, he knew why. Whenever I could, I'd have a picture and I'd say, 'This is who I'm talking to today. They're in a magazine; they're important.' Or, 'I'm going to review this show, here's a record that this person made.' So he had a real good sense of what I did. And when I could start taking him around with me, I did. He was pretty independent from an early age. I think that has a lot to do with me just dragging him around like he was my age and introducing him to people.

"It was a bartering system as far as his baby-sitting was concerned. I found a woman who was in school at the University of Illinois trying to get a degree in veterinary medicine. She was from a big family and she couldn't study in her home, so she moved in with me. She would be there when he came home from school. So I had a live-in baby-sitter in exchange for room and board and a quiet place to study."

Smith keeps an eighth-grade graduation portrait of Damon near her desk at the newspaper, along with an earlier snapshot of her son sitting on the couch. The latter, Smith says, is there "to remind me that he used to be young." Smith remembers Damon, at around age eleven, talking to her nonstop. But then, "He went to camp the summer after his eleventh year, and he came back grown up. It was like, 'Well, I really don't want to do those childlike things anymore, Mother. I'd like to get rid of all these toys and get some sophisticated electronic equipment. I don't want to hang out with you on weekends anymore. And from now on when we go to the store, I'll walk ahead in case my friends see me because I don't want them to think I'm out with my mother.'"

Now that Damon is in his midteens, Smith says, "He's like an alien: some days he's fine; other days he's full of being fifteen." She adds that he's going through a moody stage where either everything is going well or nothing is. "There's no middle ground. Last night, I started to write a poem about my son because I had gotten so upset because it didn't seem like I was getting through to him." When her son has a problem, Smith says, "He's not one of those talkative kids, so he shuts down and gets in a really bad mood. And I get upset because he's not reaching out like they do on television. My husband's going, 'Look, he's a fifteen-year-old boy. He's not going to talk to you. He doesn't think you know anything anymore.'"

Smith has written a few poems about her son, published in her second book, including "Biting Back," "Always in the Head," and "Pretending Sleep." But while her son is seldom the subject of Smith's poetry, he does share her interest in the slam. When her first book came out, Damon asked the emcee at the Green Mill in Chicago one night if he could read one of his mother's poems. Smith, who was out of town at the time, was amazed when her husband told her about the incident. Damon also writes poetry, as well as rap lyrics, and has won a couple of slams. "But I can't tell you he's done it for the artistic merit; he's done it because there's been a cash prize. He comes into a place with me, and he says, 'Is there a slam tonight?' I say, 'Yeah,' and he sits downs and writes his stuff right there, gets up on stage, reads it—and he wins." She says this with pride and amazement.

"Damon likes poetry, but he can't tell me he likes it. He won't go to readings with me anymore. I think it's the same way he feels about my working here [at the *Boston Globe*]. He likes what I do and he likes the fact that I meet people his friends would think are famous people. But he doesn't want to make too big a deal out of it because it's not too cool to make a big deal out of anything your mother does, no matter who she is.

"If I would say to Damon, 'Why don't you keep writing? This is really good stuff,' then he would stop. If I leave him alone, he'll start writing on his own. The key is just to pretend like you have no interest in what he's doing, and then he'll fire up again on his own."

Photo ©, Sid Felsen

ELIZABETH MURRAY

Elizabeth Murray

Elizabeth Murray, fifty-three, paints the world around her: coffee cups and dogs, paintbrushes and tables. Her abstracted representations, painted in vivid oils, have an infectious joie de vivre. Although her works are part of a still-life tradition that includes Juan Gris and Paul Cézanne, "the life in her paintings is anything but still," writes art critic Roberta Smith in her essay "Moving Pictures," in the book Elizabeth Murray: Paintings and Drawings.

A native of Illinois, Murray received her BFA from the Art Institute of Chicago in 1962 and, thirty years later, an honorary doctorate from the same institution. Considered one of the most important contemporary American painters to emerge in the 1980s, Murray is a member of the American Institute of Arts and Letters, and her work is in the collections of such major institutions as the Whitney Museum of American Art and the Metropolitan Museum of Art.

The artist has a twenty-four-year-old son, Dakota, from her first marriage, which ended in 1973. After nine years as a single parent, Murray married poet Bob Holman in 1982. The couple live with their two daughters, Daisy, eleven, and Sophie, eight, in New York City.

RECOGNIZED AS AN IMPORTANT CONTEMPORARY PAINTER, Elizabeth Murray has achieved her success with a singular style that is at once abstract and representational. When she talks about her success, Murray sounds a bit surprised, saying about her work, "For some reason, which I'll never understand, it's appealed to enough people so that [they] have looked at it and found it interesting and paid money for it."

Happily married to her second husband, with her son grown, two daughters at home, and a successful career, Murray says, "I have a really great life right now. I just try not to feel guilty about it."

But her life has not always been so easy. Driven to succeed, at least in part to compensate for her parents' failures, this modest, likable woman talks about the difficult years as she struggled to raise her son, first in an unsupportive marriage and then alone, while at the same time establishing herself as an artist.

Elizabeth Murray always knew that she wanted to be an artist. Her mother had studied art in school, and both of her parents respected and very much encouraged her interest in art. Murray attended the Art Institute of Chicago and then went to graduate school at Mills College. Equipped with her MFA and two years of teaching experience upstate, the twenty-six-year-old artist and her sculptor husband, Don Sunseri, arrived in New York City in 1967. Minimalism was in and critics were proclaiming the death of painting.

Determined to paint, Murray proceeded to do so and, in the process, helped revitalize contemporary American painting.

Her drive to succeed has a lot to do with her background, Murray says. After a nervous ailment destroyed her father's career as a lawyer, her family moved in with her grandmother. Her mother, unable to find work as a commercial artist, painted porcelain miniatures at home. "I had to make something of myself and, in retrospect, I feel like I had to make up for my parents' failures."

Two years after her arrival in New York, in 1969, Murray gave birth to her son, Dakota. "The enormity of what I had done really hit me, almost instantaneously. I was twenty-eight years old, I didn't know anything. But I never thought of [motherhood] as something that was going to stop me." She adds, "I really never thought of 'motherhood' period. If I did, it was that it was a definite no-no if you wanted to be an artist."

Murray taught at least three or four days a week from the time Dakota was six months old. Then in the evening, after putting her son to bed, she would paint until two or three o'clock in the morning. "I don't even know how I did it now, but I was driven to do my work." One of the most positive aspects of becoming a mother, Murray says, "was that I realized how much I needed to make my work.

"The other thing that Dakota brought into my life was the idea of unselfish love, some little glimmer that I was not the only person in the world." Murray says she was too self-involved to realize "that I could have stopped for a while and everything would have been fine."

She says, "The hardest part was the psychological anguish, at times, of feeling torn. I was not capable of saying, 'Okay, I'm not going to work for a period of time' or 'I can just relax; things will develop.' I could never relax.

"I don't know how he survived," Murray says, but quickly adds, "I'm not saying that I neglected him, because I didn't neglect him. Until he was four or five years old, I was a pretty good mother. It came naturally to me. But when I split from his father, I really lost my bearings. I could go on forever about the mistakes I made through just inexperience and being too self-absorbed to really pay attention to what was going on with him." She adds, "He's okay, by the way; he survived it."

At the same time that her marriage was ending, Murray was beginning to receive attention for her work. In 1972, she participated in her first group show in a major museum—considered a milestone in an artist's career: the Whitney Annual exhibition; the following year, she was included in the Whitney Biennial, another prestigious debut.

Murray taught full time until 1978, when Dakota was about nine years old; she continued teaching on a part-time basis until 1984. Murray says she never resented having to teach, but rather, enjoyed it and, if she had more time, would like to teach again.

Being a single parent, however, was difficult for Murray. "That was fun for about two days," she says. While her relationship with her husband was unhappy and she has never really regretted the breakup, "after a few years of being alone, I definitely felt that it was a hardship, and I could see how difficult it was for my son." However, with the increased number of divorces and separations in the 1970s, "there were a lot more single parents around all of a sudden. I don't think my son felt completely isolated by being from a separated family," she says.

But for all the difficulties, Murray says that when she became a mother, "I remember how it was the first time in my life—and I couldn't have articulated it then—that I felt like a normal person. Like, oh, I can get pregnant and have a baby."

In retrospect, she realizes the cultural conditioning or "brainwashing" inherent in the idea that "you weren't a real woman unless you had a baby." And yet, she says she wouldn't have wanted to miss the physical experience of pregnancy and birth. "It's like a million tabs of LSD to have a kid."

None of her close friends had children when Dakota was born, and most of the women and men artists she knew didn't believe that it was possible to combine a career as a serious artist with raising children. "I remember one of my women friends coming to my studio and saying, 'Well, what can *you* do anymore.' I was shocked by that.

"Having a child made me reach out in ways I never would have reached out to other women. I was such a snob, I didn't want to have anything to do with anybody who wasn't an artist in some way. I was one of those types who was completely constricted into my own little world of a few people, from insecurity. But I had to get down there and go out in the world and meet some people who weren't artists," she says.

Although her artist friends did not have children, her dealer, Paula Cooper, had two children around the same age as Dakota and was also separated from her husband. "So we had a kind of connection. She did a lot for me and my work." Murray had her first solo show at Cooper's gallery in 1976, at age thirty-six. Since then, she hasn't had to market her own work.

In terms of her career, Murray says, "I've been really lucky." Although she felt there was sympathy toward her as a mother, she didn't want to be perceived as "artist with kids. I wanted to be Artist."

Although she enjoys her children, Murray is no longer sure that motherhood is an essential experience, as her generation of women were raised to believe. She recalls her sadness when women friends who entered menopause in the early 1980s voiced regrets that they had not had children and that they felt devalued because they were too old to procreate.

But at the same time that her friends were coming to terms with their childlessness, Murray's life was heading in a different direction. For years Murray had wanted a second child, but knew that she did not want to raise another child alone.

Then in 1982, when she was forty-two years old, Murray married poet Bob Holman. "There was a lot of attraction and excitement" in their relationship, and Murray says she felt, "How could I not have a child with this person?" She gave birth to her daughter Sophie in 1982, followed by Daisy in 1985. Although Murray and Holman were initially planning on having only one child together, Murray says that when Sophie was born, "the minute she came out, I thought, I am going to do this again. I knew right away I didn't want to have another only child."

Her son was thirteen in 1982 when his first sister was born, and at the time, Murray says, she thought that having a sibling was "the best thing that could have happened to Dakota." In retrospect, Murray says that in focusing her attention on the new family she was creating with Holman, she neglected her son, who needed her as much in adolescence as he had earlier. After Sophie's birth, Murray says, "He went off, by choice, to live with his father," a change in living arrangements which both Dakota and his father wanted and which she reluctantly agreed to.

She also regrets that she did not encourage her son, whom she describes as "very talented," to pursue his interest in art. "I think I unconsciously did not want him to be an artist," she says, adding that perhaps his father felt the same way. However, Murray notes that Dakota is now following his artistic interests in the film world, working as a freelance production assistant. Because of his parents' occupations, Dakota is "a little cynical about the art world," but also "he's very sophisticated about art. There was a point where he absolutely refused to go to a gallery or a museum. Now he loves to go, and we go together and it's a lot of fun," Murray says.

While she was a struggling artist when Dakota was young, by the time her daughters were born, she says, "I was showing my work, I was starting to make some money, so I could have my kids and have my work."

She has worked out many of the practical issues of childrearing, not only because she is a good organizer, but also, Murray says, "because I can afford it." She is also somewhat more relaxed about taking time off from work to be with her children; for example, she doesn't go into the studio on weekends.

When she was younger, Murray remembers needing a lot of time to get her ideas going, "to conflict" before she could actually start painting. She was also much more anxious about her work, Murray says, because "you don't understand when you're younger that it's going to work out, that it's just a question of time. That if you keep at it, it'll come together." Now when she has to leave the studio, Murray says, "I just know I'll come back, unless some horrible thing befalls me."

Until recently, Murray has always had a studio in her home. When Dakota was little, she considered herself lucky to have a loft with enough space to work as well as live in. "There was a basketball hoop at one end and I didn't care. And then gradually as Dakota got bigger, I wanted more and more privacy, so I built a wall that separated my studio."

When her daughters were born, the family was still living in this loft with the studio in the front, an arrangement that worked well for the first few years, until she again wanted her own space. When Holman and Murray bought a house in the West Village area of Manhattan, she moved into a studio five minutes away, while he now shares an office at a film studio where he is working on poetry videos.

In terms of the division of household labor between herself and her husband, Murray says, "I feel like I do everything, but that's not true." But she sees the question of who does the dishes or who does the cooking as a matter of technical details. The most important difference between her and her husband, Murray says, has to do with the fact that her husband feels free to continue working even after he has come home for the evening, while she would feel too guilty if she tried to work past 5:00 P.M.

Since moving into her new studio, Murray has begun to feel the urge to work longer hours. "Right now I feel like I could be here from six in the morning till six at night. And I would love to work at night again—that's the one thing I miss about not having my studio at the house."

Despite financial success and critical acclaim, she is not about to rest on her laurels. For one thing, she needs to work. "If I can get four hours of work done, I'm fine. It's when I can't get a certain amount of time in that I begin to crack up and get crazy," Murray says.

She is also driven by a sense that she has more to accomplish in her art. When she looks at a given piece, she often doesn't know what the work means. "It's all unconscious fantasy, and I would like to find something more concrete."

Her paintings are difficult to describe, and sometimes even art critics reviewing the same exhibition do not always agree on what is being depicted. The objects in her paintings are elongated, or both elongated and foreshortened, as in paintings by Picasso, so that the subject matter is not always immediately apparent at first glance. After a few minutes of studying a piece (and reading the title), the viewer realizes that the rectangle and splayed legs are a table, or that the circle with a long handle is, in fact, a spoon.

Murray seldom executes her paintings on a traditional flat canvas. Instead, she builds, with the help of assistants, an irregular-shaped, three-dimensional plywood structure, which may incorporate protrusions and indentations, and then covers the entire structure with canvas before applying paint. Although her works are, first and foremost, paintings, the underlying three-dimensional structure gives a sculptural quality to her pieces.

More Than You Know (1983) illustrates the emotional depth of her work and the way she frequently incorporates allusions to the works of earlier artists. Painted after a visit to her dying mother, *More Than You Know* contains such familiar elements as a room, a table, a bedstead, a letter, but at the center of the painting is an anguished kidney-shaped face, with red eyes and mouth, which clearly alludes to the howling visage in Edvard Munch's painting *The Scream*.

When asked how the content of her art is affected by her life, Murray says, "I find that a very strange question." She is clearly annoyed that some critics interpret her work as feminine simply because she frequently paints interior scenes, household objects, and people. "I think that's just so narrow," she says with a touch of exasperation. Murray is quick to point out that Degas, Cézanne, and Manet all dealt with interiors in their work, that Monet painted his family, and that contemporary artist Eric Fischel paints psychodramas that take place within rooms. "There's been such a division between the sexes and such a genderizing of the way people look at work. I just think painting is about life. What else would I paint about?"

"I've been painting a lot of dogs lately," she says. "The idea of a bounding dog really appeals to me." Exemplifying both the lively tone and the innovative structure seen in many of Murray's works is *Sunshine* (1993), a three-dimensional oil painting roughly in the shape of a dog sitting up. A ray of light seems to enter the upturned nose of the sea-green terrier, animating its red spirit. Red tubes loop through the body, connecting with a large hole where the dog's stomach might be. Although the dog is in a sitting position, there is a sense of excitement and motion about the painting; the animal seems to be craning her neck to see her tail, and her short feet seem to point in different directions.

Bounding Dog (1993–94) is one of the few paintings that Murray has done in recent years on a traditional, flat canvas. A leaping, brick-red dog, outlined in blue, with cartoonish, balloon-like limbs, takes up most of the picture space. An energetic ribbon of blue bisects the foreground; the background is a creamy yellow, with squiggles that could be heat waves; a thin blue tree, a green hill, a red ball, and several yellow leaves complete the idyllic scene.

The image of a bounding dog, Murray says, "feels like freedom, like this rush into something. Actually, I've always used dogs as images in my work. So it's not like it's anything new. It seems to come in and out of my work. What, exactly, the dog symbolizes for me or what it's a metaphor for, ultimately I don't know. That's why I keep working," she says. "I'm trying to be more conscious in my work and really say something."

Murray hopes that she has not yet reached her full potential as a painter. "In a few more years, as my daughters get older, I'll finally be able to devote myself entirely to my painting. So I'm looking forward to it, and it's scary at the same time. On the other hand—and this is very important for me—I don't think for a second that having kids has done anything but open and widen the potential for my art. Even though it's taken away time, I don't think it stopped one painting from happening."

Photo ©, J.P. Ostriker

ALICIA SUSKIN OSTRIKER

Alicia Suskin Ostriker

As a poet and as a literary critic, Alicia Suskin Ostriker, fifty-four, is at the fore-front of a new movement in American poetry, which she defines in Stealing the Language: The Emergence of Women's Poetry in America *as "explicitly female in the sense that the writers have chosen to explore experiences central to their sex and to find forms and styles appropriate to their exploration."*

Ostriker is the author of seven books of poetry: Songs *(1969),* Once More Out of Darkness and Other Poems *(1974),* A Dream of Springtime *(1979),* The Mother/Child Papers *(1980),* A Woman under the Surface: Poems and Prose Poems *(1982),* The Imaginary Lover *(1986), and* Green Age *(1989). Educated at Brandeis University and the University of Wisconsin, Ostriker is a professor of English at Rutgers University and an expert on the poet William Blake. In addition to editing Blake's complete poems, she has written four criti-cal books, including* Vision and Verse in William Blake *(1965),* Writing Like a Woman *(1983),* Stealing the Language: The Emergence of Women's Poetry in America *(1986), and* Feminist Revision and the Bible *(1993), part of the Buck-nell Series in Literary Theory. Among the honors she has received are fellow-ships from the National Endowment for the Arts, the Guggenheim Foundation, and the MacDowell Colony.*

Ostriker is the mother of three children: Rebecca, twenty-seven, Eve, twenty-six, and Gabriel, twenty-one. She lives with her husband of thirty-three years, Jeremiah P. Ostriker, a professor of astrophysics, in Princeton, New Jersey.

ALICIA SUSKIN OSTRIKER WAS ONE OF THE FIRST WOMEN IN America to publish poems about her experience as a mother. "I started writing about motherhood almost as soon as I was a mother." During her second pregnancy in 1964–65, Ostriker began composing the title poem of the chapbook, *Once More Out of Darkness,* a poem that origi-nated in "jottings I'd made during my first two pregnancies, which were eighteen months apart. At that time, I was writing because writing was what I did. It didn't occur to me that I hadn't seen any poetry about pregnancy and childbirth until I was well along in shaping that poem. That was a radicalizing moment for me as a writer."

Her first child, Rebecca, was due the same week Ostriker handed in her PhD dissertation at the University of Wisconsin, but actually arrived a few days later, in August 1963. Her second daughter, Eve, was born in February 1965; six months after that, Ostriker began teaching at Rutgers. Three factors influenced Ostriker's decision to combine career and children in an era when few women did both: ambition, a desire to organize her life differently from her mother's, and a husband who half-jokingly said that he would divorce her if she ever turned into a housewife.

When her children were small, Ostriker recalls, "It was pillar to post. I constantly felt guilty for not doing enough for my freshmen, not doing enough for my children, not having time to write, and so on. This is a very familiar story: there were never enough minutes in the day; I was always exhausted. But I was keenly aware and proud that this was my choice. I didn't know anybody else who was trying to have babies and a career simultaneously. I did have the support of my husband, so the exhaustion and the craziness and the guilt were balanced by my strong sense of intentionality. This was a life I was choosing, and I didn't want to give up any piece of it.

"Being a college teacher was something I'd wanted to do for years—that's why I went to graduate school. Writing my dissertation, on the other hand, was complete hell. I swore I would never write another critical book after that one. Later I changed my mind on that score."

Ostriker's dissertation initiated her career as a Blake scholar. "One reason I worked on Blake, who was my guru and my main man for many years, is that his writing is so revolutionary. He was a protofeminist; he explores the meaning of maternity and paternity in our culture more deeply than any previous poet, and he writes about the experience and the significance of sexuality more interestingly and more powerfully than any poet before D. H. Lawrence."

In the midst of her busy life as professor, wife, and mother, Ostriker continued to write poetry, as she had since childhood. She had neither a specific time nor a particular place set aside for that writing. "Poetry was always in the interstices of everything else, the nooks and crannies. It was always time stolen from other responsibilities. Everything else in my life was being done for someone or something else: someone needed me to do it or I was being paid to do it. Poetry was the one thing that I did for myself alone with the sense that no one on earth except myself gave a damn whether I did it or not. In my early years, I didn't make other things move over very much for it; it was always on the run.

"Where did I write? Oh, I wrote everywhere. I wrote while I was driving, I wrote sitting on buses, I wrote on the living room sofa, I wrote in bed. I even used to share a desk in my husband's office, in the astrophysics department at Princeton, and worked there. I never did much writing at Rutgers because if you kept a typewriter in an office there, it would be stolen.

"For many years, it was difficult for me to do any concentrated writing at home—not counting jots and scribbles. Scribbling something down in the first place can be done anywhere because it's done spontaneously—it just happens. But the work of revising needs peace and quiet. Concentration was difficult for me at home, because home was the place where I was responsible, where I was the mom, even when someone else was ostensibly taking care of the children. I just necessarily always had an ear to everything that was going on. We had au pair girls for ten years, though by the time my son was three, we started sending him to day care. Having an au pair girl helped, but home was still the domestic space rather than the writing space."

When the family moved to its current residence in 1975, Ostriker gained a study that doubles as a guest room; in the years since her youngest child entered high school, she has been able to do more concentrated writing at home. But even then, with more time and a room of her own, Ostriker's method of writing poetry hasn't changed. "For me, the initial draft of a poem is never place-dependent because it always interrupts something else that I'm doing. I never sit down and decide to write a poem."

Ostriker illustrated the covers of two of her early books of poetry with her own woodcuts. Although she was able to write poetry whenever and wherever, graphic arts needed more time and space than she had available after her children were born. "That was the real trade-off. When I had children, I stopped putting time into art. I had taken courses in graphics and did etchings and woodcuts. That turned into annual Christmas card making with the kids, which was the only kind of sustained visual project I ever undertook after they were born. I carry sketchbooks and still enjoy drawing, but graphic art requires time and space." She hasn't gone back to graphic arts, "because the writing meanwhile expanded exponentially."

Her children have been a major theme in all of Ostriker's books after the first. She began writing *The Mother/Child Papers,* which places family life in the context of history, when her son Gabriel was born in 1970 a few days after the United States invaded Cambodia and four student protesters were shot by National Guardsmen at Kent State University. The first section of that book includes poems that juxtapose the joy of giving birth with a mother's horror at the violence of war and her fears for her son's future. Ostriker writes: "she has thrown a newspaper to the floor, her television is dark, her / intention is to possess this baby, this piece of earth, not to surrender / a boy to the ring of killers. They bring him, crying. Her throat leaps."

Among her more recent works with a maternal theme are the sequence of poems to her older daughter in *Imaginary Lover* and a suite of birthday poems to her second daughter in *Green Age.*

Asked to what extent motherhood influenced her imagery in general, Ostriker answers, "My guess is that the experience of maternity saturates every single thing I do. Maternity augments one's vision, one's sense of reality, one's sense of self. I believe that I'm maternally motivated toward the world and not just toward my children. Certainly I'm maternally motivated toward my students, who are a big part of my life. But in addition, I think my views of art, history, politics—all sorts of issues—are in part determined by that double experience that motherhood brings of idealism and practicality. Children represent at once infinite hope and stony intractability—and the world is like that too.

"I have found that the writing I've done about family, about my children, is often the work that audiences are most engaged with and most responsive to. When I read the mother-daughter poems from

Imaginary Lover, people will always come up from the audience and say, 'I'd like to have a copy of that for my mother,' or 'I'd like to have a copy of that for my daughter.' These are themes which speak universally to audiences and to readers. Though when I and others first began writing about motherhood, the literary and critical response was, of course, 'This doesn't belong in poetry; this is trivial. It's not universal enough,'" Ostriker recalls.

"One change in the literary scene since I started writing is that it has become quite normal rather than exceptional for women to write from the position of motherhood. It was almost unheard of when I started writing, and it doesn't surprise anyone now."

Does that also mean that poems on a maternal theme are accepted now within the academic world and taught in university courses? "That, of course, moves more slowly, just as any avant-garde work exists before it's accepted. Canonization obviously takes longer than production. I would say the two most important poets getting into the classroom now who write as mothers are Anne Sexton and Sharon Olds. Maxine Kumin, too. Maxine is certainly accepted, canonized, was Poetry Consultant at the Library of Congress, and is a Chancellor of the Academy of Poets. A great piece of her work consists of family poetry which she calls 'the tribal poems.'"

Another change Ostriker has seen is in the attitude her women students have toward motherhood. One class in the 1970s had such a negative reaction to the pregnancy/birth theme of her early poem, "Once More Out of Darkness," that Ostriker wrote "Propaganda Poem: Maybe for Some Young Mamas" in response. Her students today see maternity differently, "There is no longer a feminist party line opposing motherhood. That has fortunately faded away. Young women today, I believe, see motherhood as a personal option, a personal choice, rather than an ideological one. What has not changed very much, although it has changed to a certain degree, is the extent to which fathers are prepared to invest their time and souls deeply in the nurturing and raising of their children. I know some couples in which the fathers take equal care, but they are exceptional."

In her own case, although her husband has always been very supportive of her work in terms of helping out with the children, Ostriker describes him as "more supportive theoretically than practically."

Asked what advice she would give to young women on combining creative work with childrearing, Ostriker notes, "The most important thing for a young mother to remember is that children and the experiences of maternity—ranging from ecstasy to hellish depression—are valid material for art. We require artists to explore and define the significance of all human experience. The visions of motherhood which mothers will propose will obviously differ from the views of 'experts' such as male doctors, psychologists, and novelists. Mothers can use their lives as raw materials for art just the same as Monet used landscape or Dante used Florentine politics. They can record everything and turn it into metaphors.

"One of my great regrets is that I didn't write down more. You think you'll remember everything, and then you forget." The poet urges women to keep journals and use tape recorders, cameras, and video to capture those fleeting moments. "And don't be afraid to be honest," she adds. "Don't sanitize your feelings, don't be sentimental. The culture has plenty of sentimentalized versions of motherhood. What we need is reality—the whole array of realities that have never before gotten into books," including the realities of those who are not white or middle class, she adds.

In retrospect, Ostriker says of her experience in combining writing and mothering, "I'm sure that many people will tell you this: Taking care of children is a tremendous drain on your time, your spirit, your feelings, your self-image, and there's no way around that. So that's the down side. The positive side is that having children keeps you real, keeps you open and on your toes and is a continuing learning experience. [It] gives your mind and your passions a constant workout—which, if you want to keep them alive, is not a bad thing to have happen."

Ostriker's youngest child moved out three years ago; she describes being an empty nester as "terrific." Is she still able to give her passions a constant workout? "I worry about that a lot. I worry about cooling down, and I try to find other ways of keeping hot. The question of what to replace motherhood with is a real question when you've defined yourself as a writer for many years through motherhood, as I have, because I've written about my children so much. When that consuming and absorbing interest subsides, what can you find to replace it? I'm still in the process of discovering that."

Portions of this interview were previously published in the Spring 1993 issue of Belles Lettres: A Review of Books by Women.

Photo ©, Shulamith Oppenheim

JANE YOLEN

Jane Yolen

Jane Yolen, fifty-four, is best known for her literary fairy tales. Reading such stories as The Girl Who Cried Flowers, Greyling, *and* The Hundredth Dove, *with their haunting cadences and sometimes ambiguous endings, one can easily imagine the author spinning yarns by the light of the campfire, as her great-grandfather once did in his Ukrainian village. Yolen is, in fact, a member of the National Association for the Preservation and Perpetuation of Storytelling, as well as editor of Jane Yolen Books, a Harcourt Brace imprint of fantasy and science fiction novels for children.*

Describing the relationship between child reader and author, Yolen wrote in an educational journal article, "I am mother to all children who read my tales." But Yolen's work is not limited to any one age group or genre. Her oeuvre includes poetry, fiction, and nonfiction titles ranging from Picnic with Piggins *(1988), a lighthearted picture book, to* Briar Rose *(1992), an adult Holocaust novel. With 135 books published and another forty or so already under contract over the next five years, Yolen has also received such major awards as the Caldecott Medal, the World Fantasy Award, the Golden Kite Award, the Kerlan Award, and the Regina Medal.*

Educated at Smith College and the University of Massachusetts, Yolen and her husband of thirty-one years, David W. Stemple, live in the Berkshires town of Hatfield in western Massachusetts. The couple's daughter, twenty-seven-year-old Heidi, lives in Florida, while twenty-five-year-old Adam makes his home in Minnesota, and twenty-three-year-old Jason has moved to Colorado.

WHAT IS PERHAPS MOST REMARKABLE ABOUT JANE YOLEN IS not that she is so prolific but that she gets any writing done at all. At the time of this interview, Yolen has just returned from six weeks in Saint Andrews, Scotland, where she and her husband, David Stemple, have just bought a summer home. Between visiting friends, battling the flu, and lining up local tradesmen to rewire the house, Yolen says,

"The fact that I actually had time to sit and write anything, much less four stories, was amazing."

Born in 1939 in New York City, Yolen was a child of writers. "I was nine or ten before I realized that grown-ups were not all writers," she recalls. Her father worked in journalism and public relations while her mother, who made up and sold acrostics and crossword puzzles, "was a failed short story writer, having sold only one in her lifetime."

Her brother became a journalist, but Yolen ruled out that career after working as a cub reporter for the *Bridgeport Sunday Herald* the summer between her freshman and sophomore years at Smith College. "I was perfectly fine sitting in the newsroom writing the stories," Yolen says, but "I hated going out on interviews. I couldn't go and say to someone, 'How does it feel that your son was just picked up in three different pieces?'" Her stint as a reporter did, however, have a lasting effect on Yolen's writing style. Amid the noise and chaos of the newsroom, she developed the ability to concentrate intensely on her writing for short periods of time—an invaluable skill once she became a mother.

After graduating with an English degree in 1960, she worked at a variety of jobs in first magazine and then book editing. Throughout this time, Yolen used her lunch hours, evenings, and weekends to do her own writing. Her first published article, on building and flying kites (her father's hobby), appeared in *Popular Mechanics*. She ghostwrote her first book, *A Young Sportsman's Guide to Kite Flying,* for her father, Will Hyatt Yolen, before publishing *Pirates in Petticoats* (1963) under her own name. While long out of print, it is still the only nonfiction children's book devoted entirely to women pirates, Yolen notes.

In 1965, Yolen left Alfred A. Knopf, where she was an assistant children's book editor, for a year of camping in Europe with her husband. When they returned to the US, Yolen was eight-and-a-half months pregnant with their first child. The couple settled in western Massachusetts, and Yolen—who had already sold four or five books, with another dozen making the rounds—became a full-time writer.

"I'm one who writes in very short, intense spurts—which is why I think I've managed to do as much as I do," says Yolen, who produced at least one book every year while her three children were young.

"When I'm concentrating on my writing, the house could burn down around me and I might not notice."

At that time, her creative spurts could last anywhere from fifteen minutes to an hour, she says. "Now I have so much time because my children are all grown-up. I might be working on a piece, suddenly look up, and I've been there four hours, and I haven't realized how much time has gone by. Before, I concentrated like that, but if a child needed me, I could stop and leave it and come back."

Stopping because a child needed her was not frustrating, Yolen says, "because when you're writing, your head keeps going. If physically I'm not typing anymore, I'm still writing in my head. So I didn't lose anything by it. And in fact, sometimes it was a welcome relief to get up and diddle around with other things."

Being a mother has affected her creative work in good and bad ways, she says. "I tended, I think, to be more creative when I was pregnant—after the first month and a half when I wanted to sleep all the time. And when I had a little one, I was just extraordinarily prolific. I don't know if it was hormonal rush or what.

"I think any time your life is full, you have more to write about," she adds. "Certainly children have made my life very full and very complete. But the bad thing is, of course, that there's a lack of time. One has to find ways of using the little bits and pieces of time. So in a sense, when my children were young and still very much at home, my writing life was really quilted into the rest of my life in little patches here, little patches there. Once the children started going to school, I had large swatches of time that I could use. But until then, I had a husband who gave me wonderful supportive help, and we just simply made do.

"My husband was a professor, so he was able to be around more often than someone who was working a nine-to-five job. He would take the children off for an afternoon, or he would come home and do some housecleaning. He's always been my first reader. He reads everything I write, and comments and critiques. And he's always been very supportive as far as, 'You're a writer; this is what you do. What is the way I can best help you?'"

Yolen traded baby-sitting with neighbors, and her children attended play groups. When her third child was born, she was able to hire a baby-sitter to come to her house part time. "Of course, I worked in the house, so I was always there. It's just that the baby-sitter was able to be with the children, and if there were any problems, I would deal with them."

Before the youngest child started school there were "ten years of trying to figure out times that one could work. You worked when the kids were napping, you worked when they were sleeping, you got up before they did and worked. They also learned that if Mommy was sitting at the typewriter, they didn't bother her unless it was really important. So my kids are very independent. But I was always at home. If someone was sick, I was there. If someone was home from school, I was there. If someone stubbed a toe, I was there."

Yolen, however, did not attempt to write at the kitchen table. She says she thinks it's important for someone who views herself as a professional to have a place set aside for work, "even if it's only an old closet that you've turned into your own private space. That doesn't mean that people didn't come in and borrow my stuff. When the children were little, they were always coming in for pencils and pens and erasers and paper and that sort of thing."

Yolen works in a cozy two-room aerie tucked away in the attic of her home. From the desk in her writing room, she can look down on a field, now dotted with pumpkins. A red velour dragon dangles from the ceiling, one of several fantasy creatures congregating near the stairwell.

Although her husband is a computer science professor at the University of Massachusetts, Yolen continues to use a typewriter because, "When I'm getting something down for the first time, it comes in such a white heat that if the computer burped and ate it, if there was a power surge and I lost it, I could not tell you three minutes after the screen went blank what it was that I had put down. It would be gone," she says.

Asked about her involvement in the emerging technologies, Yolen confesses with a laugh, "I am a Luddite. I play on a computer network, I'm fascinated by CD ROM, but I am really computer illiterate."

She adds, "I expect that I need to learn, but if the point of computers is to make things easier, there's enough of a Puritan in me to say that writing should never be easy. And if the point of the technology is to make me faster, nobody on God's green earth wants me to be faster. They can't keep up with me as it is."

Yolen describes herself as a "jewel polisher." While she often writes a whole poem in one sitting, she then goes over it "twenty, thirty, forty times before I'm ready to let it go out into the world." Short stories typically begin in a more roundabout way, as a page or two of writing that the author sets aside until she knows what the piece is about. Yolen works on short stories, poetry, and picture books all at the same time, but "once I know where a novel is going, I tend to work on that to the exclusion of much else because of its size."

While she would like to be able to write "a Ruth Rendell mystery, an Antonia Fraser biography, a book like Jane Smiley's *Greenlanders*, or a mammoth, sprawling novel like those of James Clavell," Yolen says, "I don't think my talents lie in any of those places, at least not yet. I tend to be better in the smaller and more particular."

Yolen, who received her master's degree in education from the University of Massachusetts in 1976 and an honorary doctorate from Our Lady of the Elms, has taught at writing workshops across the country. Children's book authors Patricia MacLachlan, Shulamith Oppenheim, Barbara Diamond Goldin, and Nancy White Carlstrom are some of the students who became her colleagues.

"One day, Harcourt Brace said, 'We want to make sure we get first dibs on the people you discover,' and so they asked me to do a line of books," says Yolen, who continues to teach a master's class in children's books each summer at the Centrum writing conference. She has edited more than fifteen novels under the Jane Yolen Books imprint since the line's debut in 1988.

Yolen has also collaborated with two of her children: Adam arranged the music for seven song books while Jason illustrated three of her books with his photographs. Her daughter, Heidi, a private investigator, is starting to write a detective novel.

Being a mother has influenced the type of books she has written at different points in her career. "When my children were really little, I tended to write picture books for younger children because I was reading a lot of those books to my own children. As they grew older, I started writing to a slightly older level. But once they became teenagers, I went back to picture books," Yolen says.

Several of her books have been inspired by places and incidents in her personal life. For example, *Owl Moon,* which won the 1988 Caldecott Medal, was based on her husband taking their children birding. Her forthcoming book, *Wild Hunt,* is set in the family's home in Scotland, while the house and town in *Briar Rose* is Yolen's own Phoenix Farm and Hatfield, Massachusetts. *The Bird of Time* (1971) was written when Yolen learned her mother had cancer, and the beginning of *The Devil's Arithmetic* (1988) is based on a Passover seder at her uncle's house.

Yolen's children have appeared indirectly as characters in some of her books: *Commander Toad in Space* (1980) is about Adam, while the boy in her science fiction novel *The Boy Who Spoke Chimp* (1981) is Jason, and the girl in *The Gift of Sarah Barker* (1981) is her daughter, Heidi.

"You wouldn't know it, but I know it. What happens when you're writing fiction is that bits and pieces of real life inform what you're doing, but it's not a one-to-one absolute ratio. And probably they're all about me in the end anyway," the author says.

While elements of a given story may be influenced by her children, Yolen says, "I was a children's book writer before I was a mother. A children's book writer needs to be in touch with the child inside of herself, and I'm very much in touch with that child part. I write the books I wanted to read as a child."

The author begins her workdays playing on a computer network in the children's books, fantasy, and science fiction categories. She then writes from about 7:00 A.M. until 2:30 P.M., with a break around ten for breakfast and getting the mail. During the busiest weeks of the editing seasons, Yolen may put aside her own writing entirely, but most of the time she needs only the last two or three hours in the afternoon for her imprint.

"Everyone at Harcourt Brace says, 'How can she produce that many books for us and still do her own writing?' The reason is: I don't go to meetings. You cannot possibly get any of your actual reading and revising of manuscripts done, or even write flap copy, if you're at seventeen meetings during the week."

Working as an editor has increased her understanding of production and, Yolen adds after a moment's hesitation, given her "a better sense of how good a writer I am. I think that every writer should spend some time reading slush, and they will understand where they are in the great scheme of things."

Yolen meets weekly with five other writers of children's books who, she says, "give no quarter. When I read stuff there, boy, they let me know when I fall down. So even if I thought it was pretty good, they'll whip me into shape."

She sends her manuscripts out to whichever publisher she thinks appropriate; if that first publisher isn't interested, she turns the marketing of that manuscript over to her agent of twenty-eight years, Marilyn Marlow, at Curtis Brown. "If you get the best to begin with," says Yolen, "you just stick with them. I've known her longer than I've known my children."

Despite the demands of editing, Yolen says her writing output has speeded up over the past few years because she has learned to prioritize her ideas. When she first began writing, Yolen says, she would work on each of her ideas "with the same passion and emotion. Now I have an automatic censor that disposes of those things that are not good enough, or are ideas that I'm perhaps not skillful enough yet to deal with, or are repetitions of things that I've already done."

Yolen's advice to young women about combining writing and motherhood is to "just do it. If you have to make a choice, if you say, 'Oh, well, I'm going to put away the writing until my children are grown,' then you don't really want to be a writer. If you want to be a writer, you do your writing. You find ways to do your writing. Whether it's when everyone's asleep at night, getting up really early in the morning, doing it with the baby in a pack on your stomach, in a pack on your back, you do it. And if you don't do it, you probably don't really want to be a writer, you just want to have written and be famous—which is very different."

What kind of changes would make it easier for writing mothers? "I just think the awareness that men are partners in raising children is certainly going to help. It will mean that the women are not going to be the absolute primary caregivers. I also think that the fax machine and the computer and all that sort of stuff which makes it easier to be in contact with your publisher will make it easier. But the problem of sitting down, inventing a story, and getting it down still remains hard, and that's never going to change.

"Just simply being a mother, as I have been for the last twenty-seven years, has been so much a part of my life that I don't see it as not being there. But I've been writing for at least thirty years. And the two things are so intertwined, I just couldn't see doing without either one of them."

Photo ©, Douglas Kent Hall

LINDA HOGAN

Linda Hogan

The stories Linda Hogan tells are the stories of the land and those who dwell upon it. Descended from Europeans on her mother's side and the Chickasaw Indian tribe on her father's, the forty-six-year-old author carries within her the legacies of two peoples whose destinies collided on this continent. In her writing, which celebrates the power and mystery of the natural world, Hogan also grapples with the greed of those who plunder, and honors the love of those who protect the earth.

Hogan is the author of a novel, Mean Spirit *(1993), which received the Oklahoma Book Award for fiction and was a Pulitzer finalist; several books of poetry, including* Seeing Through the Sun *(1985),* Savings *(1988), and* The Book of Medicines *(1993); a collection of short fiction,* Red Clay: Poems and Stories *(1983); and is coeditor of* The Stories We Hold Secret. *Hogan was educated at the University of Colorado, receiving her BA in psychology in 1972 and her MA in English and creative writing in 1978. In addition to grants and fellowships from the National Endowment for the Arts, the Guggenheim Foundation, and the Minnesota Arts Board, Hogan has also received The Five Civilized Tribes Museum playwriting award.*

Hogan now teaches creative writing as an associate professor at the University of Colorado, Boulder. She is the divorced mother of two adopted children of the Oglala Lakota tribe: nineteen-year-old Tanya and twenty-five-year-old Marie.

"I BEGAN AND GREW AS A WRITER AT THE SAME TIME THAT I began and grew as a mother," says Linda Hogan, who started writing in her late twenties.

Hogan was working as a teacher's aide when she discovered a book of poetry by Kenneth Rexroth. "I was really excited. I had never read any contemporary literature or poetry. About half a year later, I decided that I was interested in learning more about writing poetry, so I went back to school. Within the first year that I returned to school, I started publishing and I was hooked. I loved writing and I still do."

In 1978, Hogan graduated with a master's degree in English and creative writing from the University of Colorado, Boulder, and published her first book of poetry, *Calling Myself Home,* later reissued as *Red Clay: Poems and Stories.*

That first book of poems "was really about my own family and my own personal history," Hogan says. "They are home speaking through me," she writes in the introduction to *Calling Myself Home.* "These poems grew out of the Oklahoma terrain resonant with the calls of frogs, my grandfather's horse and wagon, my grandmother's uncut braids worn wrapped about her head in the traditional Chickasaw manner, the firefly-lit nights we sat outside and heard stories, including the one of the gunstocks made from our stolen black walnut trees. In these poems live red land and light."

The same year as her first book was published, Hogan became a mother when she and her husband adopted ten-year-old Marie and five-year-old Tanya, two half sisters who shared the same birth mother.

For Hogan, the decision to adopt was both personal and political. The poet was working for an Indian rights group, Denver Native Americans United, when the Indian Child Welfare Act passed. That law emphasized that Native American children in the foster care and adoption system be placed if at all possible in Indian families, preferably from their own tribe. "Before that, Indian families were not seen as families that were desirable for adoptive placement in the eyes of social service employees," Hogan says. "Up to that time, almost all the native children who were taken away or relinquished voluntarily were children who were lost to their own communities."

When the new law passed, there were about six hundred children in the Denver area who needed Indian families, says Hogan. "I had a spare room, and I always wanted to have a couple of children or more—actually, I used to be ambitious enough to want eight.

"I felt like adopting was both an important and urgent thing to do in order that children from Indian families not grow up away from their own community. Most of us who are tribal believe that having children assimilated into the white world or growing up in a family where they don't know who and what they are is a travesty.

"We were in severe crisis from the time the girls came," Hogan says. "The children were both abused in foster care and their records were 'lost,' according to Denver County social services, yet the family that had them continued to receive money. My younger daughter— the foster family *gave* her away to somebody else to raise while they collected the money," says Hogan, her voice breaking. "When Tanya came to live with us, she was five years old and weighed only twenty-four pounds and wore a size two toddler's. Her teeth were all rotted out of her head and she did not speak yet. She was severely neglected."

The older girl, Marie, had cigarette and hot-wire burn scars all over her body. She had been not only physically but also sexually abused in foster care and "had probably been sexually abused since infancy with her birth mother," Hogan says.

"I had always believed that becoming a mother by choice, out of care and love—that love could conquer everything. This is something we really want to believe. And I did not comprehend at all that there are people who cannot heal."

After a year and a half of struggle, Hogan says, "I lost Marie. I had to give her up because she was so extremely violent. She sexually molested the younger girl, and she killed one of our household pets. She did not have a conscience. It wasn't her fault; that is what made the choice to place her in residential care so difficult."

Hogan still has occasional contact with Marie. "She's in and out of jail quite a bit, so I hear from her when she wants to get out. She's still very violent; she recently attacked a man and put his eye out."

"Having that failed adoption has been a kind of ongoing mourning and grief that isn't easily acknowledged by others because people think that you only have deep grief if you lose your child to death. And then there are also people who think that you only have a connection with children who are your birth children and not with your adopted children." But, Hogan asserts, "There is a love that comes from somewhere else besides the blood."

The younger girl, Tanya, was a failure-to-thrive child, abandoned as an infant by her birth mother. "She was *found*—I like that word— she is still a miracle person. She's a survivor to the utmost degree. That she lived through the hunger, despair, and violence and turned out to be a beautiful person is amazing to me."

At the time Marie left, Hogan's marriage collapsed. "My ex-husband's way of dealing with things was not like mine. Mine was to get active and fight. His was to withdraw. I ended up doing everything alone, and he was too depressed to function. He still has not escaped that depression, nor have I.

"My ex-husband and I are friends, and sometimes we talk about Marie. It's still very painful to both of us, particularly having to make the decision about Marie and having in some way had heart-full expectations that didn't come into reality."

Hogan says she still feels anger toward her ex-husband at times. "I think this is true for other women as well; what we thought about men is so far from what we've discovered they in reality are. My father was the kind of person who could do everything, I thought. He could fix the plumbing and take care of a crisis. If there was a drunk in the neighborhood that was having DTs, my dad would take care of him. If a car accident took place, he'd take care of the people," says Hogan, who described just such a father in her short story, "Friends and Fortunes."

"I grew up thinking this was what men were like: they had the energy and the power to take care of situations. As it's turned out, in my experience, it's the women who do that, not the men."

Hogan sees the abuse her daughters suffered in foster care, in a larger context, as "tribal wounds" inflicted not only by individuals but by a historical legacy of evil and hatred, of greed. "In my writing, I am trying to make the connection between how our tribes, our people, were abused and broken and how what has happened historically moves into the present; it shows up in our lives now, in the present. When people are injured and warred against and hated, it takes generations to break that pain, to draw it out of the body and soul. Part of being a mother, for Indian families anyway, is having your children understand what has happened in a way that allows them to find wholeness and a return to ways that work better for us than the dominant culture's ways.

"Being a person whose ancestors came over the Trail of Tears [the forced migration westward of thousands of Native Americans], I think about how my ancestors survived that so that I could one day live. I was carried in their bodies; I am made out of their blood. I'm a survivor of the long tragic walk," says Hogan.

From the European-American side of her family, Hogan has a journal written by her maternal great-grandfather, Bower, which spans the years 1848 to 1934. He writes about how, after his crops were destroyed by locusts, he worked for the government, killing buffalo to feed the starving settlers. In her autobiographical essay, "The Two Lives" collected in the book *I Tell You Now,* Hogan acknowledges the desperate struggle for survival that European immigrants faced. "Their lack of regard for the land and life came, in part, out of that desperation," she writes.

Hogan seeks not only to understand the connections between the past and present, between landscape and history, but also to communicate her understanding. "I think for those of us who pass between the worlds," says the author, referring to her mixed ancestry, "that in some ways we do make connections for other people as well. Our lives are lived in a margin—not in the sense of being totally marginalized, but we live in the membrane between the two skins. We communicate and hear with both sides."

While struggling to make sense of her own history and the history of the American continent, Hogan clearly identifies more with her Indian heritage. In contemporary terms, one reason may be that her mother's relatives are not in close contact with each other; and, therefore, "their influence on me has been minimalized," Hogan says. Her father's family has had a much stronger influence on her because they are "such a close-knit family; there are so many of us and we journey long distances to get together. The difference, I believe, is a difference in the capacity for love."

Hogan's identification with her Native American roots informs not only her poetry, but also her fiction. Her novel, *Mean Spirit,* is told from the perspective of the Osage and some Chickasaw people whose oil-rich land was stolen by whites. Set in the 1920s, the novel reveals the cultural chasm that divided the whites and the Native Americans. "It was a story that I felt I had to write. This happened in all parts of Oklahoma," including the area where her paternal grandparents lived, "not just in the northeast, where it's set."

Hogan says, "Even though I love writing poetry, I felt I had to look at other genres, particularly fiction. Because so few people read poetry, I think fiction carries more potential to create and reach an emotional state and resonance that allows for people to make change from their bodies outward. I am still idealistic enough to believe that the world can change. We need to find images and words and powers that will allow for that. Writing is only one way to do it, but sometimes a strong one."

When asked how she found time to write, Hogan says, "I don't know!" In the first months and years of motherhood, she says, "One of the things I did—when there wasn't a crisis—was to have office hours at home when I would have time to write." She also worked at night while her daughters were sleeping.

At that time, Hogan was writing poems, a number of which dealt with her experience as a mother. "I suppose they're love poems in a general way," she says. An example is her poem "Daughters Sleeping," from the book *Seeing Through the Sun*. Hogan writes, "Beauties, I want to curve into your skin / while you sleep, / to suspend myself in you / and tell you it is a warm world."

That poem was inspired by daily life. "When is the best time to be able to look at how precious somebody is? When they're asleep," Hogan says.

"I still write daughter poems. I write about children and their relationship with their mother. I feel that the relationship between a mother and her child is one of the strongest and most holy bonds in existence because in some way, part of the word 'mother' has to do with being the origin or the creator of something. I'm not sure that the mother is the creator, but I think that mother and child have a creative bond and a creative energy that forms and shapes both of them."

While her writing has sustained Hogan spiritually, it has not paid the bills. She had to teach full time to make ends meet while raising Tanya alone and, in the process, lost her health.

"I worked myself into exhaustion trying to get enough writing done so that I could apply for some kind of support," says Hogan, who received a National Endowment for the Arts grant in 1986 and a

Guggenheim Foundation fellowship in 1992. "The paradox of the situation is that the only way you can get support is to do the work. And often the only way you can do the work is to get the support. I don't see that there are any alternatives except to stop writing. There are times even now when I consider this because so much energy is spent in trying to do my paid work, and everything else, in order to get time to write.

"The conflict wouldn't be there if I weren't so interested in using the language, in writing stories, and using the writing to interpret the world for myself. But writing is the way I process and understand what's happening in the world and clarify my own thinking."

Writing a novel has brought a degree of practical support that poetry has not. "I know if I hadn't done *Mean Spirit,* I would never have gotten a Guggenheim," Hogan says. But despite the fact that the novel was on the short list of 1991 Pulitzer Prize nominations, the author has found that publishers are still more reluctant to spend money to buy and promote works by women, especially middle-aged women.

Hogan is currently working on *Solar Storms,* a novel about adoption. For years, Hogan has wanted to write about her experience adopting Tanya and Marie. The birth of her granddaughter, five years ago, gave new urgency to the idea. "The renewed work on this book came about when I was concerned about my granddaughter, Marie's daughter, because I knew that if she stayed with her mother, she would possibly be killed, would certainly be abused." Hogan spent two years writing letters and talking with officials from the county and Congressional representatives to try to get help for Marie, to alert social services workers to the danger the infant faced.

"In the first two years of Danielle's life, I had contact with her. It was a sad situation, a new life come into the world, open and waiting to accept and receive love and care. And then to have it not be there. I was in a position to witness what was happening and yet not able to do anything about it. It's one of the saddest things I've ever seen.

"Early on I considered adopting her and finally realized that she would not be safe here. If I had adopted her, we would have had to go someplace and live anonymously. Having to make that kind of choice once again, being in the same situation all over again, as I was with

Marie, was very painful—and Marie, always threatening the baby, saying, 'She's not really mine. My baby died.'

"After Danielle was adopted, I decided to write this book for children to find their way back to their blood and land origins," says Hogan. "Maybe it would be a pathway that would allow people to discover something that would help them to heal. The main character, the speaker in the book, goes to find her birth family when she is seventeen years old. The story begins there, when she goes back."

In writing *Solar Storms,* Hogan has found that her work habits have changed. "I've never been a night person," says Hogan, who is used to writing first thing in the morning, but with this novel, "I usually don't even start until later in the day, and I've been working on this at night. I don't know if it's because of my own psyche trying to avoid dealing with the issues that are in this book, but it's a completely different process than anything I've done before.

"I'm fortunate if I can have a four-hour stretch," says Hogan about finding time free for writing. She doesn't require any rituals to get started. "I have learned how to work any time I have the chance. I sometimes overdose on caffeine when I'm working," she says. "But usually, I like to just start when my mind is fresh.

"My writing precedes my thinking. I feel, in some ways, the writing is a teacher. I don't know where it comes from. I know that my writing is a lot more intelligent than I am," Hogan says with a laugh. "And it's wiser than I am. So paying attention to the work is, in some way, paying attention to the deepest part of my own self, my own spirit. I also feel that when I'm working well, the land itself speaks through me. I become the medium for a greater knowledge and a greater intelligence than just mine."

When she's writing, Hogan says, "I go into an altered state, and so a lot of times I can talk to people and not even remember what we said." In an effort to protect her writing time, she says, "I go through periods of time where I just do not answer the phone for a few weeks. You have to protect yourself as a writer, and you have to do your work. On some levels, the work is a part of spirituality, it's part of a deep soul growth, and to sacrifice it means you sacrifice your integrity and the honor of your own life and language.

"One of the things I've decided women writers need to do and to know is that we don't have to be nice to everybody, and we don't have to answer every phone call and do everything that's asked of us. We're trained to be too giving. There's a point in our lives at which our generosity becomes a loss for us. I see this in women of all age groups, so I know it's not just my generation."

A number of Hogan's students at the University of Colorado are mature women with children who ask her advice about combining writing and mothering. Hogan says, "In most situations, children thrive when their mothers thrive; it's a good idea for the mothers to do their own work.

"The mothers I know who did not do their own work ended up having children who did not do very well because the resentment and the sacrifice that the mothers felt were carried over to the feelings of their children. It's an essential thing for them to have their children respect them and what they do. We're trained to not do that. We're trained to be self-sacrificing in all situations and that's just not healthy."

At this point in her life, with her daughter Tanya married and expecting her first child, Hogan is enjoying her freedom. She lives in the country but goes into Boulder to meet with friends and to teach two days a week. "This year is my first time not being a mother. I do spend a great deal of time doing chores; I mean, it takes time to go to the grocery store and to cook for myself and do dishes. But nobody knows how dirty the house is; sometimes I neglect chores for weeks on end. And then one day I'll clean it all up and take care of everything and then start all over again. I reached a point where I thought, 'I either have to accept this kind of clutter or give up writing.'

Hogan says, "When I look at the dishes or when I look at what needs to be cleaned or organized, I think: 'I could do this or I could work on my book.' And I will take my book every time."

Photo ©, Keith Carter

ROSELLEN BROWN

Rosellen Brown

In her novels, Rosellen Brown writes about the deeper, darker sides of family life. She explores how ordinary people are changed by the freak accidents and sudden violence of fate. At midcareer, the fifty-three-year-old Brown is the author of nine books, including four novels: The Autobiography of My Mother *(1976),* Tender Mercies *(1978),* Civil Wars *(1984), and* Before and After *(1992); three collections of poetry:* Some Deaths in the Delta and Other Poems *(1970),* Cora Fry *(1977), and* Cora Fry's Pillow Book *(1994); a short story collection:* Street Games *(1976); and* The Rosellen Brown Reader *(1992). She is also the coauthor, with her English-teacher husband, Marvin Hoffman, and several others, of* The Whole Word Catalog: Creative Writing Ideas for Elementary and Secondary Schools *(1972).*

Born in Philadelphia in 1939, Brown moved frequently as a child, growing up in places as diverse as Los Angeles and New York's Westchester County. She began writing full time in 1962, after earning a BA from Barnard College and an MA at Brandeis University.

Brown has won many honors for her work, including an award from the American Academy and Institute of Arts and Letters, two grants from the National Endowment for the Arts, and fellowships from the Radcliffe Institute, the MacDowell Colony, and the Guggenheim Foundation. In 1984, Civil Wars *won the Janet Heidinger Kafka award for the best novel by an American woman. And in 1985, Brown was honored as one of* Ms. *magazine's Women of the Year. A professor in the creative writing department at the University of Houston since 1982, Brown is the mother of two daughters: Adina, twenty-five, and Elana, twenty-two.*

ROSELLEN BROWN KNEW FROM THE TIME SHE WAS NINE years old that she would be a writer and a mother. Like many other women who came of age at the end of the 1950s, she thought of motherhood in terms of when—not if—she would have children. But at the same time, she says, "I had done the one thing most needful for a woman artist—maybe a woman doing anything along the way—and that was that when I married, I made sure I married somebody who bloody well understood how important my writing was going to be to me.

"I got married in 1963 and it was not shameful, or even something that you thought much about at that point, to marry somebody who was going to support you. I had a 'patron of the arts' who was supporting me at the rate of about fifty-five bucks a week, but it was good enough."

In 1965, in the midst of the civil rights struggle, Brown and her husband, Marvin Hoffman, went to Mississippi, where they taught for two years at the predominately black Tougaloo College in a program sponsored by the Woodrow Wilson Foundation.

"It was total-immersion teaching. It was a very incendiary time, obviously, and the campus was a thorn in the side of Jackson, Mississippi—it was on the outskirts of Jackson—for having been integrated for many years. It was a civil rights haven; and, therefore, you couldn't live off the campus because you might get your house firebombed. So we lived on campus, and that meant we were on call twenty-four hours a day, bailing our students out of jail and dealing with their emotional problems at three in the morning." Brown would draw on her observations of the South for her first book of poems, *Some Deaths in the Delta,* and later for her novel *Civil Wars.*

The couple's first daughter, Adina, was born in 1967, during their third and final year in Mississippi. "I wrote much of my first book of poetry after I had Adina. She napped well, so I remember managing to have time. It's a good thing I was writing poetry at the time because that actually is something you can do in a more fragmented way than fiction, or certainly than the novel. I'm not sure it would have gone quite so well if I had been trying to write a novel, which is so labor-intensive that twenty-four hours a day is hardly time enough for it."

Motherhood required an adjustment in her internal clock, Brown says. "I used to be a night person—and I've gone back to that to some extent now. But when you've got little children around, there's no way that you're going to write at three in the morning.

"I don't think I had any help with Adina until she was about two. I would be with the baby in the mornings, and then this high school kid would come in at one or two and stay with her all afternoon in the house—which was sometimes hard for me because I'd be upstairs writing. Every time I heard her [Adina] scream, I'd jump, but rarely allowed myself to enter the fray to find out what was happening because I thought she was in pretty competent hands." The family had moved to New York in 1968 after Adina's birth. Brown began writing fiction during this period, setting the stories in *Street Games* in an ethnically mixed Brooklyn neighborhood not unlike her own. Several of the stories in that collection won O. Henry prizes or were included in the annual *Best American Short Stories*.

Brown's second daughter, Elana, was born in 1970. The writer recalls, "I have a memory of worrying about whether or not I was going to be able to manage as well with two children as I did with one. My baby-sitter, the high school girl, was a hippie. She said, 'Oh, let's do the I-Ching and ask it how you're going to do; that's what I go to with all my questions.'

"First, I asked the I-Ching what sex the baby was going to be. It refused to commit itself: it came out with a perfect balance of yin and yang, as if to say, 'Don't ask impertinent questions.'"

To her second question—"Am I going to be able to manage having two kids?"—the mystical device "gave me two responses, both of which seemed very pertinent. One was about the taming power of the small, and I thought, 'Uh-oh, I'm going to be tamed; this is going to be a problem.' But the other one was something about the corners of the mouth seeking nourishment. It's a wonderful part about how there are all kinds of actions and then there are words, and about how your life can be a balance of both of them. So I rested a little bit more easy, thinking, 'Well, this thing has told me that I'm going to be able to manage motherhood and words at the same time.'

"Then, just to prove that it was going to be true, when I was in the hospital my first story to be published, which was coming out in *TriQuarterly,* arrived in galleys. My baby was right next to me, and I thought, 'This is everything, all here in the same room at the same time.'

"And it did work out. I think the reason I again didn't miss a beat when the baby was born was that I already knew myself as a writer—I knew this was the thing that I did. It was my job, and I got up every day to do it just as surely as my husband went off to his job.

"Just as I can't imagine my life without children and have never really regretted them—except in those wild moments in which you regret every choice you ever made, when you can't take another minute of it—I can't imagine what my writing would be without having had children. Now, obviously, I would have written about something if it hadn't been kids, or maybe I would have been one of those people who could write very well about kids without having had them. But I feel as if so much of what I know about the world somehow has come from having had children that the idea that I might not have had them in order to preserve myself for my work just seems like the most absurd, self-defeating protection imaginable.

"I feel as if my children have kept me in the world. You learn a lot about what's happening: you know about music, about movies, about popular culture. I remember Anne Tyler once saying that her kids dragged popular culture over the threshold to her, and that there were a lot of things that she just wouldn't have paid any attention to if it hadn't been for them. Living this pure life without kids mucking it up is a great loss in the end; you don't participate fully in the life around you."

Brown dedicated her first novel, *The Autobiography of My Mother,* to her children in spite of its horrific ending because, "I didn't know if I was going to have another book, so I gave them what I could." As in that first novel, much of her work concerns nightmares that happen to ordinary people. "I write the things that I don't want to happen."

Her fourth and newest novel, *Before and After,* is about a family whose seventeen-year-old son has accidentally murdered a young woman. The subtext of this new book is not so much about murder, Brown says, as about "how you cease to know your children very well after a certain point, or as well as you think you know them anyway. It's about the terror that perhaps you don't know what your children really are like. So there's a case where having children and thinking about motherhood and fatherhood has totally informed the work as it's informed my life. And I've written the book out of that total experience of parenthood over time."

Brown's third novel, *Civil Wars,* is another example of how motherhood has influenced her fiction. Although the book is about many other things, she says, the child characters "were very crucial to the whole idea of how one is educated morally, which was very close to the center of the book." When their segregationist parents are killed in a car accident, Helen and O'Neill move in with their aunt and uncle, both civil rights activists. "The whole idea for that book came to me from contemplating how it is that children get their moral underpinnings and their sense of the world, both politically and morally, not to mention emotionally.

"So, somehow, without being conscious of it, not ever setting out to do another book about children, obviously a great deal of my being has been spent thinking and worrying about children—mine and others," Brown explains.

Her short story, "Good Housekeeping," in *The Rosellen Brown Reader,* captures the frustration that Brown sometimes felt when her children interrupted her writing. The story begins with a woman photographer taking a picture of her baby's behind and then searching through the house for subjects for a domestic series. The baby starts crying and she goes to him, very angry at being interrupted. "This is, of course, coming right out of my own experience because not everything's been smooth. When I talk about how easy the experience was of motherhood and writing, there were plenty of moments when it wasn't easy.

"Having a supportive husband was very important because he was the one who would say to me, 'How dare you even ask whether you have a right to do what you do? I do what I do, you do what you do, and you should not take any kind of guilt on yourself for this.'"

Brown recalls an incident when her feelings of guilt were quelled by her older daughter, then six. The family had moved to New Hampshire in 1971, and during the eleven years they lived there, Brown wrote in the mornings and early afternoons, stopping around 3:00 P.M. when the school bus arrived. "I remember that when Adina was in the first grade, she came home one day and I was typing something up that I had written—I write by hand, but I was putting it on the typewriter. She came in and I was just finishing, and so I said, 'Honey, I'll be there in a second; just give me a minute to finish this.' And I went on typing and she stood next to me, looking at me, and I began to feel like, 'Oh, God, I always told myself I would not let this keep me from my kids, and I feel really bad about this.' I said, 'Look, take off your snowsuit, and I'll be there in a second.' And she just stood and looked at me. And I finally said, 'Oh, God, go get yourself some milk and cookies in the refrigerator. I'm sorry. I'm really sorry; I'll be there.'

"And she said to me, 'But Mommy, I want to see what you're doing. I want to see what your work looks like.'" Now, twenty years later, Adina is pursuing that same career as a writer in San Francisco.

Although Brown often felt reluctant to stop writing when the school bus arrived, there was a hidden benefit, she says. "I really do believe that you tend to have an easier time starting up the next day if you stop before you're finished for the day than if you actually come to the end of something. If you're writing continually, it's a little bit like a marriage in that you know—or hope, anyway—that it is ongoing. You figure, well, you're going to be back at the notebook tomorrow, so you don't have to finish it today."

Frequently, Brown worked after dinner on ancillary tasks such as writing reviews, reading, or judging contests. "I often have acted out my conflicts about where I should be as a mother by plunking myself down at the dining room table in the middle of the action and then getting frustrated by how hard it was to concentrate, but not being able to remove myself and go to my room when the kids were home.

"There were also times that I remember very clearly when everybody got out of my way." One December, her husband took their daughters for a week to visit family so that she would have time alone to work on the final revisions of a novel. Brown not only met her deadline, but started another book, *Cora Fry*. "I never would have been able to begin it that way without that perfect concentration, and I felt as if I'd been given it like a gift. Again, that goes back to having a husband who really understood that from time to time I needed some kind of silence."

Her daughters were also supportive of her need for time alone. They had lived near the MacDowell Colony, a retreat for artists and writers in New Hampshire, and were familiar with the Colony's customs. Brown recalls that her daughters "knew that one of the wonderful things that they [the Colony] did for you was that they bring you your lunch in a basket and put it on the steps of your studio, so that you don't have to stop and see people and ruin your concentration. During Christmas vacation that first year that we lived in Houston, I borrowed a friend's house so that I could go and work on revisions of *Civil Wars.* My kids, who were then about eleven and thirteen, brought over a basket lunch for me every day because they wanted to be my MacDowell Colony. This was a great coup for them because they felt like they were really doing something to help me along.

"People ask me, 'How do you discipline yourself?' Disciplining myself was easy because what I wanted was to write. The problem was disciplining everybody else to stay out of my way. I think my kids grew up simply knowing that when I was working, they tried not to bother me unless it was very important."

Another aspect of discipline is "when you do your housework," Brown says. "You have to be suspicious of yourself all the time. And I think the people who allow themselves to be interrupted by housework—of all things—either want to be interrupted because they're looking for an excuse [not to work] or they have truly allowed themselves to be sold a bill of goods by the dusters and vacuumers of the world who will never get anything done—they'll vacuum their houses a million times."

Brown has a poem about this issue in her book *Cora Fry.* A novel in poetic form, *Cora Fry* is the story of a born-and-bred New Hampshire woman, the kind of small town insider Brown met while living in that milieu from 1971 to 1982. "Now this is Cora talking, and she's talking about me:

"'I have a neighbor / who is always deep / in a book or two. / High tides of clutter / rise in her kitchen. / Which last longer, words, / words in her bent head, / or the clean spaces / between one perfect / dusting and the next?'"

The poet adds, "High tides of clutter do not rise in my kitchen; it's a great exaggeration. But the question is there to be asked among artists, writers: Which lasts longer—the words or the perfect dusting?

And I do not opt for the perfect dusting. The house is clean enough, it's neat enough, but I do it around the edges. Nothing else would have got done if I'd done that first, believe me.

"The part where the discipline comes in is that you have to take yourself so damn seriously in order to get other people to take you seriously. People crumble because they're just too embarrassed to really insist. The one thing that was lucky for me was that I started publishing fairly early and I've won prizes. And with every one of those things, aside from the fact that it was good for my ego, was the sense that it bought me some community respect.

"Even when you've published many books and you've won many awards, it's still easier to be in the world than it is to be home alone with a piece of paper. Every demand that's made on me to serve on a committee at school or whatever, to do any public thing—whether I like doing it or don't like it, find it easy or find it difficult—every bit of it is easier than the one thing I have to do: which is sit down in front of a blank piece of paper every day.

"The only technique that I ever came up with for helping me to concentrate was that I never begin my writing in the morning without reading for a while." In the early years, Brown read to unclutter her mind of the sounds of the early morning rush to get the kids dressed and off to school. "I had to get beyond words at their most functional and get into a different rhythm. So I always gave myself a few minutes to read before I began and then, little by little—it never failed—as I read I began to get this tremendous impatience, and I'd feel myself saying, 'Oh, I can do that; I want to do that.' And I'd put the book down, pick up my own book and go on writing. But I rarely just plunged into it." Now Brown walks every morning before working, listening to novels on audio tape.

The older she gets, Brown says, "in some ways, I think I am getting less done rather than more. Now, some of this may come from age and less of a sense of urgency; some of it may also come from the very many more distractions around me. I am teaching regularly now [and] there are many more demands on my time than when I was a much younger writer and nobody knew me.

"But I think a lot of it really does have to do with the necessity to get yourself together and produce when you have time. I look back at the time when I lived in Brooklyn and my babies were very young. I had this baby-sitter in the house, and I just had to do it from two to five [o'clock] or I couldn't get it done, and that was that. Some of the stringency has gone out of my life, and I feel like I've got more time than I probably do have. It's really a great shame in a lot of ways. I'm not sure that I can say that I miss being in a great hurry all the time, but I think there are losses that go along with the gains, a kind of relaxation, like middle-age spread, that takes place in your head as well as your body, and I kind of regret it.

"I find myself envying terribly people who have young children around. I feel a sense of extraordinary loss at this point, which a mother of young children will not be able to even imagine for many, many years. It was devastating to us for our children to leave. I would have thought once upon a time that it was only mothers who didn't do anything but mother their children who felt that empty-nest syndrome people talk about.

"Writer friends of mine who have children have enrolled them in an [fictitious] organization that we call COW, Children of Writers. They have certain specific problems in common." Her daughter, Adina, is a struggling writer and "going through a stage of desperate need for independence from me. She used to show me her work and we would talk about it. We were very collegial. At this point—very painfully for me, although I understand it entirely, intellectually anyway—she's not showing me her work at all.

"My other daughter [Elana] is staying as far from all that as she possibly can. At this point, she gets along with us much better because she's not in competition in any way, shape, or form." When Elana was a freshman in college, Brown recalls, "She wrote me a letter that just moves me to tears every time I read it, about how proud she is of me and how wonderful it is that I've done what I've done. And I just say to myself, 'God, can I really consider that this child was hurt in any way by the fact that she knew that her mother was concentrating very hard on something?'"

Brown is convinced that choosing the right mate is essential to combining writing and mothering. She tells her students, "Insofar as it's within one's capacity to do so, you better be plenty sure you marry someone who's more than supportive, someone who understands that your work is as important as his work."

Teaching only occasionally while establishing herself as a writer, Brown was dependent for many years on her husband's income. "Early on, we had very little money, but we always made sure we had money for the day care or the baby-sitter," she recalls. The financial payoff was a long time coming: Brown received a total of five thousand dollars for her first short story collection and her first novel, despite having already published a book of poems.

Brown says that she realizes that it is psychologically, as well as practically, harder for a young writer today to be supported by a spouse. But she believes that writers and their partners need to make financial decisions that will support the writing.

"People make a lot of choices about where their money is going to go without even realizing they're choices. I have a lot of students who say, 'Oh, well, yes, I got my master's in writing and I wish I was writing the way I was being trained to write, but I had to go get a job because we just couldn't manage without it, and so I'm not writing anymore.' And I get very upset when I hear that because I have a feeling that there is a huge sense of entitlement that a lot of young writers have these days. What they consider the absolute minimum that they need to get along is one hell of a lot higher than I think it has to be. I think a lot of people need to redefine what they mean by need.

"We've never owned a house; we drive pretty old cars; I dress from thrift shops mostly. I remember here in Houston there was a new Macy's that opened up, and a lot of my graduate students flocked there to see the place and came back with a lot of stuff. I was astonished because they cry poor all the time and they say they're not going to be able to support themselves as writers, and they were buying clothes that I wouldn't dream of buying at Macy's.

"This may sound trivial, but it matters if it's going to keep you from writing in the end because you feel like you can't do it. You've got to have a job and if you've got kids, then that really is going to take all your time and energy, and the last thing in the world you're going to have time for is writing."

Brown is proud that her daughter Adina, who lives in San Francisco, has learned to budget her priorities to support her writing. "It's quite wonderful for me to see that she is somebody who really lives on next to nothing in a very expensive city. She used to think that she was going to be an actress, and I think that she trained herself then to live very ascetically.

"And I feel as if that's the way one has to be—one has to at least be flexible enough to be able to be ascetic if you're going to write, unless you happen to have a lot of money or marry a rich man or be lucky enough to get some huge advance for a book. I hate to see how many people, especially women with children, feel like they can't take on one more thing, and then they'll take a job rather than protect the writing because they feel as though they need the money."

Portions of this interview previously appeared in Publishers Weekly, *August 31, 1992.*

Photo ©, Sarah Putnam

MAY STEVENS

May Stevens

The personal is political in May Stevens's life and work. For example, in her "Big Daddy" series of paintings from the late 1960s to the mid-1970s, she articulates the tension between the love she felt for her father as an individual and her feminist outrage at the racism, sexism, and militarism he embodied. A founding member of the feminist Heresies Collective, the sixty-eight-year-old artist is perhaps best known for her "Ordinary/ Extraordinary" series, which explores the life and death of the artist's mother and the revolutionary Rosa Luxemburg.

Her work is in the collections of the Museum of Modern Art, the Whitney Museum of American Art, the Museum of Fine Arts in Boston, and the San Francisco Museum of Modern Art, among others. In the past decade alone, Stevens has received Guggenheim, Bunting Institute, and MacDowell Colony fellowships as well as a National Endowment for the Arts grant and a National Institute of Arts and Letters purchase award.

Born in 1924, Stevens graduated with her BFA from Massachusetts College of Art in 1946 and moved to New York City. Two years later, she married Rudolf Baranik, a fellow painter. Stevens and her husband had one child, Steven Baranik, who died at age thirty-two. Stevens and Baranik live in New York City, where she teaches at the School of Visual Arts.

DEATH IS THE UNSPOKEN FEAR AT THE HEART OF PARENTING, especially the fear of surviving one's child. Painter May Stevens lost her adult son in 1981.

A graduate of Massachusetts College of Art, Stevens was twenty-four years old when her son, Steven Baranik, was born in 1948 in Paris, France, where her husband, painter Rudolf Baranik, was studying art on the GI Bill. Recalling those early years when she stayed home with her son and painted, Stevens, now sixty-eight, says, "We lived in the suburbs of Paris. We rented half a house from a couple who gave French lessons and used part of the house as a boarding school for English girls who came to get 'finished' in Paris. There was a beautiful big garden behind a wall on the edge of a forest. Steven would be in a playpen on the hill and I would be in the house, watching him from my window while I painted in the studio. It was easy, in a way, when he was small, to paint. I loved watching him and I loved painting."

She had her first gallery show during the family's three years in Paris; her son was the main subject of her paintings at that time. "We felt when he was small that we were watching, as parents always do, a replay of the history of mankind, watching how one grasps the world, makes sense of it, figures it out, little by little, and slowly comes into a realization of the world. It was breathtaking and I recorded some of those moments.

"But I think that my closeness and involvement with Steven and my separation from the art world and from what was going on in art made those paintings very much about being a mother and watching my child develop. I had no distance at all." Her skills were not yet fully developed, Stevens says, and the paintings of her son, while appealing, are not in the same category as her later works, which deal with wider, more political themes.

Stevens doesn't remember consciously deciding to have only one child. "I guess it just worked out that way. We didn't have any money and we were very concentrated on our work, and I think we felt really good about our threesome. We went everywhere together; we were together all the time." The family referred to themselves with the French phrase *tout les trois*, meaning "all three of us."

From the time he was a very young child, Steven imitated and emulated his parents, occupying himself with drawing and painting. "Wherever we lived, we'd take the largest room in the house and divide it so that I worked in one side of the room and Rudolf would work in the other. Steven grew up with people making art all around him.

"We thought of ourselves as three artists. Steven's father was as involved, almost more involved, than I. His father was very, very interested in being a father. In some ways, our roles were almost reversed. I can remember walking with Steven down a path in the woods when he was small. I would say, 'Steven, there's a tree. Why don't you climb it?' And Rudolf would say, 'Watch out! You'll fall.'"

The two painters shared equally in the domestic chores. "Diapers, cooking, shopping—absolutely. I taught him to read, that was something that I did. I wanted him to love reading and love books as I do. His father told him stories to put him to sleep at night. He'd make up stories in which Steven would be the hero. The story would end by saying, *'Et soudainment Steva est venu!'* ('And suddenly Steven arrived'), you know, and saved the day.

"I remember that I was very conscious of wanting him to understand that women are people who do things." At mealtimes, the family played a game in which one player was a famous personality and the other players tried to guess who by asking up to twenty questions. May Stevens always chose to be woman, such as Joan of Arc or Marie Curie. A teacher at New York's School of Visual Arts since 1961, she says, "I was probably didactic as a mother."

When the family returned from Paris in the early 1950s, they settled outside of New York City, "so that Steven could have the pleasure of walking out of the house into a field." Both husband and wife were showing in galleries, but as young, little-known artists living in the suburbs, they were somewhat isolated from the art world for a number of years.

That changed in the early '60s when the family moved to Manhattan where Steven attended the High School of Music and Art. "At that point we were able to get more connected to the art world and become more involved, and naturally it had an effect on the work. Then when I finally moved into a large loft space in Soho [in 1968], my paintings became larger and I tackled larger themes."

Her "Big Daddy" series of paintings from the late 1960s to the mid-1970s is an example of how the personal became the political in Stevens's work. In that series, her father, whom she loved, evolved into a patriarchal symbol of American imperialism and racism. "I painted out of love for those lower-middle-class Americans I came from and out of a great anger for what had happened to them and what they were letting happen, making happen, in the South and in Vietnam." In addition to her painting and teaching, Stevens was a founding member of the Heresies Collective, a group of New York artists that began publishing a feminist journal of art and politics in the late 1970s.

Meanwhile, Steven had grown up. He attended the State University of New York, Binghamton, and City College of New York, majoring in art with a minor in psychology. A child of the '60s, he was a conscientious objector during the Vietnam War, traveled through Europe, and later supported himself by driving a taxi in New York while he worked at making paintings and taking photographs.

Stevens recalls the only painting she did of her son as an adult, when he was in his late twenties. This small work, about two feet high and maybe ten inches across, "wasn't part of any major effort, it was just a little thing I did for him. It showed him jumping in the air in a moment of exuberance."

Although he was trained as a painter, Steven began to concentrate on photography. "He didn't talk to us much about it, and he didn't show it to us. And he didn't really professionalize himself in a sense. He didn't study photography formally, but he picked it up and made it his own," his mother remembers. "He wasn't a very practical person. I think he found painting very demanding. You know, painting is demanding and photography, I think, goes a little faster. He didn't spend enough time on the photography to take it very far, although he had the sensitivity and the talent. He was at the beginning, I think, of an artistic career that might have developed very strongly if he had gone on with it."

But Steven did not live long enough to fulfill his potential. After his death, his parents found a cache of photographs which they assembled into an artist's book, *Burning Horses: Photographs by Steven Baranik* (Ram Press, 1982). He had set fire to toy plastic horses, then quickly photographed them in black and white. He had never discussed the series with his parents, so the original impulse for the pictures remains a mystery. But one source can clearly be traced to a childhood fascination with fire.

"Steven always liked to play with fire; he and his father used to burn things together. It was a game they played. The two of them would build fires and burn things and watch what happens—like putting a wooden wheel we found in the fireplace and watching how the wheel catches fire and how the image changes. There was an aesthetic excitement to fire."

Reluctant to discuss her son's suicide, Stevens says only that he was ill. In the biographical statement at the end of the *Burning Horses* book, she writes: "He loved his friends. He died on October 26, 1981, near the river, under the bridge. He was thirty-two years old. He left a message: Thanks, earth. Namaste."

Explaining her reaction, Stevens says, "When something like this happens, there's a kind of incredulity—you don't believe it. You know the fact, but it doesn't register. For a while, you go around in a state of unreality. It's only when all the things, the places, and the times that the relationship should be there for you—and it isn't—and every time it hurts until finally [there is] a totality, and you know it's never going to be different."

At the time, Stevens was working on "Ordinary/ Extraordinary," a series she had begun in the late 1970s. The series explores the similarities and differences between the lives of the artist's elderly American mother, Alice Stevens, and the artist's intellectual heroine, murdered Polish revolutionary Rosa Luxemburg, by juxtaposing collaged and painted images of the two women.

Two years after her son died, Stevens produced three paintings on the subject of death. *Voices* and *Procession* portray the funeral of Rosa Luxemburg, while *Go Gentle* focuses on the approaching death of the artist's mother. In an essay on the "Ordinary/ Extraordinary" series, art critic Lucy R. Lippard notes that these paintings, while seeming to have little in common, all deal with "the politics of mortality."

Lippard describes the Luxemburg funeral paintings, in particular, as demonstrating both grief and renewal, "Like political demonstrations themselves, these paintings are symbols of continuing resistance, demonstrations of outrage and solidarity by which we counter the morbidity and futility connected with death—the death of ideals as well as of people."

The artist says these paintings were "totally informed" by her grieving for her son. "I had heard that it isn't until about two years later [that] you really have the full impact [of the loss], and that's the way it was with me. By the time I got to '83, when these three large paintings were done, I had full access to all of my feelings; I was all the way home. There were friends who saw my Rosa Luxemburg funeral paintings for the first time and put their arms around me and wept with me because they understood the genesis of the powerful feeling that made them."

Stevens continued on the "Ordinary/ Extraordinary" series over the next five years. During a year-long fellowship at Radcliffe College's Bunting Institute in 1988–89, she exhibited some of the last works in the series in a solo show called "The Canal and the Garden." She painted her mother, Alice, as a distant figure in a wide green field and her heroine, Rosa, in the waters of the canal. "Rosa's passionate activist life was marked by the canal—which like a road leads somewhere; Alice's stilled life, with its intense feelings turned inward, was marked by a *huis clos,* a walled garden," the painter notes.

It was while at the Bunting that Stevens met sculptor Civia Rosenberg, another bereaved mother, at an informal "loss group" organized by Ann Bookman, then assistant director at the Institute. Stevens was initially reluctant to join the group. "My son had died in 1981 and this was 1988, and I didn't think I wanted to open up all that again. This was in September and the day that my son died was in October, so it was coming to that time of year. It turned out to be important to have a place where I could go and talk about some of the feelings that came up because of the time of year.

"I don't know whether it was Civia or someone else who gave me ginkgo leaves—we had great armfuls of yellow ginkgo leaves at Steven's memorial. I pasted the yellow ginkgo leaves to the window of my studio at the Bunting. Having the leaves upstairs in my studio and being able to go to the loss group and get to know Civia and her work made a difference, cleared something for me," Stevens says.

Daniel Rosenberg had also been a photographer before he died, just one month prior to the beginning of his mother's fellowship at the Bunting. Overwhelmed by the loss of her twenty-two-year-old son, the sculptor abandoned her previously submitted proposal and began to work through her grief. The resulting exhibit was titled "The Death of a Son: A Collaboration and Response to His Art."

Stevens recalls her reaction to that exhibit: "When Civia put her show up at the Bunting, she included words about what she was doing and what it meant to her. Civia's use of words was so very fine. Her show was excruciatingly painful. It seemed to me utterly naked and it moved me terribly. I was not accustomed to seeing anyone so open and vulnerable as she was in her work. I had not ever directly addressed my son's death in my work. To see Civia do this so close to the time of Daniel's going was very shocking, almost frightening."

Civia Rosenberg and her physician/scientist husband, Irwin Rosenberg, subsequently published *Museum Studies,* a posthumous artist's book of their son's photographs. Inspired by those photographs and by her own son's photographs of burning horses, Stevens called her friend in August 1990 and proposed a collaboration.

Rosenberg remembers that telephone call: "I think May had a very large reproduction of one of Steven's photographs, one of the burning horses. She said it was over the desk and she was ready to respond."

Stevens describes her son's photographs and why she chose those particular images: "The animal forms are mutated by fire—they melt, elongate, shrink, join other forms to make new patterns—they become animals of a species never seen on earth. They prance on three legs or on one leg; their heads disappear or take on a shape that doesn't match the body—as though a crocodile mated with a tiger. All this in an eerie indoor light, or set into a grainy rut of dried mud along the river. They are hauntingly beautiful and strange."

She adds, "The main thing that motivated me was wanting the vision, the ideas, the art of these two young artists to become known, to continue, and be developed. I wanted to see what could be done by carrying their images and ideas forward."

The result was "Crossings," a powerful, moving expression not only of maternal grief and sorrow but also of the transcendence of art. Curated by Rachel Rosenfeld Lafo, "Crossings" was exhibited at the DeCordova Art Museum in Lincoln, Massachusetts, in the fall of 1991.

All artists hope their work will outlive them; in this exhibit, Daniel Rosenberg and Steven Baranik's black-and-white photographs became the basis for new work exploring the connection between life and death. The two mothers incorporated photocopies of Rosenberg's museum studies and Baranik's burning horses series into their own paintings, charcoal drawings, collages, and sculpture.

Sometimes the mothers changed the original images by adding other images, free-associating, or they expanded on them by changing the medium, scale, or tone. Stevens notes that the circle of toy horses lit by fire became, in her mind, a witches's sabbath, while the stuffed deer behind glass that Rosenberg photographed breathes again in his mother's drawings.

Stevens initially imagined that she would begin a piece and then mail it to Rosenberg to finish and vice versa. But she found that once started, "I couldn't leave it unfinished and when I finished it, I wouldn't let anyone touch it." Instead, the two women evolved ways of working independently, keeping in close contact and encouraging each other whenever the process became too painful, or got stalled in any way.

The works Stevens produced for the "Crossings" exhibition were a departure from her other series. She produced more, smaller pieces faster: about forty works on paper and two six-foot paintings in six months. It was a period of freer experimentation in which she tried out not only different media and techniques, but also, she says, "I was trying on somebody else's mind, someone else's thoughts, someone else's work. I was getting into their mode, as I apprehended it, and I felt at home with it and felt like working within their views, having some sense of where they wanted their work to go. So even though I was only working with the work and not talking with them, it was like having an intense conversation and growing with it and because of it."

Touching Fire—the show's largest and most powerful piece—exemplifies this sense of connection. At the center is Stevens's black-and-white painting of burning horses, surrounded by a circle of wooden hands sculpted by Rosenberg. The hands, some of which clutch a tongue of flame or reach for a charred horse, seem to be extended to the sons, who have crossed over into death.

In the end, Stevens says, "We made an opening. My studio is permeated by the currents of their ideas and by the stirring up of feelings that are then put to use. We put back together and sustained a connection which had been so painfully broken."

Portions of this interview were previously published in the May 1993 issue of Sojourner.

Photo ©, Meg McLean

TRINA SCHART HYMAN

Trina Schart Hyman

Trina Schart Hyman, fifty-three, has illustrated dozens of children's books in her thirty years in the field, but she is best known for her pictorial interpretations of classic fairy tales, including Little Red Riding Hood, Snow White, Swan Lake, Sleeping Beauty, Rapunzel, *and* Saint George and the Dragon. *In these works, she captures the mysterious and magical world of stone castles, fiery dragons, wrathful fairies, and haunted forests in exquisite detail.*

Hyman has written as well as illustrated half a dozen books, including How Six Found Christmas *(1969; reissued 1992),* A Little Alphabet *(1980),* Self-Portrait: Trina Schart Hyman *(1981),* The Enchanted Forest *(1984), and retellings of* Sleeping Beauty *(1977) and* Little Red Riding Hood *(1983). Art director of the children's literary magazine* Cricket *for eight years in the 1970s, Hyman won the Caldecott Medal in 1985 and Caldecott Honor Medals in 1984 and 1990, as well as two Golden Kite awards from the Society of Children's Book Writers.*

Hyman lives quietly in an old farmhouse outside of Lyme, New Hampshire, together with one cat, two dogs, and four sheep. She has one child, thirty-year-old Katrin, and a three-year-old grandson, Michou.

GROWING UP IN RURAL PENNSYLVANIA, TRINA SCHART HYMAN was fascinated by fairy tales. She would dress up as Little Red Riding Hood and entertain her younger sister, Karleen, with games and stories involving the fairies she crafted from dime-store dolls and snippets of her mother's red hair. Later, she went to art school at the Philadelphia Museum of Art, and in 1959, at age twenty, married Harris Hyman, a mechanical engineer. She followed her husband first to Boston and then to Stockholm, where he studied mathematics while she continued taking art courses.

Hyman got her first break as an artist while living in Sweden, when editor and renowned author Astrid Lindgren assigned her to illustrate *Toffee and the Little Car* by Hertha VonGebhardt. After their year abroad, the couple returned to Boston, where their daughter, Katrin, was born in 1963.

"I knew I wanted to continue working—I was in the middle of doing one of my first trade books when she was born, as a matter of fact—so I knew I needed help. And Harris, my husband, was not a help." Although her husband is now, ironically, raising three school-age children from a later marriage single-handedly, Hyman says, "When Katrin was born, I think he wasn't in the mood for being a dad; his mind was on his work, period. He was an absent kind of father, which in those days most guys were."

The artist hired first her sister and then a succession of Boston University students to baby-sit a few afternoons a week in exchange for room and board. The family moved to New York City in 1965, and Gun, the daughter of friends in Sweden, came over to work as an au pair.

Then a year later, Hyman's life changed dramatically. "I fell in love with my husband's best friend's wife." She separated from and later divorced Harris and moved to New Hampshire with Katrin, Nancie, and Nancie's twin daughters, who were the same age as Katrin. The acrimonious divorces plunged the two women and their children into an economic nightmare. "These guys were mad at us, and they weren't going to give us any money—nothing for the kids and nothing for us. And we didn't want their money anyway—there were fingers flipped in both directions," Hyman recalls.

Because her skills were more marketable, Hyman became the breadwinner, while Nancie, a painter, took care of the three little girls. "We had no money. I wasn't well known at the time. I just had to take any job I could get and hustle for work, and I did. I was working twelve, fourteen hours a day. And many times we were living on credit at the grocery store. Nancie made a big garden every summer, and we lived off produce from the garden and we kept chickens. We were really poor for awhile." Five years passed before Hyman had enough regular work to make ends meet.

Their situation was difficult emotionally as well as financially. "I was a lesbian, single mom in the days before it was okay, so we had to be extremely circumspect. We were not 'out' to our community or our families or anybody except ex-husbands and some friends." Hyman still worries that their secretive life was hard on Katrin, "although my daughter says no. And [it was] hard because there was no support; we felt very alone." But living with another woman is always easier for her than living with a man, Hyman adds.

Not until Katrin had graduated from college did Hyman come out as a lesbian to her extended family and her community. But, Hyman says, "the children always knew it was okay for two women or two men to love each other and be a family. That was okay with them. But we did say to them that it's not everyone's tradition, so you'd better cool it about coming out with this at school."

In her autobiography for children, *Self Portrait: Trina Schart Hyman*, she mentions the "good friends" she's lived with, but again had to be "extremely circumspect" about her lesbian identity, "saying it without saying it." Hyman adds, "If I were to write that book again today, I'd come out with it, because it's right. But I didn't want Nancie's and my children to be hurt by society because of me."

In 1971, Nancie and her twins left for California. That same year, Hyman began her eight-year tenure as art director for *Cricket Magazine*, a children's literary journal. Whereas Hyman had previously worked until two or three in the morning, sleeping in while Nancie got the girls off to school, she now settled into a work schedule based on Katrin's school hours. Hyman would do household chores first thing in the morning, and then work at the drawing board from ten o'clock until the school bus brought Katrin home. After taking a couple of hours off to be with her daughter and have dinner, Hyman returned to the drawing board. She would take another hour off to read bedtime stories, but otherwise continued working until midnight or 1:00 A.M.

Nowadays, Hyman works from ten to five, breaks for an hour to take a walk, then works another couple of hours until dinner and bed. "I can't work ten-hour days anymore; my eyesight isn't up to it," she says.

For many years, Hyman worked in the room closest to the front door, so that she would be instantly available if needed. In retrospect, she says that working that way, with small children around, "teaches you resilience and toughness and flexibility. Accidents happen around children; things get spilled on [what] you've been working on for two weeks. You learn to improvise, you learn great patience, you learn to adopt a philosophical attitude about things, and I think that's good for any artist."

Hyman was able to work despite the commotion, in part because she needed the money and in part because she was able to psychologically isolate herself, albeit at a price. She recalls, "My greatest aid to being able to concentrate, to close out what was going on, was whiskey. I always had a little glass of bourbon by my side on the drawing board. And it was for exactly that reason: alcohol is a great isolator. And I wound up—by the time Katrin had graduated from high school—with a real drinking problem.

"I hadn't realized that a by-product of that constant little infusion of bourbon was also courage, creative courage. So when I stopped drinking, I was faced with a blank piece of paper and a lot of self-doubt and fear; that was the most difficult to overcome. And it's still a problem for me; I work constantly on giving myself pep talks."

Despite her difficulties facing the blank page, Hyman received a Caldecott Honor Medal in 1984 for *Little Red Riding Hood,* which she both retold and illustrated. The following year, Hyman received the most prestigious award in children's book illustration, the Caldecott Medal, for *Saint George and the Dragon.* But despite her success, by 1988 Hyman had become "desperately unhappy" with her profession.

Hyman describes the dilemma she has faced as an adult producing books for children. "My children's books are mostly a personal statement, but it's the personal statement of a compartment of myself. Because it's children's literature, it can't be the really disturbing or wrenching thoughts—private thoughts that I have. I think, 'This is why I am an artist—I can express these things—and what am I doing not expressing them?'"

Until she found other avenues of expressing these darker, more complex thoughts, Hyman says, "I felt like I was losing myself as an artist. Being a children's book artist is a lot like being a woman, in this way: you're doing it for someone else, you're not doing this art for yourself. There's always the author to consider, the publisher, the children, the parents, the teachers—there's always someone else looking over your shoulder while you're doing this. You're not just doing art that's truthful and that comes from the gut, and that's what I think was making me unhappy.

"I would go sit down at my desk in the morning to go to work and just sit there and weep. I was so frustrated and angry and upset, and I didn't know how to get out of it. I thought that if I saw another fucking insipid princess with long blonde hair, I'd just vomit. Or a stupid, dumb knight in shining armor on a horse; if I had to draw one more horse in that context, I would just die of boredom and rage. Meanwhile, that was all anybody wanted from me. And it's in my nature to please—anything to make everybody happy," she says.

The dissonance between the world she created on paper, filled with princesses waiting to be rescued, and her real life as a struggling lesbian mother also became increasingly apparent. She had left her husband for another woman, a radical act in the days when lesbian mothers were considered almost criminals. But in terms of her awareness of feminist theory, Hyman says, "My consciousness has been raised incrementally over the years. In 1966, I was living this radical feminist existence, and I didn't even know it."

The classic European fairy tales are good stories, Hyman says. "They are our mythology, our culture, our heritage, and in that way they ring a lot of bells for me. But they're also part of what is so wrong with our culture and our society—they're so fucking patriarchal, these stories, and the women in them are mostly users or used. And that got to me, perpetrating this whole thing."

She gives the example of *Snow White* as a powerful story. "The reason why it is powerful is because it's a mother-daughter relationship, and the mother goes mad. But I didn't know that then. I was still seeing the dwarfs and the prince as this young woman's rescuers; they were her saviors. I suppose that I always wanted seven dwarfs to save me too. I didn't realize then that the seven dwarfs had no interest in saving her; they just wanted a housekeeper."

Hyman adds that if she had realized all of that, the book would have been much different and "too skewed. But you can only do so many of those stories without it sinking in that, 'Hey, wait a minute, there's something not being said here.

In her search for stories that were more meaningful than the classic fairy tales, Hyman turned to folktales, such as *Herschel and the Hanukkah Goblins,* for which she won a Caldecott Honor Medal.

Her daughter's marriage to a man from Cameroon and the birth of their child, Michou, in 1989, forced Hyman to confront the issue of race in her work. Although she had varied the color of her princesses' hair, their skin was always white. Hyman became acutely aware of the need for multicultural children's literature, and of how embedded her own work was in the European aesthetic.

The Fortune Tellers (1992), a story originally set in medieval Europe, became the unlikely vehicle for her entry into multicultural children's books. Although Hyman and her friend of twenty years, writer Lloyd Alexander, had always wanted to do a book together, Alexander seldom writes picture books. "But he found this manuscript that he'd written years before, sent it to his publisher, and his publisher contacted me. When I read the story, I thought it was a neat little story, but it didn't grab me the way that I would like a story to. To illustrate a book is, for me, a nine-month-to-a-year project, and I have to really like the story," Hyman says.

Her daughter read the manuscript and said that it reminded her of a Sufi tale and could be set in North Africa. Inspired, Hyman suggested changing the story's setting to Cameroon, where her daughter had lived for four years. Hyman had visited Katrin there twice, once while her daughter was in the Peace Corps and then for her wedding. "I just went crazy for this country—I was bitten by the bug that gets to some of those who go to Africa and fall in love with the landscape and the people. So this was an opportunity for me to get all that visual stuff out that I had been storing up and illustrate Lloyd's story all in one blow." Alexander was amenable to the idea; only five nouns needed to be changed in the manuscript.

"I made the hero, the carpenter, my son-in-law, and I put my daughter and my grandson in cameo roles. But all the people I had met in my two visits and everything that had struck me [as] being beautiful about [the] country went into this book. It was a real work of love," the artist says.

But moving away from traditional European fairy tales was only part of the solution to Hyman's work crisis. Together with two friends, she rented a studio in nearby Bradford, Vermont, where they spent one day a week painting from life. "We thought if we hired a model, that would make us do it—no excuses. And that saved my life. It was fun and it was really hard—I hadn't done any oil painting since I was a student."

After three years of painting from life, Hyman recently decided to paint from internal inspirations, visions, and dreams. "The painting I'm working on now is an angel. But what I would like to do is spirits; I feel like women's souls are being killed all the time, and I'd like to paint those souls. I have a lot to say about women's suffering."

At this point in her life, Hyman says, painting is "all I want to do; that's where I want to be. I could easily move in there and paint my heart out. But I can't, because I still have children's book deadlines. So I guess [one is] always torn, and I'm not sure why. I'm not sure what's stopping me from doing that, except for the contracts that I signed and my own sense that, if it's not the kids, now I've got the dogs and the sheep and the house. What's making me not just say, 'Hey, I'm over fifty years old; I can go and live in that studio if I want to and paint my heart out?'"

Although her daughter is grown and herself a mother, Hyman still struggles with domestic issues. "Even though there are no kids, there's still a house to be taken care of. I'm a nest-maker. I have had this conversation with every woman artist I know: How do you do your work and your home and your children and your relationships? And we've all come to the conclusion that that's why there aren't more women artists; it's why all the really big creative forces were men— because women are split; they're just schizophrenic about [how] they've got to take care of home, children, meals, their husbands or lovers. How to put that all in perspective—how to slot your life—takes up a lot of energy that you could be putting into your work, should be putting into your work. We all feel it and we don't know what to do about it."

To illustrate her point, Hyman describes how her family decided to come to her house for Thanksgiving dinner. Hyman and her then-partner spent three days shopping, cooking, and cleaning (despite having a regular cleaning lady). "One part of my head is screaming, 'I should be working, I'm behind on my work.' And if I shouldn't be working in this studio, I have a painting studio in another town up north, and that's where I want to be. I don't want to be standing here cooking that fucking turkey, but I do it because it's programmed into my genes," she says, laughing.

Asked how her grandson, Michou, might influence future projects, Hyman says, "When my daughter and the twins were small, I did books mostly for small children. As the children grew older, my books got older, too. And now that everybody's grown up, I'm doing children's books but in a rather grown-up way. I think that having Michou around will automatically remind me to put a toddler's point of view in there. Even if the book I'm working on isn't for little kids, there's nothing like having little kids around to remind you they're part of the world."

For example, the artist recalls an incident that happened in her painting studio last summer, when her grandson Michou was two. She had been working on a portrait, which was nearly finished. "My little grandson came into the studio and walked over to my work area, picked out a brush and dipped it in ultramarine blue, and walked right up to the canvas and started painting on it." Although her daughter and the other adults present worried about how she would react, Hyman says, "I was so happy that this child was painting. I just incorporated his blue; it was in a great spot. And I thought, that's the nice part of having been a mom and working around kids—I can use this."

Still, Hyman would advise a young woman serious about her art either not to have children or to make sure she has financial as well as emotional support from parents or the child's father. "If you want to paint, I don't think you can be a mom, be a waitress to make money, and paint. It's hard enough to be a mom and paint. I think you need help with your children, even if you only have one child." She adds that her daughter is trying to write and is finding it very difficult, despite having a husband willing to share half of the child care.

"There are lots of women who have their children and say, 'Well, I'll wait till the children are grown, and then I'll go back to my career.' They just suffer agonies. You can't put being an artist on hold; you have to do it every day. You can't just say, 'I'm going to take ten years off and then go back to it.' Some women can if they're extremely determined and very strong, but most of them just want to and don't know how. I get lots of letters from women like that: 'My kids are in school, I had fine arts training, I've always wanted to be an artist or an illustrator, now what do I do?' My advice is, 'You'd better go back to art school and get yourself in the swing of creating, of doing that full time.' And it's hard to then switch over to being a part-time mom and a full-time artist."

Hyman recalled that when she announced her plans to marry while still in art school, a painter on the faculty came up to her one day and said, "Don't get married. If you get married, you will never paint. You're too good to throw it all away just for sex." Hyman says, "It stuck with me my whole life long. Basically, she was right. I did it anyway, and I kept her words with me like a challenge through my life: I'm going to do it, I can have it all. But the fact is, it's very difficult to have it all.

"On the other hand, if you're a woman, how can you not have children? I don't mean that to be as flip as it sounds; I mean, it's an opportunity, it's such an immense experience. It's one of the ultimate acts of creation, and I wouldn't have not done that for the world. But it sure makes your life as an artist difficult."

BETYE SAAR

Betye Saar

In her work, Betye Saar, sixty-seven, gives new meaning to the word recycle. *The raw materials for her intricate three-dimensional collages, or assemblages, include everything from vintage photographs and Mexican amulets to moss and discarded circuit boards. Saar transforms the detritus of material culture into art imbued with mystery and layered meaning. An African-American with Irish and Native American ancestors, Saar's multicultural and pan-religious work expresses her spirituality and her personal history. She uses the symbols we share—sun, moon, stars, hearts, eyes—to show how connected we really are.*

Born in 1926 in Pasadena, California, Saar studied design at Pasadena City College and UCLA, from which she received her bachelor's degree in 1949. She later studied printmaking at California State University at Long Beach and in 1992 was awarded an honorary doctorate by Massachusetts College of Art. Recipient of two National Endowment for the Arts awards and grants from the Getty and Guggenheim Foundations, Saar has exhibited and lectured around the world.

She married Richard Saar, an artist and art conservator, in 1952 and has three daughters: Lezley, born in 1953, followed by Alison in 1956, and Tracye in 1961. She is also a grandmother to Lezley's two daughters, four-year-old Sóla and two-year-old Geneva, and Alison's children, four-year-old Kyle and infant daughter, Maddy. Divorced since 1968, Betye Saar lives and works in her Los Angeles home.

OVER THE PAST TWENTY-FIVE YEARS, BETYE SAAR HAS CRE-ated an impressive oeuvre while working at home within the confines of family life. When a television interviewer in the late 1970s asked how she balanced art and family, Saar responded, "What's the difference?" She feels the same way today, "Childrearing can be very creative. Since my daughters are women now—the eldest will be forty this year—I think it works out," she says with a laugh.

"I've always been a kitchen artist. Basically, I worked around the family and things got done. You can have this schedule in your mind, but if your child has the measles, you take care of the kid."

Whenever circumstances impede her ability to work in the studio, Saar turns her attention to whatever she *can* do: sketching, gathering materials, or scouting for new ideas. This ability to "refocus" seems to be one of the keys to Saar's success. Because she is not driven to succeed, Saar says, the work remains a pleasure rather than a chore. The work itself sustains her interest, engaging her imagination and love of materials, and that interest runs like a thread through the artist's life.

Betye Saar's own mother was a seamstress, and the artist remembers making doll clothes as a child. She studied design in college and three years after graduation, married an artist, Richard Saar, who ran a ceramics business. She worked from home, making and selling enamel jewelry, and then began producing a line of studio greeting cards when her eldest daughter, Lezley, was born in 1953. Her second child, Alison, was born three years later, when Saar was thirty years old.

"I didn't really think about making art until Alison was almost five. I was working on a teaching credential at [California State University] Long Beach and was seduced by printmaking. I started taking printmaking classes; that was my introduction into fine arts.

"Around that time, when Alison was starting school, I became pregnant with Tracye, my youngest daughter. Actually, I was making a print on the day that she was born. I have a serigraph called *Anticipation,* which is a pregnant woman sitting in a chair, and several about the birth experience, like *Lost Travail* (1961), a color etching. It was really interesting because when Tracye was born, her face looked so much like this baby's face [in *Lost Travail*], it was really a surprise to me." Saar says, "I kept doing printmaking but not as frequently because I wasn't able to go to a facility where I could use the press. I would make a woodcut or a serigraph that I could do at home.

"If you have children, you know it takes a good two years before you get your energy back—when they take a nap, you take a nap." Once her energy returned, the artist worked while Tracye napped. One day, when her youngest daughter was two or three years old, Saar began drawing Tracye as she sat watching television. "I started making lots of drawings of her while she was sitting in this chair because she was fairly still. I would draw her and we could still be together. I didn't want to work with the [printmaking] acids when she was around because I couldn't really concentrate on both of those things. On the weekends, my husband was at home or the older girls were at home, and they could watch her and I could do prints then."

A few years after Tracye's birth, the family moved to the Laurel Canyon area of Los Angeles, where one of their new neighbors had a printing press. Saar recalls, "I would work on her press and do very small etchings, but they were mostly about nature and the three children. That's what my interest was then, the home and children, and they were right here. I did not have a car and I lived in a very rural area, so the fact that I had a neighbor who had a small press and we could just walk up there and I could do my printmaking made it all easier."

Although the acids and sharp tools used in etching and woodcutting were too dangerous for her children to handle, Saar did involve them in other art projects such as making potato stamps or simple block printing. In the summers, she would organize an art class for children in the neighborhood.

In the mid-1960s, Saar's work took a new direction as she began to combine her etchings and drawings and frame them with old windows, resulting in such work as her 1966 piece, *Mystic Window for Leo*.

Mysticism and an interest in other cultures have always been important elements in the artist's life. Saar, who remembers being psychic and clairvoyant until her father died when she was six years old, says, "As a child, I was always fascinated by palmistry charts that were at the storefront of gypsy fortune-telling booths. We lived in Pasadena; there was a park in South Pasadena where every year they [the gypsies] would have their camp, and our family would drive by there out of curiosity. They would have the old caravans, sometimes even with horses. That whole lifestyle really fascinated me.

"In the '60s, when the hippie movement, metaphysics, and the occult were really popular, there were these coffeehouses with bookshops that had books about palmistry charts and phrenology charts and Egyptian mythology. So I would buy these books and look at these old charts, and they would work their way into my work."

In 1967, Saar attended an exhibition of assemblage artist Joseph Cornell's work. Instead of using windows to frame collages, Cornell used boxes to house assemblages of two- and three-dimensional objects. Inspired, Saar spent the next couple of years "going to flea markets and thrift stores and estate sales, concentrating on gathering materials because I really wanted to make those boxes."

Although it was Cornell's exhibit that awakened Saar to the possibilities of assemblage, she was also inspired by childhood memories of the Watts Towers. While visiting her paternal grandmother who lived in then-rural Watts, Saar had watched as Simon Rodia, an Italian immigrant, built his fantastic sculpture, Watts Towers—several spiraling hundred-foot-high structures constructed of steel and covered with cement and with thousands of seashells, bits of broken china, tile, and glass.

One of Saar's earliest assemblages, *Black Girl's Window,* shows the confluence of the metaphysical, autobiographical, and ethnic threads that run through much of the artist's work. In the upper half of the piece are nine boxes with suns, crescents, stars, a phrenology chart, and a tintype of a white woman—expressions of the artist's interest in the occult and an allusion to her mixed ancestry. A skeleton is in the center box. The work, like many later pieces, is marked by death, just as Saar's childhood was marked by the death of her father.

The bottom half of the piece is filled with the face of a young black girl pressed against the glass of the window that frames the work. On a personal level, the silhouette of the girl represents the artist. On a political level, the girl can be seen as representing black people in general; the work was created in 1969, after the Watts riots and the 1968 murder of civil rights leader Dr. Martin Luther King Jr.

Saar collected derogatory images of blacks and used them in some of her earliest assemblages, such as *The Liberation of Aunt Jemima* (1972), in which the artist juxtaposes vintage and modern images of smiling Jemimas with a three-dimensional Jemima holding both a broom and a gun. The piece is an example of Saar's "homeopathic use of stereotypes as weapons to attack the racism that produced them," writes art critic Lucy Lippard in her book, *Mixed Blessings.*

Saar says, "With the nostalgia series, I used photographs of African-Americans. I love photography, and I collect vintage photographs, especially of African-Americans because they're just so rare to find. The ritual series goes back to our ancestral history. It goes back to Africa, but it also goes back to Egypt and Oceania and any[where] that is indigenous, that is non-Western, non-European. So that ethnic tie has always been part of my work."

Although her African-American heritage is an important thread in her work, racial politics is not a major theme. "My art is about things that mean something special to me personally—[my] interest in the occult, in my family and children, in nature.

"My ex-husband is from Ohio and he is German-English, so our friends were always mixed racially. We never lived in the ghetto, we always lived in a middle-class neighborhood that was a mixed neighborhood. Those are the neighborhoods I grew up in. I would meet racial discrimination every once in a while, and I was always sort of surprised."

At the same time that Saar's work was changing from printmaking to assemblages, her personal life was also moving in new directions. Her divorce in 1969 "meant I had to get a job job, other than making art at home or designing cards. My first job was at this theater, which is called the Inner City Cultural Center, and I became the costume designer there. It was a theater that had a grant to do productions for high school kids, so that meant it was a job from September to June." In the summer, Saar took her daughters to northern California where she designed costumes for the Napa Valley Theater Company.

Although she had little time to pursue her own art over the next couple of years, the costume design jobs did provide "a creative outlet because it involved sketches and then shopping for materials and putting materials together."

Saar began teaching in 1971 and continued until the mid-1980s, working for varying lengths of time at UCLA, the University of Alaska, the Otis Art Institute, and other schools. Her first teaching stint, in the fall of 1971, was at California State University, Hayward, several hundred miles away from her home in Los Angeles. "It was hard because I had to be separated from my children. At that time, Lezley had finished high school and she was spending the year in Europe. Their father, even though we were divorced, moved into the house and took care of the younger daughters. The girls came up for Thanksgiving and we talked [on the phone] or I would drive down to see them. I could make a little art but it was mostly drawing and sketching and gathering materials.

"But I would just refocus: 'Okay, I physically can't make art, so I will gather materials, or I will go to museums and look at things, or I will make sketchbooks.' That's the way it is now too—like when my downstairs was torn up [for] remodeling. I have a two-story house and in the upstairs part I have a little table. The table became my studio and I just did collages.

"I've always felt that my house was like this big assemblage. There would be bookshelves where I would put different objects or flower arrangements or stones or shells or things that I've collected." Saar, whose current hobby is gardening, says, "I love lavenders so it's mostly a lavender garden, but the garden itself is very sculptural. As soon as I finish this remodeling, I plan to build a grotto with broken crockery. That definitely is a throwback to the Watts Towers."

Were there times when she wished her studio was out of the house? Saar replies, "I still do, just for space. I'm in the process of building a garage with a studio over it, which hopefully will be completed this year. But I like working at home, and I don't like to get in my car to go someplace to do it because I don't function with that kind of discipline. I don't get up and go into the studio to work. Sometimes I work at the desk because a lot of it's paperwork. Sometimes I work in the field, going to flea markets or estate sales or thrift stores, gathering materials. And sometimes I just do research, reading or looking at picture books or catalogs or going to art exhibitions. The museums that I prefer are natural history museums; that's where I get the most inspiration."

An artist-in-residence stint at the Massachusetts Institute of Technology in 1987 sparked Saar's interest in "technology as magic." She says, "The interesting thing about technology is that as soon as it's complete, it's obsolete, so I give it a second life.

"When I started working at MIT, these circuit boards charged my imagination. They became these ritualistic things by adding objects to them." The colored glass beads in the circuit board she used in *Sanctuary's Edge* (1988) reminded Saar of Egyptian beads, so she added a miniature Egyptian sarcophagus, along with *milagros,* Mexican amulets in the shape of various body parts.

While Saar relies on her intuition to guide her in choosing which objects to purchase in the field and which to use for a particular piece, her design training accounts for the importance of symmetry in her work, "There's always a center and something at both ends," she says.

"The way that I get started working is sort of like cleaning up and tidying up, examining the boxes that hold my things. I have all my things in boxes, plastic shoe boxes to sweater boxes to large plastic containers down to small ones that hold nails and screws. I just start sorting through things. Or I'll find something that triggers my imagination and pull out a box and pull out everything that makes me think of what I want to do.

"I also have lots of stories. Sometimes I think of myself as a *griotte;* it's an African word meaning the historian, storyteller. Every time I find a special box or a special set of materials, a new story comes out. I'm just never out of ideas."

When her great-aunt Hattie died in the mid-1970s, Saar did a series of works about the women of her family, using old photographs and objects (such as a pair of black gloves) that belonged to them, to tell stories about their lives. Many of those pieces were small works contained in boxes, although the series also included *In My Solitude* (1983), an installation piece.

Saar describes *In My Solitude* as installed in a dim room, with dried flowers on the floor. "The kitchen chair had a moss seat with candles that became a ritual object. The elements that belonged to my great-aunt were a pair of party shoes from the '30s and a black chiffon dress. It seemed like wherever I did this installation, [the dress] was hanging by an air vent, so there was movement to the dress; it was like a ghost. When they went into that space, people felt very sad and had feelings of grief, and when I would talk to them, they would say, 'It made me think of my father who passed [away] last year, or my mother.'"

In retrospect, the artist, whose own mother died in 1985, sees *In My Solitude* as the beginning of her current work, which she calls creative grieving, "a way of dealing with those feelings through an installation with light and sound as well as visual elements. I did a piece at the University of Colorado at Boulder, where I designed a set and then the audience could participate in a performance." In a ritual gesture before entering the space, visitors evoke the sound of falling rain by turning a rain stick, a hollow wooden stick filled with bits of bamboo and stones. Inside the space, "I provided a box that was three feet by three feet, filled with white sand on the floor. They write the name of the departed person, and then as they exit, they turn the rain stick on the other side.

An element of spirituality is one of the threads in Saar's work. Noting that a viewer referred to her in the comment book at one recent exhibition as "Satan's Mother," Saar says, "I don't want to offend anyone's religion."

Rather, her aim is "that when you look at what I do, I hope that you feel—I can't say elevated—but curious about something in yourself that you weren't aware of before. I'm finding that the most effective way to do that is with an installation so the viewer enters the space. As soon as you step into that space, a different mood hits you, a meditative mood."

Her three daughters have all grown up to be artists. Lezley Saar, a book designer and illustrator, works with her drafting table set up in a corner of the bedroom her two daughters share. In contrast, Alison Saar produces her large-scale sculptures in a studio outside her home while a baby-sitter cares for her two young children. Tracye Saar, who does not have children, currently works three days a week for her father and two days a week as her mother's assistant, in addition to doing her own freelance projects.

Saar and her middle daughter collaborated on *House of Gris-Gris* (1990), a mixed-media installation and the centerpiece of "Secrets, Dialogues, and Revelations: The Art of Betye and Alison Saar," a touring exhibition sponsored by UCLA's Wight Art Gallery. This seven-feet long, five-feet wide, six-feet high "house of good magic," made of wood and aviary wire stuffed with feathers, moss, and eucalyptus leaves, is the first piece the two artists have jointly created.

The elder Saar says, " The house as an image and as a symbol was really important to us. She [Alison] was raised in our house. And our first planning meeting was soon after the birth of her [Alison's] young son, so she was in, as she likes to phrase it, 'a nesting mode.'" Alison contributed the corrugated tin roof and the windows, while Betye did the floor, on which she painted a Haitian *veve* heart symbol; an altar inside the house; and above the door, a "spirit tree" hung with bottles to attract positive and repel negative spirits.

Curator Elizabeth Shepherd writes about the piece in the introduction to the exhibition catalog: "Entitled *House of Gris-Gris*, it refers to grey magic—neither black nor white—and it charts the progression of the spirit from its mortal state to its heavenly ascent. In it, the artists conjure up a sensory environment that alludes to the 'nest' as the site of artistic creativity and procreativity."

Photo ©, Marian Kolisch

URSULA K. LE GUIN

Ursula K. Le Guin

*Considered one of the most distinguished writers of science fiction and fantasy,
Ursula K. Le Guin, sixty-four, creates worlds where intelligent beings, separated
by gender, race, age, culture, and even species, reach across the abyss to build
relationships. Although her novels, short stories, and poems are often set on
faraway planets in the distant future, her characters face very human dilemmas
as they struggle for harmony, with each other and with the natural environment.*

*Le Guin graduated from Radcliffe College in 1951 and, a year later, received
her master's degree in Italian and French Literature from Columbia University.
Le Guin is the author of more than forty books, including seventeen novels,
eight children's books, several books of critical essays, three short story collections, and half a dozen volumes of poetry. She has received a number of honors
for her work, including three Hugo Awards given by the International Science
Fiction Association, four Nebula Awards from the Science Fiction Writers Association, a National Book Award, and the Janet Heidinger Kafka Prize for Fiction.*

*Le Guin has lived most of her adult life in the house on Thurman Street in
Portland, Oregon, which she shares with her husband of forty years, historian
Charles Le Guin, now Professor Emeritus at Portland State University. The couple
have three children: thirty-six-year-old Elisabeth, thirty-four-year-old Caroline,
and twenty-nine-year-old Theodore; and two grandchildren: nine-year-old Lyra
Sofia Howell and four-month-old India Downes-Le Guin.*

IN "THE FISHERWOMAN'S DAUGHTER," ONE OF HER MOST
influential critical essays, Ursula K. Le Guin considers the question of
whether a woman can combine books and babies. Gathering quotes
from a variety of literary sources, Le Guin weaves these together with
her own experience to envision a woman who calmly balances both children and writing. Indeed, balance is a theme in Le Guin's life and work.

"The whole principle of keeping a balance became a sort of mo-
tif; you can find it in practically everything I write," says Le Guin, who

was drawn as a young teen to the Chinese philosophy of Taoism, which emphasizes the need for balance and harmony. "This romantic ideal of the male artist standing in total isolation from his society—that is an unbalanced, eccentric idea which I reject because that's not how you get good work done. To me, an art grows organically out of its society at its best, so you don't cut the connection. And if your connections happen to be family ones—to your ancestors, to your descendants, to your lateral kinfolk—then that's your world," she says.

While Le Guin's writing is informed by her relationships, she is not a particularly autobiographical writer. In fact, much of her writing is not personal at all. For example, her story "Intracom" seems to be about an argument between the various crew members whose spaceship has just been invaded by an alien. The story can also be read as a metaphor for conception with the spaceship symbolizing a woman and the alien a sperm. "That's about as autobiographical as I get," Le Guin says with a laugh. "I distance and disguise, and am slightly unwilling to confess which is the made-up experience and which is the real one."

Although Le Guin hasn't written about her family in her fiction, her parents, both of whom worked in the field of anthropology, clearly influenced her writing. In her novels and short stories, Le Guin travels through time and space, creating entire civilizations just as her parents traveled to worlds beyond their own, documenting other cultures in their books. Her father was the pioneering anthropologist Alfred L. Kroeber, who established the anthropology department at the University of California and directed the anthropology museum there, in addition to writing a number of books. His research focused on the native peoples of California, although he also did fieldwork among Indian tribes in Mexico, New Mexico, and Peru. Her mother, Theodora Kroeber, is best known for her nonfiction book *Ishi in Two Worlds* (1961), the true story of a Native American who was the last surviving member of the Yahi tribe.

Le Guin absorbed not only an interest in other cultures from her parents but also a respect for the solitude of a working writer. She recalls, "My father wrote all my life. He had a study, and when he was in his study, we did not interrupt him for any frivolous reason. It wasn't scary or rigid, but you just knew, don't knock on the door unless it's important because he's writing. So I grew up with this fact-of-life kind of respect for somebody who's working, and I had no difficulty, no guilt, about instilling that in my kids."

From an early age, Le Guin wanted to be a writer. She began writing poetry at the age of five and then several years later, short stories. By the time she left her hometown of Berkeley, California, to attend Radcliffe College, she was submitting poems and short stories to literary magazines. After graduating in 1951, Le Guin entered Columbia University to study medieval Romance languages with the intention of supporting her writing by teaching. She finished her master's degree a year later and received a Fulbright scholarship to spend a year in Paris. On the voyage across the Atlantic, she met another doctoral student, Charles Le Guin; the two were married in France in 1953.

Charles Le Guin had already started writing his dissertation, so both husband and wife had some experience of what the life of a writer entailed. "I told him, 'Now look, I want to write. I'm getting a college degree so that I can support myself by teaching so that I can write, and nothing is going to change that.' And he said, 'Fine.'" After a couple of years, Le Guin quit graduate school to concentrate on her writing, teaching French part time while her husband finished his studies.

Although Le Guin published some poetry in her twenties, the four or five novels she wrote during that decade were rejected. "I just kept writing; I didn't stop for any long time at any point," she says.

Le Guin found a colleague in her mother, who had begun writing in her fifties, after raising her four children. Le Guin says, "I was rather jealous of her for a while because she was getting published while I was still getting rejected. But it was really fun because as she became a writer, we could talk shop, talk editors and publishers. Although she published before I did, she considered me more experienced, which I was—I'd been writing longer, although I was only in my twenties.

"Once she started writing, she never stopped. When she was about eighty, she said to me—just once—'I wish I had started a lot sooner because I'm just learning how to write novels now and it's too late.' That kind of broke my heart," says Le Guin, whose mother died at eighty-three.

Unlike her mother, Le Guin wrote during the years she was home with her three children, who were born in 1957, 1959, and 1964. But becoming a mother did have a dramatic impact on her writing schedule.

"I very seldom tried to write while I was on duty taking care of them," she says. Although she considers herself a "morning worker," who thinks best in the early part of the day, for the first decade of motherhood, Le Guin wrote mostly at night, after the children went to bed. Her husband "kept an ear out" for the children so that she could concentrate. Once all three were in school, Le Guin was able to return to working during her preferred morning hours.

Her persistence paid off with the publication of her first short story in 1962, followed by the publication of two novels, *Planet of Exile* and *Rocannon's World,* in 1966, when Le Guin was thirty-six years old. Since then, she has published a new novel or story collection every year or two, in addition to children's books, poetry collections, and several volumes of critical essays.

"I'm amazed now with how much I wrote when they were all young and when I was doing so much else, with them, for them, and also being politically active. I was extremely strong when I was young, and I could do lots of things at once," Le Guin says.

Having children affected not only her writing time but the form her writing took. She remembers the frustration "particularly with short stories, where the story catches you up and wants to be written right now, imperatively, but you can't, and you have to put it away till tomorrow.

"Whereas a poem, and often a short story, need to be grabbed while they're flying past," Le Guin says, "a novel has its own momentum, and you can put it away until tomorrow without losing it. Novels were definitely my way of getting through the interrupted phase. Once you get it going, you do live in the novel, to some extent, for twenty-four hours a day, but not to an extent that I felt made me ineffective for motherhood and other duties. The part of your mind that's busy with the novel goes glunking away, halfway underground. But then you are ready to go in the morning because that half-conscious stuff has been going on."

While Le Guin altered her work habits and the type of writing she did to meet the demands of childrearing, "I can't say that I see any difference in either what I wrote about or the quality of my writing in the years when I had kids home and after they left."

Throughout, Le Guin has received both material and moral support from her husband, "which at least in my generation, was fairly rare," she says. The theme of balance can also be seen in her marriage, with each partner providing a supportive environment for the other. Le Guin says, "To a large extent, our lives, Charles's and mine, have been a kind of collaboration. We have collaborated in each other's work in the sense of making it possible." Indeed, Le Guin has dedicated several of her books to her husband; the dedication page in *The Left Hand of Darkness* reads, "For Charles, *sine quo non*," or "without whom nothing."

For many years while her writing income was "tiny or zilch," her husband supported the family financially. Raised in a working-class Southern family, he both expected and wanted to be the breadwinner. And Le Guin had grown up with similar expectations. "My mother never had a paid job when I knew her. I didn't feel imprisoned or helpless or patronized or anything like that by living off him. I did hope that I would be able to fetch some money in and, sure enough, when I started fetching it in, then I fetched it in in a big way for us. And Charles has had absolutely no problem living off my income the last few years.

"For one thing, it was always our money—it wasn't his money or my money," she says. The only exception was when Le Guin sold her first short story and used the money to buy a pair of pants. "That was *my* thirty dollars. But after that, it went into the kitty."

When she speaks to aspiring young writers, Le Guin says, "I tell them either make money or marry it. Get yourself some kind of skill other than your art that you can either fall back on or work part time at or support yourself with so that you are not dependent on your editor's whim, so that you can do your work in your time. If you don't have any financial independence, life is going to be so damn hard. It's nice to tell people, marry a supportive spouse or find a supportive partner, but that's a matter of luck. But obviously, the partner is often the key to the whole thing."

At the same time, Le Guin says, "I'm a little anxious to avoid making it sound like you have to have a partner in order to be an artist. You don't. And yet there's something important to me in realizing how our partnership has been a collaboration in three different kinds of work—counting housework and kids—because of the myth of the solitary artist, who must work alone and must sacrifice maybe kids, maybe normal human relationships. I think perhaps this kind of sacrificial solitude may be even counterproductive in the long run. It certainly leads to a kind of arrogance about the relationships that are so important in most people's lives—which are your blood kin, your neighbors, and the people you work with. An artist who is working in grand isolation doesn't know anything about all that, is aloof from it, and this may impoverish the novel."

Much of Le Guin's own writing deals with relationships. Separated by gender, race, culture, or even species, her characters reach out and experience "some kind of emotional breakthrough to which they then hold," remaining loyal to each other despite trying circumstances.

In her novel *The Left Hand of Darkness,* the friendship that develops between Genly Ai, a man from Earth, and Lord Estraven, a Gethenian, is an example of Le Guin's concern with relationships. The novel can also be seen as an example of how the theme of balance permeates Le Guin's work. In this case, she balances male and female by creating a world in which everyone is androgynous.

Genly Ai, the narrator of *The Left Hand of Darkness,* is the first envoy to make formal contact with the faraway world of Gethen. He is both repelled and fascinated by the fact that each Gethenian has the ability to quickly develop either male or female sexual characteristics during the monthly mating period but is otherwise androgynous. A Gethenian who is the mother of several children may be the father of several more.

The fact that all Gethenians of reproductive age are equally likely to be tied down by childbearing "implies that no one is quite so thoroughly 'tied down' here as women, elsewhere, are likely to be—psychologically or physically," the character Genly Ai writes in his field notes. And conversely, he adds, "nobody here is quite so free as a free male anywhere else."

The Earthman does not know how to relate to a people who do not see themselves as men or women. "One is respected and judged only as a human being. It is an appalling experience," the character comments.

When Le Guin wrote the novel in 1967, the current wave of feminism was just beginning. "I began to want to define and understand the meaning of sexuality and the meaning of gender, in my life and in our society," she writes in her essay "Is Gender Necessary?" (1976).

Le Guin notes that she was not proposing Gethen as a model for humanity but rather using the invention as a heuristic device, a thought experiment, to explore "what, besides purely physiological form and function, truly differentiates men and women." She goes on to suggest that "One of the essential functions of science fiction, I think, is precisely this kind of question-asking: reversals of a habitual way of thinking, metaphors for what our language has no words for as yet, experiments in imagination."

In retrospect, Le Guin says, "I see where in that book I could have shown androgynous behavior much more clearly." Although the novel includes a pregnant king, the characters, particularly Lord Estraven, do seem to be more masculine than feminine, a perception that is perhaps reinforced by the heroic quest elements of the plot.

In her essay "The Fisherwoman's Daughter," Le Guin writes that "it seems to me a pity" that so many women have narrowed their perception and written "as if their sexuality were limited to copulation, as if they knew nothing about pregnancy, birth, nursing, mothering, puberty, menstruation, menopause, except what men are willing to hear."

Looking back on that passage today, she observes, "I was scolding myself. I wrote like a man for years, as we were taught to do. I have learned late, and I'm still learning how to write fully as a woman. It can be very hard; there are not all that many models.

"It's like we have nine million books about fathers and sons, and we're just beginning to get the novels about mothers and daughters, about motherhood and daughterhood, which is endlessly fascinating and a very difficult subject," Le Guin says. "And motherhood as perceived not by the child but by the mother—there are not a whole lot of books about that. In other words, books from a grown-up point of view. There's still lots to be done."

The novel in which Le Guin most completely rearranges gender roles, in the social rather than the biological sense, is *Always Coming Home* (1985). Le Guin says that although the main society in that book has been repeatedly referred to as a matriarchy, "it's nothing of the kind. It's a woman-centered book, but it's not a female-dominated book—and that seems to be a distinction which (particularly male) reviewers are unable to make."

The book is set in California's Napa Valley, one of the author's favorite places, where she spent childhood summers listening to the stories told by her father's Native American friends. In *Always Coming Home*, Le Guin portrays the Kesh, a people from a very distant future, whose society is stable and in ecological balance. Interspersed with the main story are not only poems, legends, and myths, but also ethnographic essays, explaining Kesh funerary rites, clothing, religious rituals, and other customs.

Le Guin has written eight children's books, including *A Ride on the Red Mare's Back* (1992), a picture book dedicated to her granddaughter Lyra who loves horses. As in the case of her poetry and short stories, Le Guin says, "I cannot plan a kid's book. I can only sit and wait and hope that one might happen. They come all of a piece, and I write them down real fast and there they are—waiting to be revised. And like poetry, of course, in a kid's book, every word had better be just right because you haven't got all that many." Like her poems, the children's books arrive unexpectedly, as "gifts," the author says. "I get handed this big present which says, 'Write me.'"

The biggest change in her writing life in recent years has had nothing to do with her role as a mother, but with her role as a public figure. "As I became better known, my correspondence grew and grew," she observes. "This began to eat into my time along about the time the kids were getting older and going off to college. And now, it could be as time-devouring as they ever were, if not more so, and very much less rewarding."

Part of her bind, Le Guin says, is that as someone who has written science fiction, she is part of the community, or subculture, of science fiction enthusiasts who keep in touch with each other. "Most of them are doing it by E-mail now, which I won't touch because I know it would be a total black hole."

While she knows that some writers ignore their mail, she has no desire to imitate them. "The ones I've heard about that don't answer letters are artists whom I dislike anyway." On the other hand, she says, "I could spend my life answering letters. And there's a temptation to do so because it's easier than writing in some respects. It's a kind of false writing."

As she gets older and her energy decreases, the need to balance competing demands becomes more acute. Le Guin says, "There's a kind of drawing in and weakening of your forces, so that you have to be kind to yourself and not reach out too much, or you find yourself completely frittered away. This happens to me so easily now."

Although as a younger woman she was able to write anywhere under any circumstances, her ability to work in the midst of distraction has diminished with age. These days, for her to reach that state of being "in a vortex," or completely throwing herself into her work, she says, "I have to be literally alone in the house. I do not seem to be able to do that when I'm with people."

Previously her attitude toward the idea of a writing retreat was, "What do you need that for? Now I understand; now I'm humble," she says. For the past six years, the Le Guins have had their own writing retreat, a beach house on the Oregon coast, which they take turns using for a week at a time. "It's become very important to both of us as this need to get away from all distractions in order to work grows on us." Providing a way to balance their need for solitude with their need for companionship, Le Guin says, "that place has become just wonderful for both of us."

Photo ©, Faith Ringgold, Inc.

FAITH RINGGOLD

Faith Ringgold

In her paintings, soft sculptures, story quilts, and picture books, Faith Ringgold, sixty-two, conveys both the vitality and the pain of the African-American community, and in particular, African-American women. From her political paintings of the late 1960s to her current "French Collection" series of story quilts, Ringgold creates work that emphatically expresses her tripartite identity: female, black, American.

Educated at City College of New York, from which she received her bachelor's degree in education in 1955 and her master's degree in art in 1959, Ringgold taught art in the New York public schools for seventeen years. She has received awards from the National Endowment for the Arts, the Guggenheim Foundation, and other institutions, and a twenty-five-year retrospective exhibition of her work toured more than thirteen US cities in the early 1990s. Ringgold has also written and illustrated three children's books: Tar Beach (1991), which won a Caldecott Honor Medal; Aunt Harriet's Underground Railroad in the Sky *(1992); and* Dinner at Aunt Connie's House *(1993).*

Ringgold divides her time between the New York area and San Diego, where she is a professor of art at the University of California. Married since 1962 to her second husband, Burdette Ringgold, she is the mother of writer Michele Faith Wallace, forty-two, and teacher Barbara Faith Wallace, forty-one, and grandmother to her daughter Barbara's three children: ten-year-old Faith, nine-year-old Teddy, and four-year-old Martha.

A THIN, ELEGANT, MIDDLE-AGED BLACK WOMAN SITS BY THE sea talking with her teenage son in Faith Ringgold's story quilt, *On the Beach at Saint Tropez* (1991), the last in "The French Collection: Part One" series. The words which border the painting tell Willia Marie Simone's story. The sixteen-year-old Simone was on her way to Paris to be an artist when she met her husband Pierre on the boat from New York. After Pierre's early death, she decided to send her son and daughter back to America, while she stayed in France. She says to her son, "I fought hard for what I have as an artist. There is no one here giving out careers.... You are such a beautiful boy, my son, and if you want to judge me it is your choice to do so. But it will only make us both sad. I cannot change my past or yours."

Ringgold has called Willia Marie, the central character of "The French Collection" series, her alter ego. Ringgold's daughter, cultural critic Michele Wallace, describes the recurring theme of that series as "what a young, ambitious black woman might have become if not for marriage and children."

But in her own life, Ringgold did not choose between art and family: she struggled to combine them. She doesn't pull any punches, though, about the difficulty of trying to have it all. "It's hard when they're little, it's hard when they're big, it's hard when they're grown—it's difficult for women to be artists, period, when they have families. It's hard because you have to be alone, you have to isolate yourself and have your time to think about what it is you're doing, to resolve it, to develop it, to do it. You must have that time and, somehow or another, nobody thinks women should have that time.

"They want us all to just have jobs. You go on your job, you work from nine to five, you come home, and then you take care of everybody else. But an artist doesn't do that. You need all your time—you really need twenty-four hours a day—to just concentrate on what it is you're doing. That's the kind of thing that's reserved for men who are scientists or famous artists or musicians. That's what it takes, complete absorption, twenty-four hours a day. And that is just not something that most people think mommies should have," Ringgold says with a laugh.

Born in Harlem in 1930, Ringgold draws inspiration from her happy memories of that community. As a child, she entertained herself with art projects while resting after her frequent asthma attacks. Although her teachers discouraged her interest in art, Ringgold found a role model in her mother, fashion designer Willi Posey. In 1950, while still in college, Ringgold married Robert Earl Wallace, a classical and jazz pianist, and had two daughters. She left Wallace in 1954 and spent the next eight years as a single parent. After graduating with her BA from City College of New York in 1955, Ringgold taught art full time in the New York City public school system. She continued teaching after her remarriage so that her daughters could attend private school.

Ringgold recalls that during those years, "I was exhausted all the time. I used to get up at the crack of dawn and try to get a little painting in before I woke them [her daughters] up, and then I'd do some on the weekends and I'd do some in the summers." But she did not have long, uninterrupted stretches of time for her art. Although she had help from both her husband's and her own family, Ringgold says that she felt she should be with her children whenever possible during their waking hours.

Consequently, Ringgold's development as an artist was delayed for a number of years. "When they were very little, I didn't work on real projects in art. I mean, I didn't really develop. I couldn't go from A to B to C because I never knew when I could work and when I couldn't. So I would just try and do things. Like, I'd do some watercolors or I'd do some drawings or I'd work with this material or that material. I just explored. But I wasn't able to really develop ideas because I just never had the time," Ringgold says.

She completed her master's degree in 1959, and then, two years later, traveled to Europe for the first time, accompanied by her mother and daughters, to see the works of art she had studied in college. Ringgold returned home more determined than ever to succeed as a professional artist.

A turning point in her attempt to balance art and mothering came in the summer of 1963. Throughout their childhood, Ringgold and her daughters often spent part of the summer away from Manhattan, on Martha's Vineyard and in Cape Cod's Provincetown; at age twelve and thirteen, the girls were finally able to keep themselves entertained and safe while their mother painted. That was the year Ringgold began her "American People" series, which she considers her first mature work.

By then, the artist was thirty-two years old and, having finally begun her career, she says, "I was desperate not to stop working. I was determined I would not stop because I had started so late, I was playing heavy-duty catch-up. I just didn't want the time to get away from me.

"And I knew that one day, they would be grown up and they would be gone, and then I would be needing a life to have. So I was not about to devote my life only to them. I think that is a terrible mistake, and parents who do that will live to regret it. If you raise them properly, they will grow up and leave you. And if you have set your life up for them, and they leave you, well, then you're going to feel deserted, abandoned. So you have to build your [own] life all the time [you're] trying to give them everything they need."

But she was not yet able to work nonstop on her art. As her daughters moved into a new, more difficult phase of adolescence, Ringgold says, "I couldn't concentrate on my work because I was being aggravated by kids trying to grow up. Then I became an activist in the '60s, and that helped because it was such a positive way to spend my time. Instead of just worrying about my kids, I had to worry about the world and try to do something about [it]. I tried to involve them [in activism] too because I thought it was good for kids to feel they could do something about the world."

The summer of 1967 was another turning point in Ringgold's career: for the first time she could devote herself to her art while her mother took seventeen-year-old Michele and sixteen-year-old Barbara to Europe. Although she had remarried in 1962, Ringgold stayed at her mother's house that summer, rather than with her husband, so that she wouldn't have to do any housework. "I had the first summer of my whole life where I could wake up in the morning and I didn't have to please anybody: no parents, no husband, no children. It was great, and I've been constantly trying to get back there. It's like somebody who takes drugs; they take that first high and they keep trying to get back to that—I'm still trying to get back to that first summer," she says, laughing.

Each morning, she woke up and went down to her studio in a gallery. "I would paint all day, and I'd make a date to meet a friend and we would go and have dinner and we could sit there and talk. I didn't have to be home, I didn't have to pick up anything, I didn't have to do anything.

"And then I realized that most of my friends, they had that [freedom] all the time. They didn't even know what I was talking about because their whole life was like that. People who don't have children, who aren't married, they have that all the time, right? Their whole thing is their own self. A lot of them don't do a damned thing with it," she says.

"I feel that sometimes people who don't have children can be a little shortsighted, a little unaware of what it is to put someone else first, because that's what you learn to do when you're a mother: you have to put somebody else first." But, she adds, "It's also nice when you don't have to do that anymore, when the kids grow up and go."

During those months alone, Ringgold painted the large murals in her "American People" series: *The Flag Is Bleeding, Die,* and *U.S. Postage Stamp Commemorating the Advent of Black Power. Die* is one of her most graphic depictions of the racial violence that swept the country during the late 1960s: thirteen figures of men, women, and children, black and white, all spattered with blood, some attacking, others fleeing, still others dead and dying. At the center of the canvas, a little white boy and a little black girl clutch each other, their faces, like the others', wild-eyed with terror.

The next year, the artist's daughters spent the summer in Mexico, and then, in 1971, Ringgold took a year-long sabbatical from her job. "There was no stopping me because I'd had a taste. And then I just kept moving toward more and more freedom; I just kept trying more and more to get the yoke off me so that I could be my own woman. Actually, that's the name of my unpublished [autobiographical] manuscript, *Being My Own Woman.*"

Two years after her sabbatical, Ringgold was finally able to quit her teaching job when her daughters decided they wanted to go to a public rather than a private university. "Then I really could work. I had all these projects in my head. I used to just make little notes of what I would do if I had the time, all these different things that I would do. And I'd fantasize, oh god, it would just be so great—I would do this and I would do that." When the opportunity finally came, Ringgold says, "I was so eager to get started."

Ringgold's work took several new directions in the early '70s. Instead of painting with oils on canvas, she began to use acrylic paints on fabric panels. These were framed with *tankas,* borders of pieced cloth, which Ringgold developed after seeing a Tibetan art exhibit in Amsterdam in 1972. That year she began her "Slave Rape" series, dealing with a subject that at that time was seldom discussed in public. Painted on fabric with a patchwork frame, the pieces in this series were the precursors to her later story quilts.

Ringgold also began making masks and soft sculpture during this period, such as the "Witch Mask" series which spans the years 1973–89. One of those masks, *Weeping Woman #4,* has a life-sized face of gold, black, red, and green beads and long raffia hair, dyed saffron, reddish-pink, and bright green. The breasts, gold-painted gourds, hang on the outside of the costume, which is a length of ornate floral fabric with a center patchwork panel, decorated with gold thread. There are holes for the eyes and mouth, outlined in black beads, for Ringgold wore the masks in performance pieces. Other masks in the series have leather faces with the features outlined in colorful thread and braids of yarn, sometimes black but more often green, blue, red, or yellow, and caftan-style costumes. On her first trip to Africa in 1976, Ringgold exhibited some of her masks in Nigeria to great acclaim.

Ringgold portrays both the joyful and the painful aspects of life in her works. *Three in a Bed* (1981), for example, is a lighthearted soft sculpture, in which three girls and a teddy bear are tucked into a sofa bed, listening to their mother read a bedtime story titled *Do You Love Me*. But that same year, Ringgold created *Screaming Woman,* which expresses the artist's maternal grief over the serial killings of twenty-one black children. The life-sized cloth figure in that piece holds a poster which reads, "Save Our Children in Atlanta," and includes the names, ages, and photographs of the victims. The woman has dropped her bag of groceries, and her worn handbag, with its spilled contents, lies at her feet.

In the 1980s, Ringgold began making the story quilts for which she is perhaps best known. At the center of these works is a painting that is surrounded by a patchwork frame. The text of the story is printed by hand onto numbered muslin squares that are incorporated into the pieced border.

The five-part "Bitter Nest" quilt series (1988), for example, tells a multigenerational story of love and power, beginning when a middle-aged dentist meets a fourteen-year-old girl, CeeCee, the event chronicled in the first quilt. Pregnant within a year of their marriage, CeeCee is struck dumb after the birth.

In the second quilt, *Harlem Renaissance Party,* CeeCee entertains her husband's illustrious guests, wearing strange costumes and dancing to music only she can hear. Her daughter, Celia, grows up to become a doctor. But while on vacation in Paris, Celia falls in love with a married man (the third quilt: *Lovers in Paris),* becomes pregnant, and is later forced by her father to give up the child.

In *The Letter,* the fourth quilt of the series, Celia's now-grown son, Percival, discovers the truth about his parents when he finds a cache of love letters. The story ends, after the dentist's death, on a reconciliatory note in the vibrantly patterned fifth quilt, *The Homecoming.*

Although the African-American family is one of her dominant subjects, the artist has seldom depicted her own family in her work. One of the few early paintings inspired by her daughters was *Hide and Seek.* "It's a picture I sold many years ago of some little kids playing hide-and-seek through some leaves," Ringgold recalls. However, her current series, "The French Collection," which places African-American women in French Impressionist settings, includes portraits of her family. Barbara Wallace and her three children appear in *Dancing in the Louvre,* while Michele Wallace is included in *The Picnic at Giverny* quilt. The artist's mother, together with eighteen other deceased relatives, sits at the center of *Matisse's Chapel.*

Her oldest grandchild and namesake, Faith, inspired a quilt series called, "Baby Faith and Willi." The artist says, "My mother died and my grandchild was born within months. So I did this series as a tribute to both of them. And then the 'Dah' series also relates to my grandchild, Faith, who actually named the series." Both of these series are painted in an abstract style, unlike most of Ringgold's other work.

Members of her family have, on occasion, collaborated with Ringgold. For example, in the 1970s, her mother made the cloth frames for Ringgold's paintings and the costumes for her masks. Their last project was the quilt *Echoes of Harlem,* produced the year before Posey's death in 1980. Michele Wallace has written about her mother's career in her essay collection, *Invisibility Blues: From Pop to Theory,* and in several exhibition catalogs, while Ringgold's younger daughter, Barbara Wallace, did historical research for *Aunt Harriet's Underground Railroad in the Sky.*

Although her children are grown, the artist still feels the tug of family obligations. Ringgold says, "I'm constantly thinking, 'Am I giving them too much time? Don't give them too much time.' It's a struggle, a constant day-to-day struggle for one's own autonomy, one's own identity. As far as I can see, it never really resolves itself, unless you totally separate yourself from them—and I think that's also a mistake. You need your family because, if you've trained them properly, they'll be supportive of you, and you need that support system. But you have to be careful that you don't stop doing your thing and start doing their thing. You have got to keep your mind on what it is that you are about."

She particularly warns women artists to be vigilant of their men. "You have to make sure that the men don't stop you because they try, very hard. They never stop trying, they always think they can stop you. Every woman I meet who says, 'Oh no, my husband is very supportive, he just loves that I'm an artist'—forget about it. He doesn't take it seriously; she's just beginning, he doesn't really believe it. You give it another ten, fifteen, twenty, twenty-five years—see if he likes it then."

Asked how she's stayed married for thirty years, Ringgold says, with a laugh, that her husband can't do anything about her art. "It's either walk away or put up with it. I'm not going to stop; I'm just going to do more. And we give each other a lot of space; we're not right on top of each other."

While Ringgold says that childless people are missing something, it's not a void she encourages them to fill, except perhaps by mothering someone else's children. With all the problems of AIDS, drugs, negative images in the media, the artist says, "a parent today really has a lot to struggle against. And for those reasons, I don't know whether it's all that great to have kids today—it's too much to guard against for them, there are too many pitfalls for them to fall into. I think if you're ready to do all the heavy-duty work and caring and loving that you need to do, then fine. But if you're not, I don't think you should do it."

Is it more difficult for African-American mothers to be artists?

"Absolutely," Ringgold says. "Because you need money, that's absolutely the bottom line. Support in every way is what you need. You need emotional support, you need sympathy, you need money, you need time—and African-American women would fall short on all of that. It's such a day-to-day struggle. And you're going to put the art there, too? That would be very hard, very hard."

Today, after years of struggling to combine art and mothering, the artist says, "I really can pretty much do as I please. I don't have any restrictions placed on me." She still rises early, around 5:00 A.M., exercises, drinks some coffee, and then starts painting, finishing around two or three o'clock in the afternoon.

Ringgold plans to continue working on "The French Collection" until 1995 and then begin another quilt series, "The American Collection," which will rewrite American art history to include black women. She hopes to finish "The American Collection" by the end of the millennium, when she turns seventy. "It's a wonderful time for me," Ringgold says. "I'm just doing what I want."

Selected Bibliography

Archuleta, Margaret, and Dr. Rennard Strickland. *Shared Visions: Native American Painters and Sculptors in the Twentieth Century*. Phoenix: The Heard Museum, 1992.

Bank, Mirra. *Anonymous Was a Woman*. New York: St. Martin's Press, 1979.

Barthes, Roland. *Mythologies*. Translated by Annette Lavers. New York: Hill and Wang, 1972; New York: Farrar, Straus & Giroux, 1972 [1957].

Brown, Betty Ann, and Arlene Raven. *Exposures: Women and Their Art*. Photographs by Kenna Love. Pasadena: New Sage Press, 1989.

Cardozo, Arlene Rossen. *Sequencing*. New York: Atheneum, 1986; New York: Macmillan, 1989.

Chesler, Phyllis. *With Child: A Diary of Motherhood*. New York: Berkeley Books, 1981.

Christensen, Kathleen. *Women and Home-Based Work: The Unspoken Contract*. New York: Henry Holt & Co., 1988.

Coltelli, Laura. *Winged Words: American Indian Writers Speak*. Lincoln, NE: University of Nebraska Press, 1990.

Costa, Peter. *Q & A: Conversations with Harvard Scholars*. Cambridge, MA: Harvard University Press, 1991. (See Mary Karr, "The rhyme and meter of life.")

Dally, Ann. *Inventing Motherhood: The Consequences of an Ideal*. New York: Schocken Books, 1982.

Fraser, Kennedy. "Feminine Fashions." *The New Yorker*, November 9, 1981.

Gardner, John. *On Becoming a Novelist*. New York: Harper & Row, 1983; New York: HarperCollins, 1985.

Garis, Leslie. "Staying Home in the '80s." *Vogue*, April 1987.

Gerson, Kathleen. *Hard Choices: How Women Decide about Work, Career, and Motherhood*. Berkeley and Los Angeles: University of California Press, 1985.

Gieve, Katherine, ed. *Balancing Acts: On Being a Mother*. London: Virago Press, 1989; North Pomfret, VT: Trafalgar, 1990.

Greene, Melissa Fay. "A Writer's Life in a Household of Children." *Ms.* magazine, May/June 1992.

Gorney, Cynthia. "Surfacing." *California Living Magazine, San Francisco Sunday Examiner & Chronicle*, December 25, 1983.

Grove, Valerie. *The Compleat Woman: Marriage, Motherhood, Career: Can She Have It All?* New York: Random House, 1989.

Hochschild, Arlie, with Anne Machung. *The Second Shift: Working Parents and the Revolution at Home.* New York: Viking Penguin, 1989; New York: Avon, 1990.

Higonnet, Anne. *Berthe Morisot: A Biography.* New York: HarperCollins, 1991.

—. *Berthe Morisot's Images of Women.* Cambridge, MA: Harvard University Press, 1992.

Jong, Erica. "Creativity vs. Generativity: The Unexamined Lie." *The New Republic*, January 13, 1979.

Kenyon, Olga, ed. *Women Writers Talk*. New York: Carroll & Graf, 1990.

Lamott, Anne. *Operating Instructions: A Journal of My Son's First Year.* New York: Pantheon, 1993.

Le Guin, Ursula K. "The Hand That Rocks the Cradle Writes the Book." *The New York Times Book Review*, January 22, 1989.

Lippard, Lucy R. *Mixed Blessings: New Art in a Multicultural America.* New York: Pantheon, 1990.

Malinowski, Patricia A., and Liz Fox, eds. *Elizabeth Murray: Drawings, 1980–1986.* Pittsburgh: Carnegie-Mellon University Press, 1986.

Michelson, Maureen R., ed. *Women and Work: Photographs and Personal Writings.* Pasadena: New Sage Press, 1986.

Olsen, Tillie. *Mother to Daughter, Daughter to Mother: Mothers on Mothering, A Day Book and Reader.* New York: The Feminist Press, 1984.

—. *Silences.* New York: Seymour Lawrence, 1978; New York: Delacorte Press, 1989.

Pavese, Edith M. *Elizabeth Murray: Paintings and Drawings.* New York: Harry N. Abrams, 1987.

Pearlman, Mickey, and Katherine Usher Henderson, eds. *Inter/View:*

Talks with America's Writing Women. Lexington, KY: University Press of Kentucky, 1990.

Pearlman, Mickey. *Listen to Their Voices: Twenty Interviews with Women Who Write*. New York: W. W. Norton & Co., 1993.

Plimpton, George, ed. *Women Writers at Work: The Paris Review Interviews*. New York: Viking Penguin, 1989.

Ramsland, Katherine. *Prism of the Night: A Biography of Anne Rice*. New York: Penguin Books, 1989; New York: NAL-Dutton, 1992.

Rich, Adrienne. *Of Woman Born: Motherhood As Experience and Institution*. 10th anniversary edition. New York: W.W. Norton & Co., 1986.

—. *On Lies, Secrets, and Silence: Selected Prose, 1966–1978*. New York: W. W. Norton & Co., 1980.

Rountree, Cathleen. *Coming Into Our Fullness: On Women Turning Forty*. Freedom, CA: The Crossing Press, 1991.

Rowland, Robyn. *Woman Herself: A Transdisciplinary Perspective on Women's Identity*. Australia: Oxford University Press, 1988; Australia: Oxford University Press, 1990.

Ruddick, Sara. *Maternal Thinking: Toward a Politics of Peace*. Boston: Beacon Press, 1989; New York: Ballantine, 1990.

Ruddick, Sara, and Pamela Daniels, eds. *Working It Out: 23 Women Writers, Artists, Scientists, and Scholars Talk About Their Lives and Work*. New York: Pantheon, 1977.

Shepherd, Elizabeth, ed. *Secrets, Dialogues, Revelations: The Art of Betye and Alison Saar*. Los Angeles: The Wight Art Gallery, University of California, Los Angeles, 1990.

Siegel, Jeanne, ed. *Art Talk: The Early '80s*. New York: Da Capo Press, 1990.

Slatkin, Wendy. *The Voices of Women Artists*. New Jersey: Prentice Hall, 1992.

Smiley, Jane. "Can Mothers Think?" *The True Subject: Writers on Life and Craft*, ed. by Kurt Brown. St. Paul: Graywolf Press, 1993.

Spender, Dale. *The Writing or the Sex?*. New York and Oxford: Pergamon Press, 1989.

Sternburg, Janet. *The Writer on Her Work*. New York: W. W. Norton & Co., 1980.

—. *The Writer on Her Work*. Vol. 2. New York: W.W. Norton & Co., 1991.

Suleiman, Susan Rubin. *Risking Who One Is: Encounters with Contem-*

porary Art and Literature. Cambridge, MA: Harvard University Press, 1994.

—."Writing and Motherhood." The (M)other Tongue: Essays in Feminist Psychoanalytic Interpretation, ed. by Shirley Nelson Garner, Claire Kahane, and Madelon Sprengnether. Ithaca and London: Cornell University Press, 1985.

—. "On Maternal Splitting: A Propos of Mary Gordon's Men and Angels." In SIGNS, Autumn 1988.

Sumrall, Amber Coverdale, ed. Write to the Heart: Wit and Wisdom of Women Writers. Freedom, CA: The Crossing Press, 1992.

Swann, Brian and Arnold Krupat, eds. I Tell You Now: Autobiographical Essays by Native American Writers. Lincoln, NE: University of Nebraska Press, 1987.

Swigart, Jane. The Myth of the Bad Mother: Parenting Without Guilt. New York: Doubleday, 1991; New York: Avon, 1992.

Theroux, Phyllis. Night Lights: Bedtime Stories for Parents in the Dark. New York: Viking Penguin, 1987; New York: Viking Penguin, 1988.

Truitt, Anne. Daybook: The Journal of an Artist. New York: Penguin Books, 1982; New York: Viking Penguin, 1984.

—. Turn: The Journal of an Artist. New York: Penguin Books, 1986.

Turner, Robyn Montana. Faith Ringgold. Portraits of Women Artists for Children series. Boston: Little, Brown and Company, 1993.

Wagner-Martin, Linda W. Sylvia Plath, A Biography. New York: St. Martin's Press, 1987; New York: St. Martin's Press, 1988.

Walker, Alice. In Search of Our Mothers' Gardens. New York: Harcourt, Brace, Jovanovich, 1967; New York: Harcourt, Brace, 1984.

Wallace, Michele. Invisibility Blues: From Pop to Theory. New York: Verso Press, 1990.

Walz, Barbra and Jill Barber. Starring Mothers. New York: Doubleday & Co., 1987.

Weigle, Marta. Creation and Procreation: Feminist Reflections on Mythologies of Cosmogony and Parturition. Philadelphia: University of Pennsylvania Press, 1989.

Winter, Nina. Interview with the Muse: Remarkable Women Speak on Creativity and Power. Berkeley: Moon Books, 1978.

Witzling, Mara R., ed. *Voicing Our Visions: Writings by Women Artists.* New York: Universe, 1991.

Woolf, Virginia, *A Room of One's Own.* New York and London: Harcourt, Brace and World, 1929; New York: Harcourt Brace, 1989.

Yalom, Marilyn. *Maternity, Mortality, and the Literature of Madness.* University Park and London: Pennsylvania State University, 1985.

Selected Fiction by Other Authors

Cooper, J. California. *Family*. New York: Doubleday, 1991.

Drabble, Margaret. *The Millstone*. New York: William Morrow & Company, 1965; New York: NAL-Dutton, 1984.

Emecheta, Buchi. *The Joys of Motherhood*. New York: George Braziller, 1979.

Gilman, Charlotte Perkins. *The Yellow Wallpaper*. Boston: Small, Maynard, 1899; New York: The Feminist Press, 1973.

Kingsolver, Barbara. *Animal Dreams*. New York: HarperCollins, 1991.

—. *The Bean Trees*. New York: Harper & Row, 1988; New York: HarperCollins, 1989.

—. *Pigs in Heaven*. New York: HarperCollins, 1993.

Lazarre, Jane. *The Mother Knot*. Boston: Beacon Press, 1976; Boston: Beacon Press, 1986.

McMillan, Terry. *Mama*. Boston: Houghton Mifflin Company, 1987; Fort Wayne, IN: PB, Co., 1991.

—. *Disappearing Acts*. New York: Simon & Schuster, 1989; New York: Viking Penguin, 1989.

—. *Waiting to Exhale*. New York: Viking Penguin, 1992.

Miller, Sue. *The Good Mother*. New York: Harper & Row, 1986; New York: Dell, 1987.

—. *Family Pictures*. New York: Harper & Row, 1991; New York: HarperCollins, 1991.

Weldon, Fay. *Puffball*. London: Hodder and Stoughton, 1980; New York: Viking Penguin, 1990.

Selected Books by Interviewed Authors

Dorothy Allison

Bastard Out of Carolina. New York: Plume, 1992.
Skin: Talking About Sex, Class & Literature. Ithaca, NY: Firebrand Books, 1994.
Trash. Ithaca, NY: Firebrand Books, 1988.
The Women Who Hate Me: Poetry 1980–1990. Ithaca, NY: Firebrand Books, 1991.

Kate Braverman

Hurricane Warnings. Los Angeles: Illuminati, 1987.
Lithium for Medea. New York: Harper & Row, 1979; New York: Viking Penguin, 1989.
Palm Latitudes. New York: Simon & Schuster, 1988; New York: Viking Penguin, 1989.
Postcard from August. Los Angeles: Illuminati, 1990.
Squandering the Blue. New York: Ballantine Books, 1990; New York: Ivy Books, 1991.
Wonders of the West. New York: Ballantine Books, 1993; New York: Fawcett Columbine, 1993.

Rosellen Brown

The Autobiography of My Mother. New York: Doubleday, 1976; New York: Ballantine, 1981.
Before and After. New York: Farrar, Straus, Giroux, 1992.
Civil Wars. New York: Alfred A. Knopf, 1984.
Cora Fry. New York: W. W. Norton & Co., 1977; Greensboro, NC: Unicorn Press, 1989.
Cora Fry's Pillow Book. New York: Farrar, Straus, Giroux, 1994.
A Rosellen Brown Reader: Selected Poetry and Prose. Hanover, NH: University Press of New England, 1992.

Street Games: A Neighborhood. New York: Doubleday, 1974; Minneapolis: Milkweed Edition, 1991.
Tender Mercies. New York: Alfred A. Knopf, 1978.

Rita Dove

Fifth Sunday. Charlottesville and London: The University Press of Virginia, 1985.
Grace Notes. New York: W. W. Norton & Company, 1989.
Museum. Pittsburgh: Carnegie-Mellon University Press, 1983.
Selected Poems. New York: Vintage Books, 1993.
Thomas and Beulah. Pittsburgh: Carnegie-Mellon University Press, 1985.
Through the Ivory Gate. New York: Pantheon Books, 1992.
The Yellow House on the Corner. Pittsburgh: Carnegie-Mellon University Press, 1980.

Cristina Garcia

Dreaming in Cuban. New York: Alfred A. Knopf, 1992.

Mary Gordon

The Company of Women. New York: Random House, 1980; New York: Ballantine, 1986.
Final Payments. New York: Random House, 1978; New York: Ballantine, 1986.
Good Boys and Dead Girls and Other Essays. New York: Viking Penguin, 1992.
Men and Angels. New York: Random House, 1985; New York: Ballantine, 1986.
The Other Side. New York: Viking Penguin, 1989.
The Rest of Life: Three Novellas. New York: Viking Penguin, 1993.
Temporary Shelter. New York: Ballantine, 1988.

Linda Hogan

The Book of Medicines. Minneapolis: Coffee House Press, 1993.
Eclipse. Los Angeles: American Studies Center, University of California, Los Angeles, 1983.

Mean Spirit. New York: Athenaeum, 1990.

Red Clay: Poems and Stories. Greenfield Center, NY: Greenfield Review Press, 1991.

Savings. Minneapolis: Coffee House Press, 1988.

Seeing Through the Sun. Amherst, MA: University of Massachusetts Press, 1985.

Trina Schart Hyman (books written or retold by)

How Six Found Christmas. New York: Holiday House, 1991.

Little Red Riding Hood. New York: Holiday House, 1983.

Self-Portrait: Trina Schart Hyman. New York: Harper & Row, 1989; New York: HarperCollins Children's Books: 1989.

The Sleeping Beauty. New York: Little, Brown, 1983.

Perri Klass

Baby Doctor. New York: Random House, 1992.

I Am Having an Adventure. New York: G.P. Putnam's Sons, 1986.

A Not Entirely Benign Procedure: Four Years As a Medical Student. New York: G.P. Putnam's Sons, 1987; New York: NAL-Dutton, 1988.

Other Women's Children. New York: Random House, 1990.

Recombinations. New York: G.P. Putnam's Sons, 1985. New York: NAL-Dutton, 1991.

Ursula K. Le Guin

Always Coming Home. New York: Harper & Row, 1985; New York: Bantam, 1987.

Dancing at the Edge of the World: Thoughts on Words, Women, Places. New York: Harper & Row, 1989; New York: HarperCollins, 1990.

The Farthest Shore. New York: Athenaeum, 1972; Bantam, 1984.

Going Out with Peacocks and Other Poems. HarperCollins, 1994.

The Language of the Night: Essays on Fantasy and Science Fiction. Edited by Susan Wood. New York: G.P. Putnam's Sons, 1978; New York: HarperCollins, 1993.

The Lathe of Heaven. New York: Scribner, 1971; New York:Avon, 1976.

The Left Hand of Darkness. New York: Ace Books, 1969; New York: Ace

Books, 1983.

A Ride on the Red Mare's Back. New York: Orchard, 1992.

Tehanu: The Last Book of Earthsea. New York: Athenaeum, 1990; New York: Macmillan Children's Group, 1990.

The Tombs of Atuan. New York: Athenaeum, 1970; New York: Bantam, 1975.

A Wizard of Earthsea. Boston: Houghton Mifflin, 1978; New York: Bantam, 1984.

Joyce Maynard

Baby Love. New York: Alfred A. Knopf, 1981.

Domestic Affairs: Enduring the Pleasures of Motherhood and Family Life. New York: McGraw-Hill, 1987; New York: Random House, 1987.

Looking Back: A Chronicle of Growing Up Old in the Sixties. New York: Doubleday, 1973.

To Die For. New York: NAL-Dutton, 1992.

Mary Morris

The Bus of Dreams and Other Stories. Boston: Houghton Mifflin, 1985; New York: Viking Penguin, 1986.

Crossroads. Boston: Houghton Mifflin, 1983.

Maiden Voyages: Writings of Women Travelers. (Edited, with Larry O'Connor.) New York: Vintage Books, 1993.

A Mother's Love. New York: Doubleday, 1993.

Nothing to Declare: Memoirs of a Woman Traveling Alone. Boston: Houghton Mifflin, 1988; New York: Viking Penguin, 1989.

Vanishing Animals and Other Stories. New York: David R. Godine, 1979; New York:Viking Penguin, 1991.

The Waiting Room. New York: Doubleday, 1989.

Wall to Wall: From Beijing to Berlin by Rail. New York: Doubleday, 1991

Alicia Suskin Ostriker

A Dream of Springtime. Brooklyn, NY: The Smith, 1979.

Feminist Revision and the Bible. Bucknell Series in Literary Theory. Cambridge, MA: Blackwell Publishers, 1993.

Green Age. Pittsburgh: University of Pittsburgh Press, 1989.

The Imaginary Lover. Pittsburgh: University of Pittsburgh Press, 1986.

The Mother/Child Papers. Santa Monica, CA: Momentum, 1980; Boston: Beacon Press, 1986.

Once More Out of Darkness. Berkeley: Berkeley Poets' Cooperative, 1974.

Songs. New York: Holt, Rinehart & Winston, 1969.

Stealing the Language: The Emergence of Women's Poetry in America. Boston: Beacon Press, 1987.

A Woman Under the Surface: *Poems & Prose Poems*. Princeton, NJ: Princeton University Press, 1982.

Writing Like a Woman. Ann Arbor: University of Michigan Press, Poets on Poetry Series, 1983.

Bea Nettles

Breaking the Rules: A Photo Media Cookbook. Urbana, IL: Inky Press Productions, 1987.

Complexities. Urbana, IL: Inky Press Productions, 1992.

Corners: Grace and Bea Nettles. Urbana, IL: Inky Press Productions, 1989.

Flamingo in the Dark: Images. Urbana, IL: Inky Press Productions, 1979.

Life's Lessons: A Mother's Journal. Urbana, IL: Inky Press Productions, 1990.

The Skirted Garden: 20 Years of Images. Urbana, IL: Inky Press Productions, 1990.

Patricia Smith

Big Towns, Big Talk. Cambridge: Zoland Books, 1992.

Close to Death. Cambridge: Zoland Books, 1993.

Life According to Motown. Chicago: T'a Chucha Press, 1991.

Jane Yolen

The Boy Who Spoke Chimp. New York: Knopf, 1981.

Briar Rose. Edited by Terri Windling. New York: Tor Books, 1992.

Commander Toad in Space. New York: Coward McCann, 1980.

The Devil's Arithmetic. New York: Viking, 1988; New York: Puffin Books, 1990.

The Gift of Sarah Barker.New York: Puffin Books, 1992.

A Letter From Phoenix Farm. Katonah, New York: Richard C. Owen
    Publishers, 1992.
Owl Moon. New York: Philomel, 1987.
Pirates in Petticoats. New York: David McKay, 1963.
Touch Magic. New York: Philomel, 1992.

About the Author

Judith Pierce Rosenberg grew up in Kansas and Nevada and graduated from the University of California, Berkeley, with a BA in Middle Eastern Studies. She has been a freelance writer for more than a decade, having been published in numerous newspapers and magazines including *The Boston Globe, Ms., Publishers Weekly,* and *The Middle East Magazine.* She wrote this book because she, too, needed to read it—to learn how to balance creative work and family. She lives in Lincoln, Massachusetts, with her computer scientist husband, Carl Rosenberg, and their two school-age children, Michael and Christina.

Papier-Mache Press

At Papier-Mache Press, it is our goal to identify and successfully present important social issues through enduring works of beauty, grace, and strength. Through our work we hope to encourage empathy and respect among diverse communities, creating a bridge of understanding between the mainstream audience and those who might not otherwise be heard.

We appreciate you, our customer, and strive to earn your continued support. We also value the role of the bookseller in achieving our goals. We are especially grateful to the many independent booksellers whose presence ensures a continuing diversity of opinion, information, and literature in our communities. We encourage you to support these bookstores with your patronage.

We publish many fine books about women's experiences. We also produce lovely posters and T-shirts that complement our anthologies. Please ask your local bookstore which Papier-Mache items they carry. To receive our complete catalog, send your request to Papier-Mache Press, 135 Aviation Way, #14, Watsonville, CA 95076, or call our toll-free number, 800-927-5913.